The U.S.-Soviet Confrontation in Iran, 1945–1962

A Case in the Annals of the Cold War

Kristen Blake

UNIVERSITY PRESS OF AMERICA,® INC.
Lanham • Boulder • New York • Toronto • Plymouth, UK

Copyright © 2009 by
University Press of America,® Inc.
4501 Forbes Boulevard
Suite 200
Lanham, Maryland 20706
UPA Acquisitions Department (301) 459-3366

Estover Road
Plymouth PL6 7PY
United Kingdom

All rights reserved
Printed in the United States of America
British Library Cataloging in Publication Information Available

Library of Congress Control Number: 2009921488
ISBN: 978-0-7618-4495-2 (clothbound : alk. paper)
ISBN: 978-0-7618-4491-4 (paperback : alk. paper)
eISBN: 978-0-7618-4492-1

∞ ™ The paper used in this publication meets the minimum
requirements of American National Standard for Information
Sciences—Permanence of Paper for Printed Library Materials,
ANSI Z39.48—1984

Contents

Preface	v
Acknowledgments	vii
Abbreviations	ix
Introduction	1
Map	7
1 Prelude to the U.S.-Soviet Confrontation in Iran	9
2 The Iranian Crisis of 1945–46 and Its Role in Initiating the Cold War	28
3 The Oil Nationalization Dispute and Its Ramifications	62
4 Iran's New Pro-Western Stance	94
5 The End of Cold War Tensions in Iran	137
Conclusion	183
Bibliography	193
Index	207

Preface

Today the mention of Iran conjures the image of a hostile country embroiled in a deepening controversy with the international community over the development of its nuclear program, which it claims is for peaceful purposes. The United States is pressuring Iran to become more transparent about its nuclear agenda. Russia, on the other hand, has been supportive of Iran and its right to develop nuclear energy, and in fact helped Iran build a nuclear facility in Bushehr. Prior to the Islamic Revolution of 1979, Iran and the United States had an amicable relationship that had developed during the early years of the Cold War, when Iran became an arena for U.S.-Soviet rivalry. The United States had helped Iran resist Soviet attempts to spread its influence and control over the country. The origins of this superpower rivalry, which influenced Iran's political and economic development, is traced back to the Second World War.

During the Second World War, Iran had declared its neutrality. The German attack on the Soviet Union in the summer of 1941, however, drew Iran into a whirlpool of events that would undermine its sovereignty. Iran became the focal point of Anglo-Soviet and American war efforts against Germany for several reasons. First, Iran's geographical location and close proximity to the Soviet Union made it the suitable route through which the Allies could provide war supplies to the Soviets. Second, Iran had established strong economic ties with Germany over the years and there were German advisers and employees who were actively involved in the country. Third, the Soviets and the British had their own interests to protect with regard to Iran. The British wanted to protect their oil interests in southern Iran, and at the same time protect their interests in India, from any German encroachment. The Soviets wanted to protect their southern borders, which they shared with Iran, as well as their oil wells in Baku, which lay in close proximity to the Iranian border.

At the same time, the Soviets intended to pursue their interests in northern Iran by obtaining an oil concession from the Iranian government. The Americans, at the time, did not have well-defined interests in Iran and were only concerned with the Allied war effort.

The British and the Soviets began to pressure Reza Shah to expel the Germans from Iran. Reza Shah, however, refused and insisted on Iran's neutral stand in the war. In a coordinated effort, the two powers occupied Iran on August 25, 1941. Soviet troops took control of the northern part of Iran while British troops took control of the southern part. A neutral zone, which included the capital, Tehran, was placed under Iranian control. A year later, American advisers and troops came to Iran as part of the Allied war effort. These conditions set the stage for an unprecedented rivalry among the superpowers in Iran that eventually led to the Iranian Crisis of 1945-46, which became a major factor in the development of the Cold War between the United States and the Soviet Union. The U.S.-Soviet confrontation in Iran continued well beyond the settlement of the Iranian Crisis until the early 1960s.

This book is a study of the origins, development, and end of the U.S.-Soviet Cold War rivalry and tensions in Iran from 1945 to 1962 and its influence on the political and economic development of the country. In analyzing the U.S.-Soviet rivalry during the aforementioned period, the book will focus on the development of U.S.-Iranian relations and U.S. policy toward Iran, which was primarily concerned with preventing the spread of communism in the country. The book traces U.S. policy toward Iran through the Truman, Eisenhower, and Kennedy administrations and examines whether there were any elements of continuity among the three administrations in keeping Iran free from communism. The book also provides an in-depth analysis of the response of the Shah and the Iranian government to foreign-power rivalry in Iran.

This book is based on a number of primary sources, including: declassified U.S. government documents collected at the National Archives in College Park, Maryland; documents printed in the *Foreign Relations of the United States* series as well as the analysis and coverage of certain key events in the State Department *Bulletin*; Russian sources noted in correspondences and protocols between heads of states as recorded by the U.S. State Department and the American embassy in Iran; Russian newspapers and periodicals; British sources as cited in the *Foreign Relations of the United States* and certain secondary sources; and Iranian sources, which include memoirs of prominent Iranian statesmen, the Iranian Oral History Project conducted at Harvard University, and leading Iranian newspapers and periodicals of the period. I have tried to use these sources objectively to show how the superpower rivalry affected Iran's political and economic development from 1945 to 1962.

Acknowledgments

This book developed out of over a decade of research and study regarding the U.S.-Soviet Cold War rivalry in Iran between 1945 and 1962 that eventually culminated in my doctoral dissertation in 1999 presented to Harvard University. A new chapter has been added and the other chapters have been revised.

I owe much to my mentors whose guidance and support over the years enabled me to complete this project. First, I would like to thank Roger Owen, professor of Middle Eastern History at Harvard University, who was my dissertation adviser, for his generous support and guidance in helping me complete this manuscript. Next, I would like to thank Roy Mottahedeh, professor of Islamic History at Harvard University, who was my second adviser. I would also like to thank Oktor Skjaervo, professor of Iranian Studies at Harvard University, for his guidance and generous support during my graduate studies and research that eventually paved the way for the completion of this manuscript. I would also like to thank Beatrice Manz, professor of History at Tufts University, who reviewed part of the manuscript and provided valuable comments, for which I am extremely grateful.

I would like to thank my colleagues at Molloy College for their encouragement and support while I was completing this project. Special thanks go to Sister Francis Kammer and Sister Francis Piscatella for their support and kindness throughout the years. Professor Nicholas Fargnoli is an inspiration and he encouraged me from the very beginning to publish this manuscript. Professor Emerita Loretta Lagana, Sister Francis Kammer, Dr. Lelia Roeckell, Dr. Stephan Ethé, Dr. Paul Van Wie, Joseph Maher, Dr. Tom Ryley, and Ms. Joyce Nappo in the Department of History and Political Science were all supportive. I would like to thank the Faculty Research and Scholarship Committee at Molloy College for the grant that enabled me to complete this project. Special thanks go to the librarians at Molloy College for their help and patience: Robert Martin, Norman Weil, Winnie Chen, Patricia Sullivan, Ellen Rich, and Margaret Gough. I would especially like to thank Ann Kirschner, my copy editor, for her patience and valuable advice that helped me refine this manuscript. I am truly grateful to Judith Rothman, vice- president and director of University Press of America, Inc., Patti Belcher, Brooke Bascietto, Brian DeRocco and other members of the editorial board of UPA for their patience and support that helped me bring the manuscript to fruition. Finally, I would like to thank my parents and family for their love and support throughout the years.

Abbreviations

AID	Agency for International Development
AIOC	Anglo-Iranian Oil Company
ARAMCO	Arabian-American Oil Company
ARMISH	United States Mission to the Iranian Army
BMEO	British Middle East Office
CENTO	Central Treaty Organization
CIA	Central Intelligence Agency
CINCEUR	Commander in Chief, Europe
DLF	Development Loan Fund
ECA	Economic Cooperation Administration
FBI	Federal Bureau of Investigation
EXIM	Export Import Bank
FO	Foreign Office
GENMISH	United States Mission to the Iranian Gendarmerie
GNP	Gross National Product
GTI	Division of Greek, Turkish, and Iranian Affairs, Department of State
IBRD	International Bank for Reconstruction and Development (World Bank)
ICA	International Cooperation Administration
ICBM	Intercontinental Ballistic Missile
IMF	International Monetary Fund
IRBM	Intermediate Range Ballistic Missile
JCS	Joint Chiefs of Staff
KGB	Committee for the State Security of the Soviet Union
MAAG	Military Assistance Advisory Group
MAP	Mutual Assistance Program

MDAP	Military Defense Assistance Program
MEI	Division of Middle Eastern and Indian Affairs, Department of State
MI6	Britain's Secret Intelligence Service
MK	Morrison-Knudsen
MOSSAD	Israel's Intelligence Agency
NAC	North Atlantic Council
NATO	North Atlantic Treaty Organization
NEA	Office of Near Eastern and African Affairs, Department of of State
NIE	National Intelligence Estimate
NIOC	National Iranian Oil Company
NSC	National Security Council
OCI	Overseas Consultants Incorporated
OSS	Office of Strategic Services
PGC	Persian Gulf Command
PSF	President's Secretary's File
RG	Record Group
RSFSR	Russian Soviet Federated Socialist Republic
SACEUR	Supreme Allied Commander, Europe
SAVAK	Iran's National Information and Security Organization
SNIE	Special National Intelligence Estimate
SWNCC	State-War-Navy Coordinating Committee
TCA	Technical Cooperation Administration
TIAS	United States Treaties and Other International Act Series
UN	United Nations
UNAEC	United Nations Atomic Energy Commission
USIA	United States Information Agency
USOM	United States Operations Mission

Introduction

Historians and political scientists have been unable to reach a consensus regarding the origins and development of the Cold War. Many have ascribed this conflict to the U.S.-Soviet rivalry over Europe in the aftermath of the Second World War. A small number, aware that Iran also became an arena for U.S.-Soviet rivalry, limited their analysis to the Iranian crisis of 1945–46 in Azerbaijan, because U.S. and Soviet government documents crucial for the study of this topic remained classified for many years. They disagreed, however, over how the U.S.-Soviet confrontation in Iran began.

The traditionalists[1], who represented the orthodox school of thought, argued that the Soviet Union sought to spread its communist ideology beyond its borders, and in doing so, pursued an expansionist policy. The Soviet support of the Azeris and the Kurds in northern Iran to establish their own autonomous regimes in 1945, and their refusal to withdraw their troops from Iran in 1946, led to the U.S.-Soviet confrontation in the country. The Soviet goal was ultimately to take over the Iranian province of Azerbaijan and have it become part of the Soviet Union.

The revisionists[2] blamed the United States for the U.S.-Soviet confrontation in Iran. They argued that the confrontation had primarily resulted from the United States pursuing its economic interests in the region. The United States had sought to promote its interests in the Middle East as a solution to economic problems that had resulted from the Great Depression and by 1933 had managed to negotiate successfully an oil concession with Saudi Arabia. The United States was interested in obtaining an oil concession in Iran between 1943 and 1944, however, due to Soviet objections, the Iranian government decided not to grant concessions to any foreign powers. When the Azeri and the Kurds rebelled against the Iranian government in 1945, Russian troops stationed in northern Iran, prevented the Iranian troops from entering the Azerbaijan province to restore order. The Iranian government, in turn, filed a complaint against the Soviet Union at the United Nations in 1946. The Truman administration and the U.N. Security Council's support of the Iranian case forced the Soviet troops to withdraw from northern Iran.

The postrevisionists[3] are another group of scholars, whose analysis of the origins of the Cold War draws from both the orthodox and revisionist schools of thought. The postrevisionists agree with the orthodox view that the U.S.-Soviet confrontation in Iran resulted from Soviet ambitions to promote their interests in the region. Yet they also take into consideration U.S. attempts at promoting its strategic and oil interests in the region, as factors, which left the Soviets and the British at a disadvantage. The postrevisionists argue that the confrontation in Iran resulted from rivalry between the Soviet Union, the United States, and Great Britain.

Aside from the above three schools of thought, certain scholars have also attempted to analyze the Iranian Crisis of 1945–46 from a unique perspective. These scholars argue that the U.S.-Soviet confrontation in Iran resulted primarily from U.S. emphasis on the pursuit of its strategic interests in the region.[4] As apart of its national security policy, the United States expanded its military activities in the region, which in particular threatened the Soviets and made them reconsider their priorities in northern Iran. These scholars also discuss U.S. oil interests in the region alongside its strategic interests, and in doing so their arguments parallel the revisionist view. Following the end of the Cold War, a small number of scholars have also emerged to analyze the Iranian Crisis of 1945–46 and in particular the Soviet role using declassified documents from the former Soviet archives.[5] A closer look, however, reveals that their analysis is an amalgam of the arguments put forth by the postrevisionists.

It is not this book's contention that the Cold War between the United States and the Soviet Union originated in Iran, since scholars remain divided to this day over where the conflict began. Rather, it treats Iran as a case study, where Cold War ramifications were also manifested outside Europe. While it agrees with the postrevisionist argument that Soviet actions in northern Iran led to the U.S.-Soviet confrontation in Iran, it nonetheless attempts to maintain an objective view regarding the Soviet role after the settlement of the Iranian crisis in 1946, and takes into account U.S., British, and Iranian roles in the development of the Cold War rivalry in Iran.

This book is also different from several studies of U.S.-Iranian relations generated by the outbreak of the Islamic Revolution of 1979, when scholars rushed to analyze where and how U.S.-Iranian relations had gone wrong.[6] For the most part, these scholars discussed briefly the 1945–46 crisis in Azerbaijan and the oil nationalization crisis of 1951–53 as the highlights of the

Cold War period in Iran but seemed unaware that the Cold War tensions in Iran continued well until the early 1960s. The majority of these sources are outdated. In recent years, numerous books and articles on U.S.-Iranian relations have focused on the period since the Islamic Revolution of 1979.[7] These sources have discussed Iran's nuclear dilemma and possible U.S. responses ranging from sanctions to regime change and even war. They have for the most part left out any discussion of previous U.S.-Soviet Cold War rivalry in Iran failing to see the connection between the past and the present.

This book examines five major themes and important questions associated with the origins, development, and end of U.S.-Soviet Cold War rivalry and tensions in Iran between 1945 and 1962:

1. *The role of the Iranian crisis of 1945–46.* Was U.S. opposition to a Soviet sphere of influence the first phase of the U.S.-Soviet confrontation in Iran? Was Soviet policy in Iran a response to U.S. hostility rather than an expansionist policy?
2. *Soviet policy toward Iran in the aftermath of the Iranian Crisis.* What kind of policy did Stalin pursue toward Iran in the aftermath of the Iranian Crisis? In what ways did it lead to an escalation of Cold War tensions in Iran? Was Khrushchev's policy toward Iran a continuation of that advocated by his predecessor? How did Khrushchev's policy change the course of the superpower rivalry in Iran?
3. *U.S. policy toward Iran in the aftermath of the Iranian Crisis.* What measures did the United States take to prevent the spread of communism in Iran? Were there any similarities or differences among the Truman, Eisenhower, and Kennedy administrations in implementing their policy in Iran?
4. *British policy toward Iran in the aftermath of the Iranian crisis of 1945–46.* What measures did the British take between 1946 and 1953 to protect their interests in Iran? How did British policy affect the course of the Cold War rivalry during this period?
5. *The role of Muhammad Reza Shah and the Iranian government between 1945 and 1962.* How did the Shah and the Iranian government respond to the superpower rivalry in Iran? In what ways did their actions influence the course of the Cold War rivalry in Iran and eventually help bring an end to Cold War tensions in Iran by the end of 1962?

This book strives to present a comprehensive analysis of the origins, the development, and the end of the U.S.-Soviet Cold War rivalry and tensions in Iran. It serves as a bridge to cover the gap between studies that have been limited on the one hand to the Iranian Crisis of 1945–46 and the origins of the Cold War, to books written on U.S.-Iranian relations, the outbreak of the Islamic Revolution, and the period since that have neglected to discuss the continuation of U.S.-Soviet Cold War tensions in Iran well after the Iranian Crisis of 1945–46. It focuses on the Cold War context to provide a simultaneous analysis of the internal and external factors that drew U.S.-Soviet rivalry to Iran and how that shaped Iran's political and economic development.

Chapter 1 discusses the origins and evolution of Anglo-Russian and later Anglo-Soviet interests in Iran that culminated in the occupation of country in 1941 during the Second World War. The occupation led to U.S. involvement in Iran as part of the Allied war effort and set the stage for an unprecedented rivalry among the powers that would lead to the Iranian Crisis of 1945–46. Chapter 2 analyzes the Iranian Crisis of 1945–46 and its role in initiating the Cold War. The settlement of the crisis is discussed in detail. Chapter 3 discusses the nationalization of the Iranian oil industry by Prime Minister Muhammad Musaddiq and the ensuing dispute. The Anglo-American and Soviet reaction to this dispute will be discussed as well. Chapter 4 focuses on Iran's new pro-Western stance following the coup that overthrew Musaddiq's government. It discusses Iran's new alliance with the West and the Shah's policy of Positive Nationalism. Chapter 5 discusses the end of Cold War tensions in Iran that resulted from the Iranian government's assurances to the Soviets not to allow the establishment of any foreign missile bases in Iran, as well as the unfolding of the White Revolution, which I argue was a by-product of U.S. Cold War policies in Iran. The conclusion will summarize the main findings of this book and reflect on Iran's future prospects.

Linguists have yet to agree on a standard system of transliterating Persian characters into their Latin counterpart. I have used a modified form devised by the Library of Congress. Diacritical marks have only been used to denote the *ayn* and *hamzah* (indicated by a prime), as they appear in a word for example the proper name Ja'far. Persian words such as Tehran and proper names such as Muhammad Musaddiq are spelled, as is the case in English literature. All translations from the Persian language are by the author unless otherwise stated.

NOTES

1. Herbert Druks, *Harry S. Truman and the Russians, 1945–1953* (New York: Robert Speller and Sons, 1966), 119–29; Herbert Feis, *From Trust to Terror: The Onset of the Cold War, 1945–1950* (New York: W. W. Norton, 1970), 63–70, 81–87; Louis J. Halle, *The Cold War as History* (New York: Harper & Row, 1967), 99–100; Joseph M. Jones, *The Fifteen Weeks* (New York: Viking Press, 1955), 48–58; John

W. Spanier, *American Foreign Policy Since World War II* (New York: Frederick A. Praeger, 1960), 19–20.

2. Justus Doenecke, "Revisionists, Oil, and Cold War Diplomacy," *Iranian Studies* 3 (Winter 1970): 23–33; Doenecke, "Iran's Role in Cold War Revisionism," *Iranian Studies* 5 (Spring-Summer 1972): 96–111; Denna F. Fleming, *The Cold War and its Origins, 1917–1950*, vol. 1 (Garden City, N.Y.: Doubleday, 1961), 340–42, 344–48; Lloyd Gardner, Economic Aspects of New Deal Diplomacy (Madison: University of Wisconsin Press, 1964), 217–36; Gardner, *Architects of Illusion* (Chicago: Quadrangle, 1970), 210–15; Gabriel Kolko, *The Politics of War* (New York: Random House, 1968), 309–11.

3. Richard Cottam, "The United States, Iran, and the Cold War," *Iranian Studies* 13 (Winter 1970): 2–22; Cottam, *Iran and the United States: A Cold War Case Study* (Pittsburgh: University of Pittsburgh Press, 1988), 55–81; Louise Fawcett, *Iran and the Cold War: The Azerbaijan Crisis of 1946* (Cambridge: Cambridge University Press, 1992); Gary Hess, "The Iranian Crisis of 1945–46 and the Cold War," Political Science Quarterly 89 (March 1974): 117–46; Bruce Kuniholm, *The Origins of the Cold War in the Near East* (Princeton, N.J.: Princeton University Press, 1980); Stephen McFarland, "A Peripheral View of the Origins of the Cold War: The Crises in Iran, 1941–1947," *Diplomatic History* 4 (Fall 1980): 333–51; Richard Pfau, "Containment in Iran, 1946: The Shift to an Active Policy," *Diplomatic History* 1 (Fall 1977): 359–72; Eduard Mark, "Allied Reactions in Iran, 1941–47: The Origins of a Cold War Crisis," *Wisconsin Magazine of History* 59 (Autumn 1975): 51–63.

4. Fred Lawson, "The Iranian Crisis of 1945–46 and a Spiral Model of International Conflict," *International Journal of Middle Eastern Studies* 21 (1989): 307–26; Melvyn Leffler, A Preponderance of Power (Stanford, Calif.: Stanford University Press, 1992), 79–81.

5. Jamil Hasanli, *Iran at the Dawn of the Cold War: The Soviet-American Crisis over Iranian Azerbaijan, 1941–1946* (Lanham, Md.: Roman & Littlefield, 2006). Natalia Yegorova, *The Iranian Crisis of 1945–46: A View from the Russian Archives*, working paper no. 15, Woodrow Wilson International Center for Scholars: www.wilsoncenter.org/topics/pubs/ACFB51.pdf, accessed September 7, 2007; Fernande S. Raine, "The Iranian Crisis of 1946 and the Origins of the Cold War," in *The Origins of the Cold War: An International History*, Melvyn Leffler and David Painter, eds. (Oxon, U.K.: Routledge, 2005), 93–112.

6. James A. Bill, *The Eagle and the Lion: The Tragedy of American-Iranian Relations* (New Haven: Yale University Press, 1988); Richard Cottam, "American Policy and the Iranian Crisis," *Iranian Studies* 13 (1980): 279–305; Richard Cottam, *Iran and the United States: A Cold War Case Study*, 81–271. Mark J. Gasiorowski, *U.S. Foreign Policy and the Shah: Building a Client State in Iran* (Ithaca, N.Y.: Cornell University Press, 1991); Gasiorowski, "The 1953 Coup d' Etat in Iran," *International Journal of Middle East Studies* 19 (August 1987): 261–86; James F. Goode, *The United States and Iran, 1946–1951: The Diplomacy of Neglect* (London: Macmillan, 1989); Goode, *The United States and Iran: In the Shadow of Musaddiq* (London: Macmillan, 1997); Benson L. Grayson, *United States-Iranian Relations* (Washington,

D.C.: University Press of America, 1981); Barry Rubin, *Paved with Good Intentions: The American Experience in Iran* (Oxford: Oxford University Press, 1980); Gary Sick, *All Fall Down: America's Tragic Encounter with Iran* (New York: Random House, 1985).

7. Ali Ansari, *Confronting Iran: The Failure of American Foreign Policy and the Next Great Crisis in the Middle East* (New York: Basic Books, 2006); Ilan Berman, ed., *Taking on Tehran: Strategies for Confronting the Islamic Republic* (Lanham, Md.: Lexington Books, 2007); Babak Ganji, *Politics of Confrontation: The Foreign Policy of USA and Revolutionary Iran* (London: Tauris Academic Studies, 2006); David Houghton, *U.S. Foreign Policy and the Iran Hostage Crisis* (Cambridge: Cambridge University Press, 2001); Kenneth Pollack, *The Persian Puzzle: The Conflict Between Iran and America* (New York: Random House, 2004); Barbara Slavin, *Bitter Friends, Bosom Enemies: Iran, the United States, and the Twisted Path to Confrontation* (New York: St. Martin's Press, 2007).

Chapter One

Prelude to the U.S.-Soviet Confrontation in Iran

The origins of the U.S.-Soviet rivalry in Iran can be traced back to the Second World War period. In 1941, the British and the Soviets had entered into an alliance and occupied Iran to prevent German encroachment on the country, which could have led to subsequent attacks on the Soviet Union. The Soviets wanted to safeguard their southern borders, which they shared with Iran, as well as their oil fields in Baku, which lay in close proximity to the Iranian borders. The British wanted to protect their oil investments in southern Iran. Soviet troops occupied northern Iran, while British troops occupied the south. A neutral zone that included Tehran, the capital, was placed under Iranian control. The Anglo-Soviet occupation of Iran eventually led to the stationing of American troops in Iran in 1942 as part of the allied war effort.

Once their troops were stationed in Iran, the British and the Soviets began to interfere in Iranian affairs. The Iranian government preferred U.S. involvement in Iran to counterbalance British and Soviet influence in the country. For this reason, the Iranian government began to negotiate the terms of an oil concession with the United States between 1943 and 1944. The Soviets became furious and demanded a similar concession. Realizing that a dangerous situation had developed, the Iranian government announced that it would not negotiate any concessions with foreign powers. Between 1944 and 1945, the rivalry between the United States and the Soviet Union began to heat up in Iran and culminated in a crisis that became a contributing factor in the development of the Cold War. To understand the significance of the Anglo-Soviet occupation of Iran in 1941 that led to the U.S. involvement and the subsequent U.S.-Soviet confrontation, it is necessary to begin with the historical context of Anglo-Soviet rivalry in the country.

HISTORICAL BACKGROUND

In the nineteenth century, the British and the Russians had engaged in an unprecedented rivalry to spread their influence and control over Central Asia, which became known as the Great Game. It was within this context that Persia[1] became a pawn in the rivalry between the two powers. Russia's interest in Persia was primarily territorial, since the Russians were pursuing an expansionist policy. Once the Russians managed to occupy the Caucasus and Central Asian territory that had been formerly under Persian suzerainty, they forced the Persian Qajar monarchy to enter trade and loan agreements that were not to the country's benefit. The British initially saw Persia as a buffer state to India, which was their colony. British interest in Persia, however, changed dramatically in the early twentieth century, with the discovery of oil in the southern part of the country. Like their Russian counterparts, the British also entered into trade and loan agreements with the Qajar monarchy that were not beneficial to Persia.

The concessions granted by the Qajar monarchy to the British and the Russians included the establishment and management of Persian banks, industries, and railways. The people were outraged by these concessions and staged protests to end foreign influence. To this effect, Persian nationalists carried out a revolution in 1906 and presented the Qajar monarchy with a draft for a constitution. The Qajar monarchy acquiesced and later that year, Persia's National Assembly, the Majlis, convened for the first time.[2] Foreign influence in Persia, however, persisted.

Despite their rivalry over Persia and Central Asia, the British and the Russians decided to negotiate in order to protect their interests in the region. On August 31, 1907, the two powers concluded the Anglo-Russian Convention in St. Petersburg regarding Tibet, Afghanistan, and Persia. Tibet was regarded as a neutral buffer state. Afghanistan was considered a British protectorate. The Russians pledged to respect Tibet and Afghanistan's autonomy and refrained from any attacks. Persia was divided according to British and Russian zones of influence. The Russian zone covered northern Persia, the British zone southeastern Persia, and a neutral zone was designated at the center, which included Tehran, the capital. Despite their arrangements, the two powers agreed to respect Persia's sovereignty.[3]

There were several reasons behind the Anglo-Russian Convention of 1907. Both the British and the Russians were wary of the threat posed by Germany and its attempts to spread its influence in the Middle East and Central Asia. In 1902, the Ottomans had granted the Germans a concession to develop the Baghdad railway. The British feared that the German aim was to take control of Persia and India. The Russians feared that the Germans would gain a foothold in Central Asia, which could threaten their security.[4]

The Anglo-Russian fear of the spread of German influence into Persia and Central Asia became more apparent during the First World War. In 1915, Britain and Russia found out that the Germans were negotiating a treaty with Persia, and warned Persia not to get involved. In addition, Britain and Russia signed the Constantinople Agreement. According to this treaty, the British would allow the Russians to take control of Constantinople and the Turkish Straits once the Ottomans were defeated. The Russians, in turn, agreed that the British would take control of the neutral zone in Persia, which had been previously negotiated as part of the 1907 agreement.[5] The terms of the Constantinople Agreement, however, were never implemented.

As the First World War drew to a close, the Russians had to deal with internal strife and political turmoil from within. In February 1917, disgruntled Russians carried out a revolution that led to the abdication of Tsar Nicholas II. The Russian imperial government was replaced by a provisional government. The provisional government, in turn, was overthrown by the Bolshevik Revolution in November 1917, led by Vladimir Ilyich Lenin, who declared the founding of the Russian Soviet Federated Socialist Republic (RSFSR). The RSFSR itself became part of the Soviet Union, which was founded in 1922, with Lenin as its leader. In 1918, Leon Trotsky, the Soviet commissar of foreign affairs, informed the Persian government that the Anglo-Russian agreement of 1907 was no longer in effect. Lenin also sent a letter to the Persian government apologizing for Russia's past actions.[6]

Following the triumph of Lenin's Bolshevik Revolution in 1917, a civil war broke out which was fought between Soviet forces and members of the White Army, who were former Tsarist officers opposed to the Bolsheviks. In 1920, Soviet forces began to hunt down members of the White Army, who had begun to retreat. Some of these officers had sailed to the port of Enzeli in northern Persia. In order to capture these officers, Soviet forces occupied the Persian province of Gilan. The Persian government protested against this occupation but to no avail. Soviet forces then began to aid the Jangali movement in Gilan, which was a local pro-Soviet and anti-British movement led by Mirza Kuchik Khan. On June 4, 1920, Mirza Kuchik Khan announced the founding of the Gilan Soviet Republic.[7]

The Persian government decided to free Gilan from Soviet influence. On August 24, 1920, Persian forces led by Reza Khan Mir Panj, the commander of the Cossack Brigade, were able to free Rasht, the capital of the Gilan province. The Soviets realized that the Gilan Soviet Republic could not survive without additional Soviet troop deployment and therefore decided to negotiate a treaty with the Persian government. It took several months before the two sides concluded a treaty.

On February 21, 1921, Reza Khan carried out a military coup to bring an end to the corrupt practices of the Qajar monarchy as well as to the growing Soviet influence in the northern province of Gilan. Reza Khan was assisted by Sayyid Zia al-Din Tabataba'i, who was the editor of the *Ra'd* newspaper. Following the coup, Sayyid Zia became prime minister and Reza Khan was appointed minister of war. Reza Khan maintained this position until 1923, when he became the prime minister.[8]

On February 26, 1921, the Soviet and the Persian governments concluded a bilateral treaty. Because of this treaty, the Persian government was able to regain control over Gilan. The Soviets, however, had inserted Article VI as part of this agreement, which gave them the right to send their troops into Persia if they ever felt any threats on their southern borders.[9] The Soviets later used this article to legitimize their occupation of Iran in 1941.

As prime minister, Reza Khan began to exercise effective control over domestic and foreign affairs. He consolidated his power by building a new army, which was used to maintain order over the provinces. Furthermore, he had great influence over the cabinet and the Majlis. In 1923, Reza Khan forced the last ruling Qajar monarch, Ahmad Shah, into exile. With his dictatorial powers intact, Reza Khan then prepared to declare himself the Shah. The Majlis drafted an act declaring the end of the Qajar dynasty and granted Reza Khan supreme power. The act was approved on October 31, 1925. Reza Khan declared the founding of the Pahlavi Dynasty and took the title of Shah.[10]

In an attempt to diminish British and Soviet influence in the country, Reza Shah sought to involve a third power and utilized a Third Power Strategy.[11] He hoped that the presence of a third power would not only bring an end to British and Soviet interference in Persian affairs, but at the same time help reconstruct the economy that had been left in shambles by the Qajar dynasty. Reza Shah's choices at the time were the United States and Germany.

In 1922, before Reza Khan became the new Shah, the Persian government had asked the United States for a financial adviser. The United States sent Dr. Arthur Millspaugh as Treasurer General. Financial reform in Persia included measures that threatened the interests of many government officials, tribal chiefs, and even the clergy. Reza Khan had initially supported Millspaugh. However, once Reza Khan became the Shah, he refused to cooperate with Millspaugh and sought to reduce his powers. Millspaugh did not give in to Reza Shah's demands, and his mission came to an end in 1927.[12] Reza Shah then turned to Germany for help.

Reza Shah used German aid to reduce Persia's dependence on foreign imported goods. Persia, for example, was dependent on the Soviet Union for its import of cotton textiles. To free Persia from this dependence, Reza Shah built several textile mills near Tehran in 1931 under German supervision. Reza Shah also used German aid to improve the country's infrastructure including its road system and transportation facilities. The Germans were instrumental in building the Trans-Iranian Railway, which linked the southern part of the country to the north.[13] This railway would be used for the transport of supplies to the Soviet Union during the Second World War.

THE ALLIED OCCUPATION OF IRAN AND ITS CONSEQUENCES

In the aftermath of the First World War, Germany's main concern had been to revive its economy. It was in need of capital and natural resources for its industries. Germany was able to promote its interests in Persia by taking the third power role in that country. It began to strengthen its industries with Persia's natural resources and was able to establish a foothold in the Middle East.

By the mid-1930s, the British and the Soviets had become wary of the rise of German power in Europe and its growing influence in Iran, but they took no action at the time. The situation, however, changed during the Second World War, when Germany declared war on the Soviet Union in June 1941. As a result, the British and the Soviets entered into an alliance to prevent a German attack on the Caucasus and the Persian Gulf region. The British had to find a way to supply the Soviet Union while protecting the Iranian oil fields that were important to the war effort. Given its geographical location, Iran would be used as a route to send war supplies to the Soviet Union.

The Iranian government had declared its neutrality during the war, but it remained pro-German. Over the years, Germany had become Iran's trading partner and helped modernize the Iranian infrastructure. As a result, there were many Germans stationed in Iran. The Allies feared that these Germans would pave the way for a German invasion of the Soviet Union through Iran. As a result, Great Britain and the Soviet Union sent a letter to Reza Shah in July and again in August 1941 to expel the Germans. Reza Shah's refusal to comply led to the Anglo-Soviet occupation of Iran on August 25, 1941. The Soviets occupied the northern part of the country while the British occupied the south. The central part, which included Tehran, was declared neutral and left under the Iranian government's control. On August 27, 1940, Prime

Minister Hasan Ali Mansur resigned and was succeeded by Muhammad Ali Furughi. Shortly thereafter, on September 15, 1941, Reza Shah was forced to abdicate in favor of his son Muhammad Reza. Reza Shah left Iran and later settled in South Africa, where he died in 1944.[14]

Prime Minister Furughi pledged his government's cooperation with Allied war efforts in Iran. Sir Reader Bullard, the British minister in Iran, supported Furughi and considered him a competent politician. Bullard was under the impression that the majority of the Iranian ministers were supportive of British policies. He was even told by an Iranian politician, Ali Suhaili, who would later become prime minister, that the British could replace any Iranian minister whose performance they deemed unsatisfactory.[15] Following Reza Shah's departure from Iran, Furughi began to take inventory of the crown jewels, which had helped to support the Iranian currency. In addition, Furughi released several political prisoners who had been arrested during the reign of Reza Shah. Among these were fifty-two individuals who would form the Hizb-i Tudeh or the Tudeh Party.[16]

The origin of the Tudeh Party can be traced back to the activities of Dr. Taqi Arani, who was educated in Germany. Dr. Arani was drawn to Marxism and condemned dictatorship. While Arani advocated modernization, he wanted his country to retain its Persian character. Arani wanted the elimination of foreign words from the Persian language. He even went so far as to write an article that advocated the end of the usage of the Turkish dialect in the Iranian province of Azerbaijan, which happened to be his native province, and replacing it with the Persian language.[17]

In 1933, Arani began to publish the journal *Dunya* (World). The journal's publication ended in 1937 when Arani and fifty-two of his colleagues were jailed by Reza Shah's order. Arani died in prison, but his colleagues moved on to create the Tudeh Party once they were released in 1941. They chose the name Tudeh (Masses) so that its members would be drawn from different groups of people.[18] Even though the Tudeh Party was a communist party, it refrained from making any reference to communism in its program. This was because of a law passed in 1931 that banned any communist activities in Iran and which had led to Arani's arrest.[19]

In February 1942, the Tudeh Party published its provisional program, which emphasized the fight against dictatorship for the sake of achieving democracy, and the protection of human rights.[20] In October 1942, the Tudeh Party held its First Provisional Conference in Tehran, where a new program was announced to replace the provisional program. The new program was designed to appeal to different groups within the Iranian society.[21] A Provisional Central Committee was elected to guide the party until the convening of the First Party Congress in 1944.[22]

Meanwhile, the British, Soviet, and Iranian governments had begun to negotiate a tripartite treaty in an effort to improve relations following the Allied occupation of Iran. On January 29, 1942, Great Britain, the Soviet Union, and Iran, signed a tripartite treaty of alliance. According to this treaty, the Allied troops were given the right of passage and access to communication facilities in Iran, and that their presence was not considered a military occupation. The British and the Soviets agreed that their troops would withdraw from Iran no later than six months after war with the Axis powers had come to an end.

Prime Minister Furughi, who had been instrumental in negotiating the tripartite treaty, was unable to deal with certain problems such as the food shortages and tribal unrest in southwest Iran. He resigned and was succeeded in March 1942 by Ali Suhaili. Suhaili also had to deal with the problems of food shortages and tribal unrest in the country. In order to protect its oil interests in Iran, the British government asked Suhaili to address the grievances of the tribes that had revolted in southwest Iran.[23] To alleviate the food shortage in Iran, the British sent nearly 70,000 tons of wheat to the country.[24]

THE BEGINNING OF AMERICAN INVOLVEMENT IN IRAN

The origin of U.S.-Iranian relations is traced backed to the activities of Presbyterian missionaries, who had arrived in Persia in 1830s.[25] Even though Persia and the United States had established trade relations in 1856, official diplomatic relations did not begin until the American legation opened in Tehran in 1883.[26] In 1911, at the request of the Persian government, the United States sent Morgan Shuster to Persia as Treasurer General.[27] The Persian government had hoped to get the United States involved in its affairs to counterbalance British and Russian influence in the country. The Russians resented Shuster's presence in Persia and pressured the Persian government to terminate his services. Shuster eventually left Persia in January 1912. Russian objections to any U.S. involvement in Persia also became evident in 1921, when they forced the Persian government not to negotiate an oil concession with the Sinclair Oil Company.[28]

In 1922, the Persian government once again approached the United States and asked for a financial mission. The United States agreed and sent a financial mission led by Arthur Millspaugh.[29] This mission ran into difficulties because Reza Khan, who had just become the Shah, refused to cooperate with Millspaugh. As a result, Millspaugh's mission was terminated in 1927. A series of events between 1935 and 1937 created tensions in U.S.-Iranian relations. In 1935, the Iranian foreign minister in Washington was arrested for a traffic violation, which became a major source of embarrassment to the Iranian government.[30] In 1936, the *New York Mirror* printed an article about Reza Shah's harsh rule, referring to him as a former stable boy who had served the British legation.[31] Reza Shah responded by temporarily closing the Iranian legation in Washington. U.S.-Iranian relations survived nonetheless. In fact, in 1937, the Iranian government gave an oil concession to a subsidiary of the Seaboard Oil Company for the exploration of oil in the province of Khorasan. The company let go of the concession in 1938 due to unsuccessful exploratory drilling.[32]

In 1939, the United States maintained in Tehran a small diplomatic legation, whose main task was to prepare reports on political and economic developments in Iran. The personnel consisted of a chargé d'affaires, two secretaries who devoted their time to consular business, a clerk, and a translator.[33] In 1940, the United States sent Louis Dreyfus to serve as the first American minister in Iran. Dreyfus was a diplomat with no experience in Middle Eastern affairs. In time, he gained the trust of the Iranian people as he was sympathetic to their problems. Dreyfus was replaced by Ambassador Leland Morris in 1944, when the legation was transformed into an embassy. The Second World War and the Anglo-Soviet occupation of Iran in 1941 changed the activities of the American legation in Iran as it began to serve as an intermediary between the British, Soviet, and Iranian governments.

The Germans renewed their attacks against the Soviet Union in the spring of 1942. To aid the Soviets, the Allies sent supplies through Iran. Given the significance of this route, higher measures of security were required. Due to the weakness of the Iranian ports, and railways along with a British shortage of manpower for transport duties, the British decided that the U.S. Army should take over those operations in Iran.[34] At the same time, the British convinced the Shah and the Iranian government that it would be beneficial for Iran to utilize the services of American advisers in alleviating some of the problems the country was facing. Prime Minister Suhaili went before the Majlis and announced that he would invite American advisers to Iran.[35] In the summer of 1942, the American combined chiefs of staff met in Washington and decided that the primary responsibility for supplying the Soviet Union through Iran should be undertaken by the United States. As a result, the Persian Gulf Service Command was activated under the direction of Brigadier General Donald Connolly.[36]

In July 1942, prior to the arrival of the American advisers, Prime Minister Suhaili resigned and was replaced by Ahmad Qavam. The Soviets were pleased with Qavam's appointment because he was not supportive of British policies in Iran. The British had initially suspected Qavam of being supportive of the Soviets, but after an interview at the British legation, he was seen as being free from any Soviet influence.[37] Following this interview, Sir Reader Bullard notified the Shah of his approval of Qavam's appointment as prime minister.[38]

The American advisers began to arrive in Iran in August of 1942, prior to the arrival of the American troops. The Military Mission for the Reorganization of the Gendarmerie was led by Colonel H. Norman Schwarzkopf. It had a staff of three and was responsible for preparing the Iranian gendarmerie to promote better security in rural areas. The food adviser, Joseph P. Sheridan, and the police adviser, Stephen Timmerman arrived next. They faced several problems and had to ask the American legation for advice and mediation on their behalf with Iranian government officials.[39]

The Military Mission for the Iranian Army began its operations in the summer of 1942. It was later replaced by a more elaborate mission led by Major General Clarence Ridley to help train the Iranian Army. Finally, the financial mission to Iran was led by Dr. Arthur Millspaugh, who had previously served as Treasurer General in Iran from 1922 to 1927. The financial mission was scheduled to arrive and begin its operations in January of 1943.[40]

In September 1942, representatives from the U.S. Lend-Lease Office and the U.S. Commercial Cooperation arrived in Tehran to supervise the distribution of lend-lease materials to the Iranian government. Later that year, a representative from the Office of War Information was assigned to Iran, and an office of the War Shipping Administration was established at the Iranian port of Khoramshahr. In December 1942, nearly 20,000 American troops began to arrive at Khoramshahr to assist in delivering supplies to the Soviet Union, and improving the Iranian transportation system.[41]

In January 1943, Arthur Millspaugh returned to Iran as Treasurer General. Millspaugh knew that if he were to succeed at carrying out any financial reforms in Iran, he would have to be given special powers. He was able to acquire those powers in 1943 due to the American legation's support. Millspaugh's major reform was his income tax project. The Majlis deputies, who consisted mainly of wealthy individuals, did not want to pass any legislation that would affect their interests. Millspaugh, in turn, submitted his resignation. The American legation was able to persuade the Iranian government that it was necessary to cooperate with Millspaugh. Even though the income tax legislation was enacted and Millspaugh resumed his duties, he was unable to enforce that legislation. The Majlis and the Iranian government's opposition to Millspaugh eventually led to his final resignation in 1945.[42]

Joseph P. Sheridan, the American food adviser, also had his share of problems with Millspaugh. In the fall of 1942, Sheridan had helped the Iranian government overcome a severe food shortage with American supplies. However, Millspaugh's economic activities came to include the supervision of the harvest, which Sheridan refused to accept. As a result, Sheridan left Iran in July 1943, and his tasks were taken over by Millspaugh.[43]

In February 1943, Qavam resigned and was once again replaced by Ali Suhaili, the former prime minister. Like his predecessor, Suhaili had to deal with the problems of food shortages and inflation. During this time, the American Army in Iran continued with its Allied war efforts, as it supervised the Iranian railway and heavy trucks to deliver supplies to the Soviet Union. The American Army built a large camp in Tehran and the headquarters of the Persian Gulf Command was also moved to Tehran.[44]

In the spring of 1943, President Franklin D. Roosevelt sent General Patrick Hurley to observe and report about the activities of the American troops and the political situation in Iran. Hurley sent Roosevelt a report about the problems he witnessed. He described the ongoing British and Soviet rivalry in Iran, and recommended that the United States either continue to cooperate with the British or take a firm stance in pursuing its interests in Iran. Hurley noted that the United States' conciliatory approach to the Soviets had led to negative developments. He explained how the operations of the American Army Intelligence units in northern Iran had been rendered useless because of Soviet objections. Hurley then put forth several recommendations for the U.S. government to consider among which was the transformation of the American legation in Iran into an embassy.[45] Hurley was also critical of Louis Dreyfus for not speaking out against Anglo-Soviet interference in Iranian affairs. Roosevelt accepted Hurley's recommendations, which were implemented between 1943 and 1944.

Meanwhile, the Iranian government had been thinking about becoming a signatory to the United Nations Declaration of January 1, 1942. On July 5, 1943, the Iranian government expressed its desire in a memorandum to the American, British, and Soviet governments.[46] The United States replied that the Iranian government had to agree to certain points before hand. The most important was for Iran to give up its neutrality and declare war on Germany and the Axis powers. Iran agreed and on September 9, 1943, declared war on Germany and the Axis powers. As a result, Iran was allowed to become a signatory to the United Nations Declaration of January 1, 1942.[47]

Iran was also acknowledged for its cooperation with the Allies at the Tehran Conference that took place on December 1, 1943. This conference was attended by Franklin D. Roosevelt, Joseph Stalin, and Winston Churchill, who signed a Tripartite Declaration. Even though the conference focused primarily on the Allied war efforts, it nonetheless provided Iran with a chance to secure certain objectives. Among these were the Allies' acknowledgment of Iran's help during the war and their pledge to honor Iran's sovereignty.[48]

U.S.-SOVIET COMPETITION FOR OIL CONCESSIONS IN IRAN

Iran's oil soon led to tensions among the Allies. In 1943, the Iranian government wanted to grant an oil concession to the Standard Oil Company of New Jersey. As a result, the Iranian government began to negotiate with Standard-Vacuum Oil, which was a company operated by Standard Oil and Sinclair Oil. In the spring of 1944, Prime Minister Suhaili resigned and was replaced by Muhammad Saed. At the same time, the American companies had reached a decision and submitted their proposals to obtain an oil concession in southern Iran.[49]

The Soviets were displeased by these developments and sent Sergei Kavtaradze, their representative, to Iran to negotiate an oil concession in northern Iran with exploration to begin within five years.[50] The Soviet proposal was supported by members of the Tudeh Party, who had managed to elect nine of its candidates to the Majlis.[51] The Iranian government became alarmed at the Soviet proposal and the Tudeh Party's support. Therefore, the Iranian government notified the American, British, and Soviet embassies that negotiations for oil concessions would be postponed until the war had come to an end.

The Soviets responded with a negative propaganda attack against Prime Minister Saed and his cabinet. The Tudeh deputies in the Majlis accused Prime Minister Saed of favoring the Americans over the Soviets and declared that the Soviet Union should be allowed to compete for concessions. The Tudeh Party also organized demonstrations throughout October in support of the Soviet Union. As a result, Prime Minister Saed resigned.[52] Decades later, Nur al-Din Kianuri, a prominent Tudeh leader, stated in his memoirs that the Soviets wanted to prevent the spread of American influence in Iran, especially the northern region, which they considered their sphere of influence. Kianuri believed that the Tudeh Party had made a mistake in attacking Saed's government and should have been more cautious about Soviet proposals.[53]

On November 20, 1944, Morteza Qoli Bayat succeeded Saed as prime minister. Despite the Iranian government's announcement that it would postpone any discussion of oil concessions until the end of the war, the issue was threatening Iran's political stability. On December 2, 1944, Muhammad Musaddiq, a well-known politician, introduced a bill in the Majlis that forbid the Iranian government from concluding any agreement with a foreign government that could lead to further problems for Iran.[54]

NEGOTIATIONS FOR THE ALLIED TROOP WITHDRAWAL FROM IRAN

There were numerous negotiations regarding the question of Allied troop withdrawal from Iran. The first was the Yalta Conference, which took place in February 1945. Prior to the conference, Churchill had sent Roosevelt a telegram discussing how the Soviets had reacted over the negotiations for an oil concession in Iran. Churchill observed how the Soviets were upset over the Iranian government's decision not to grant concessions until the end of the war and how their actions had forced Prime Minister Saed to resign. Churchill added that the Soviet government had to uphold the 1943 Tehran Declaration, which emphasized the Allies' respect for Iran's sovereignty.[55] Shortly thereafter, Muhammad Shayesteh, the Iranian foreign minister, asked Edward Stettinius, the American secretary of state, to place the question of the Allied troop withdrawal from Iran on the agenda at the Yalta Conference.[56]

On February 8, 1945, Iran was discussed at the meeting of the foreign ministers at Yalta. Anthony Eden, the British foreign minister, emphasized that the Allies should not pressure Iran to negotiate any oil concessions until the war had ended. Vyacheslav Molotov, the Soviet Foreign Minister, replied that the Iranian government's decision not to grant oil concessions was contrary to what it had previously negotiated. He was displeased with Eden's suggestion of removing Anglo-Soviet troops from Iran.[57] Thus, the issue of foreign troop withdrawal from Iran remained unresolved.

Meanwhile, the Tudeh Party had organized demonstrations against the Iranian government throughout the country. On March 3, 1945, riots by the Tudeh Party in Isfahan led to clashes with the police.[58] On March 8, 1945, the Tudeh Party held demonstrations in Tabriz to protest the Iranian government's crackdown in Isfahan, which resulted in clashes with the police. The Tudeh Party then sent a telegram to the Majlis asking for the removal of the governor of Azerbaijan and the punishment of government officials involved in actions against the Tudeh Party.[59] The Iranian government ignored the Tudeh Party's demands and continued its crackdown on the party's activities.

In April 1945, the Iranian government received the news of President Roosevelt's death. Roosevelt was succeeded by his vice president, Harry Truman, who pledged to uphold the principles of the Atlantic Charter. The Truman administration would become the first U.S. administration to launch a major crusade against communism and Stalin's expansionist policies. Truman developed a greater interest in Iran and would provide strong diplomatic support for Iran in its case, which it filed with the United Nations against Soviet interference in Azerbaijan. In contrast to his predecessor, Truman would rely extensively on the State Department, which played a key role in the making of U.S. foreign policy.

The end of the war in Europe in May 1945 provided the Iranian government an opportunity to pressure the Allied powers to withdraw their troops from Iran. During this time, Prime Minister Bayat had resigned, and the Shah nominated Ibrahim Hakimi as Bayat's successor. On May 18, 1945, the Shah met with Leland Morris, the American Ambassador. The Shah told Morris that the Iranian government would inform the British and the Soviet governments to uphold the terms of the Tripartite Treaty of 1942, which specified the withdrawal of their troops six months after the end of the war. At the time, the Shah had not mentioned anything about the American troops to Morris. The Iranian government nonetheless delivered letters to the British, Soviet, and American embassies in Tehran requesting that their troops be withdrawn from Iran.[60]

The British and Soviet governments replied that their troops had the right to remain in Iran for six months following the end of the war with Japan, as specified in the Tripartite Treaty of 1942. The United States, however, agreed to withdraw its troops from Iran and announced that as of June 1, 1945, the army's supply mission from Iran to the Soviet Union would end. There were, however, two important issues that the United States wanted the Iranian government to know. First, it would take a few months before the United States could find available transportation to remove all its troops from Iran. Second, the United States preferred maintaining a small number of its military personnel in Iran to run the airbase at Abadan, which was considered a vital link to East Asia.[61]

Meanwhile, Prime Minister Hakimi's cabinet had failed to gain the approval of the Majlis. Hakimi had initially received sixty-four votes in the Majlis to form a cabinet, but the Majlis refused to accept his cabinet after much debate.[62] Therefore, Hakimi's cabinet fell apart and Muhsin Sadr was nominated as the next prime minister. On June 20, 1945, Prime Minister Sadr met with Wallace Murray, who had replaced Leland Morris. Murray had previously served as the chief of the Division of Near Eastern and African Affairs at the State Department. Prime Minister Sadr relayed his concern to Murray about the developments in Iran. Sadr thought that most of the Majlis deputies were pro-British, while a small number were pro-Soviet. Due to these circumstances, the Iranians were unable to handle their domestic affairs. Murray said that the issue of foreign interference in Iran had to be discussed at a future meeting attended by the Allied powers.[63]

The question of Allied troop withdrawal from Iran was discussed at the Potsdam Conference on July 21, 1945. Anthony Eden argued that the British and Soviet troops had to first withdraw from Tehran and then from the rest of the country. Stalin agreed to the troop withdrawal from Tehran but refused a complete withdrawal from the country. He believed that the Allied troops had to remain in Iran for six months until the war with Japan had ended. It soon became clear why Stalin was stalling. Soviet troops stationed in northern Iran had begun aiding Azeri and Kurdish rebels to set up their autonomous regimes inside Azerbaijan.[64]

Churchill did not oppose Stalin, since the British wanted to maintain control over the oil fields in southern Iran. Truman did not object to the delay in British and Soviet troop withdrawals from Iran, because he wanted to transfer American troops from Iran to East Asia.[65] Truman's position is understandable given the fact that at the time, the United States had no special interests in Iran and was aware of the British and Soviet interests there. The question of troop withdrawal from Iran remained unsolved until the London meeting of the Council of Foreign Ministers in late September.

The dropping of the U.S. atomic bomb on Hiroshima and Nagasaki, and the Japanese surrender on September 2, 1945, meant that the Allied troop withdrawal from Iran would be completed by March 2, 1946, six months after the war was over. On September 9, 1945, the Iranian government informed the Allied powers that it was setting the deadline for the evacuation of all troops on March 2, 1946.[66] The British and the Soviets agreed to Iran's deadline. The Iranian government had a major stake in the Allied troop withdrawal, since the political situation in Iran's northern provinces had began to deteriorate. The Soviets were encouraging separatist movements inside the Iranian province of Azerbaijan. Armed by the Soviets, the Azeris and the Kurds rebelled against the Iranian government and established their own autonomous regimes inside Azerbaijan; this became known as the Iranian Crisis of 1945–1946.

NOTES

1. Iran was formerly known as Persia. The name Persia is traced back to the ancient Greeks, who called the country based on one of its provinces, Fars. The West continued to use the name Persia for a long period of time. In 1935, Reza Shah officially changed the name of the country from Persia to Iran to emphasize its Indo-European heritage. I have used the name Persia to refer to the country before 1935, and Iran for the period thereafter.

2. George Lenczowski, *Russia and the West in Iran, 1918–1948: A Study in Big-Power Rivalry* (Ithaca, N.Y.: Cornell University Press, 1949), 4; Rouhollah K. Rama-

zani, *The Foreign Policy of Iran, 1500–1941* (Charlottesville: University of Virginia Press, 1966), 83–85.

3. Amin Banani, *The Modernization of Iran* (Stanford, Calif.: Stanford University Press, 1961), 8; Richard Frye, *Iran* (New York: Holt, 1953), 58; Firuz Kazemzadeh, *Russia and Britain in Persia, 1896–1914* (New Haven: Yale University Press, 1968), 498; Lenczowski, *Russia and the West in Iran*, 4; John Marlowe, *Iran* (London: Pall Mall Press, 1963), 35–36; Ramazani, *Foreign Policy of Iran, 1500–1941*, 92; A. J. P. Taylor, *Struggle for Mastery in Europe* (Oxford: Clarendon Press, 1954), 442; Richard H. Ullman, *Anglo-Soviet Relations, 1917–1921* (Princeton, N.J.: Princeton University Press, 1961–1973), vol. 1, 303.

4. Kazemzadeh, *Russia and Britain in Persia*, 593; Lenczowski, *Russia and the West in Iran*, 5; Ramazani, *Foreign Policy of Iran, 1500–1941*, 89–91; Taylor, *Struggle for Mastery in Europe*, 442–45.

5. Peter Avery, *Modern Iran* (London: Ernest Benn, 1965), 134; William Cleveland, *A History of the Modern Middle East* (Boulder, Colo.: Westview Press, 2004), 162; Kazemzadeh, *Russia and Britain in Persia*, 677–79; Bruce Kuniholm, *The Origins of the Cold War in the Near East: Great Power Conflict and Diplomacy in Iran, Turkey, and Greece* (Princeton, N.J.: Princeton University Press, 1980), 133; Lenczowski, *Russia and the West in Iran, 1918–1948*, 44; Ramazani, *Foreign Policy of Iran, 1500–1941*, 128; Malcolm Yapp, *The Making of the Modern Near East, 1792–1923* (New York: Longman, 1987), 275–76.

6. Avery, *Modern Iran*, 201; Kuniholm, *The Origins of the Cold War in the Near East*, 133, n. 8; Ramazani, *Foreign Policy of Iran, 1500–1941*, 148.

7. Cosroe Chaqueri, *The Soviet Socialist Republic of Iran, 1920–1921* (Pittsburgh: University of Pittsburgh, 1995); Kuniholm, *The Origins of the Cold War in the Near East*, 133; Lenczowski, *Russia and the West in Iran*, 51; Muhammad Ali Manshur, *Siyasat-i Dowlat-i Shoravi dar Iran* (The Soviet Policy in Iran) (Tehran: n.p., 1327/1948), 41–42; Martin Sicker, *The Bear and the Lion: Soviet Imperialism in Iran* (New York: Praeger, 1988), 41; Ullman, *Anglo-Soviet Relations*, vol. 3, 369–89; Sepehr Zabih, *The Communist Movement in Iran* (Berkeley: University of California Press, 1966), 7–40.

8. Hussein Amirsadeghi and R. Ferrier, eds., *Twentieth-Century Iran* (New York: Holmes & Meyer, 1977), 24–25; Avery, *Modern Iran*, 203–204; Amin Banani, *The Modernization of Iran, 1921–1941* (Stanford, Calif.: Stanford University Press, 1961), 36, 40–42; Cyrus Ghani, *Bar Amadan-i Reza Khan Bar Uftadan-i Qajar va Naqsh-i Ingilis-ha* (Iran: The Rise of Reza Khan, the Fall of the Qajars, and the Role of the British) (Tehran: Niloofar, 1377/1998), 186–222; Ramazani, *Foreign Policy of Iran, 1500–1941*, 66.

9. Frye, *Iran*, 72–73; George Lenczowski, ed., *Iran Under the Pahlavis* (Stanford, Calif.: Hoover Institution, 1978), xvii; Lenczowski, *Russia and the West in Iran*, 25, 52; Gunther Nollau and Hans Wiehe, *Russia's South Flank: Operations in Iran, Turkey, and Afghanistan* (New York: Praeger, 1963), 21; Sicker, *The Bear and the Lion*, 44; Zabih, *The Communist Movement in Iran*, 40–41.

10. Avery, *Modern Iran*, 152; Banani, *The Modernization of Iran*, 43; Frye, *Iran*, 73–74; Ghani, *Iran*, 396–411; Kuniholm, *The Origins of the Cold War in the Near*

East, 134; Lenczowski, *Russia and the West in Iran*, 59; Marlowe, *Iran*, 48–49; Ramazani, *Foreign Policy of Iran, 1500–1941*, 177–85; Joseph M. Upton, *The History of Modern Iran: An Interpretation* (Cambridge, Mass.: Harvard University Press, 1960), 50–51; Donald Wilber, *Iran, Past and Present* (Princeton, N.J.: Princeton University Press, 1976), 125–30; Zabih, *The Communist Movement in Iran*, 40–45.

11. The Iranian government's use of the "third power" or "Third Power Strategy" is actually traced back to the Qajar period. It was later pursued by Reza Shah and his son, Muhammad Reza as part of Iran's foreign policy. Authors who have discussed this issue extensively include: Ramazani, *Foreign Policy of Iran, 1500–1941*, 18, 25, 29, 39, 70, 203–11, 277–80; Ramazani, *Iran's Foreign Policy, 1941–1973* (Charlottesville: University of Virginia Press, 1975), 70–72; and Shaul Bakhash, "The Failure of Reform: The Premiership of Amin al-Dawla, 1897–88," in Edmond Bosworth and Carole Hillenbrand, eds., *Qajar Iran: Political, Social, and Cultural Change, 1800–1925* (Edinburgh: Edinburgh University Press, 1983), pp. 14–34. While Ramazani's analysis encompasses both the Qajar and the Pahlavi period, Bakhash's analysis is limited to the Qajar period of rule.

12. Avery, *Modern Iran*, 262–63; Banani, *The Modernization of Iran*, 115–17; Lenczowski, *Russia and the West in Iran*, 152; Arthur Millspaugh, *Americans in Persia* (Washington, D.C.: Brookings Institution, 1946), 22–26; Ramazani, *Foreign Policy of Iran, 1500–1941*, 209–10.

13. Avery, *Modern Iran*, 302–303; Banani, *The Modernization of Iran*, 131–37; John DeNovo, *American Interests and Policies in the Middle East, 1900–1939* (Minneapolis: University of Minnesota Press, 1963), 297–302; Frye, *Iran*, 226; Kuniholm, *The Origins of the Cold War in the Near East*, 137; Lenczowski, *Russia and the West in Iran*, 152–55; T. H. Vail Motter, *The United States Army in World War II: The Middle East Theater: The Persian Corridor and Aid to Russia* (Washington, D.C.: Department of the Army, 1952), 331; Ramazani, *Foreign Policy of Iran, 1500–1941*, 284–85.

14. Avery, *Modern Iran*, 327–28; Fakhreddin Azimi, *Iran: The Crisis of Democracy, 1941–1953* (London: Tauris, 1989), 35; Sir Reader Bullard, *The Camels Must Go* (London: Faber and Faber, 1961), 227; Winston Churchill, *The Grand Alliance* (London: Cassell, 1950), 484–85; Kuniholm, *The Origins of the Cold War in the Near East*, 140; Lenczowski, *Russia and the West in Iran*, 168–71; Mark Lytle, *The Origins of the Iranian-American Alliance, 1941–1953*, 10; Muhammad Reza Pahlavi, *Mission For My Country* (London: Hutchinson, 1960), 70–72; Rouhollah Ramazani, *Iran's Foreign Policy, 1941–1973*, 30–32.

15. Bullard to FO, 22 September 1941, FO 371 EP 27158 as cited in Azimi, *Iran: The Crisis of Democracy, 1941–1953*, 40.

16. U.S. Embassy in Tehran, "War History Report," 25 September 1945, RG 84, Box 9, Confidential Files 1940–1952, File No. 124.06/9-2545, 8, National Archives, College Park, Md.

17. Ervand Abrahamian, "Communism and Communalism in Iran: The Tudeh and the Firqah-i Dimukrat," *International Journal of Middle Eastern Studies* 1 (1970): 297–98.

18. Ervand Abrahamian, "Communism and Communalism in Iran: The Tudeh and the Firqah-i Dimukrat," *International Journal of Middle Eastern Studies* 1 (1970): 298–300; Ervand Abrahamian, *Iran Between Two Revolutions* (Princeton, N.J.: Princeton University Press, 1982), 281–83; Buzurg Alavi, *Panjah va Seh Nafar* (The Fifty Three Individuals) (Tehran: Amir Kabir, 1357/1978), 191; Kianuri, Nur al-Din, *Khatirat-i Nur al-Din Kianuri* (The Memoirs of Nur al-Din Kianuri) (Tehran: Ittila'at, 1371/1992), 67. Kianuri had been a member of the Tudeh Party for over Forty years and was chosen as First Secretary in 1978. Following the Islamic Revolution of 1979, Kianuri was imprisoned for ten years. Shortly after his release, the Didgah Research Institute interviewed Kianuri from 16 May 1991 through 27 April 1992 at his home in Tehran. The present work is a collection of his memoirs. Anvar Khamahi, *Panjah Nafar va Seh Nafar, Khatirat-i Anvar Khamahi* (Fifty and Three Individuals, the Memoirs of Anvar Khamahi) (Tehran: Hafteh, 1363/1984), 10–11.

19. Iraj Iskandari, "Histoire de Parti Toudeh," *Moyen-Orient* 6 (December 1949): 9, as quoted in Zabih, *The Communist Movement in Iran*, 73–74; Faramarz Fatemi, *The U.S.S.R. in Iran* (London: Thomas Yoseloff, 1980), 8; L. P. Elwell-Sutton, "Political Parties in Iran," *Middle East Journal* 3 (January 1949): 47.

20. Abrahamian, *Iran Between Two Revolutions*, 282. A full discussion of Tudeh's program is provided by Ahmad Qasemi, *Hizb-i Tudeh-yi Iran chi Miguyad va chi Mikhahad?* (What Does the Tudeh Party Say and What Does it Want?) (Tehran: Tudeh Press, 1322/1943).

21. Tudeh Party, "Party Program," *Rahbar*, 12 February 1943, as cited in Abrahamian, *Iran Between Two Revolutions*, 284.

22. Abrahamian, *Iran Between Two Revolutions*, 286.

23. Bullard to FO, 6 March 1942, FO 371 EP31390, as cited in Azimi, *Iran: The Crisis of Democracy*, 55.

24. Azimi, *Iran: The Crisis of Democracy*, 56.

25. Abraham Yeselson, *United States–Persian Diplomatic Relations, 1883–1921* (New Brunswick, N.J.: Rutgers University Press, 1956), 8–11.

26. Yeselson, *United States-Persian Diplomatic Relations*, 20–26.

27. Morgan Shuster, *The Strangling of Persia* (Washington, D.C.: Mage, 1987), 3–15.

28. U.S. Embassy in Tehran, "Memorandum Prepared for the Conference in Istanbul," 12 December 1949, RG 84, Box 22, Confidential General Records 1940–1952, National Archives, College Park, Md.

29. U.S. Embassy in Tehran, "Memorandum Prepared for the Conference in Istanbul."

30. Mark Lytle, *The Origins of the Iranian-American Alliance, 1941–1953* (New York: Holmes & Meyer, 1987), 6.

31. Richard Cottam, *Iran and the United States: A Cold War Case Study*, (Pittsburgh: University of Pittsburgh Press, 1988), 53; Lytle, *The Origins of the Iranian-American Alliance*, 6.

32. U.S. Embassy in Tehran, "Memorandum Prepared for the Conference in Istanbul."

33. U.S. Embassy in Tehran, "War History Report," 25 September 1945, RG 84, Box 9, Confidential Files 1940–1952, File No. 124.06/9-2545, 3–4, National Archives, College Park, Md.

34. Lytle, *The Origins of the Iranian-American Alliance*, 27.

35. *Muzakerat-i Majlis*, 19 April 1942, as cited in Azimi, *Iran: The Crisis of Democracy*, 58.

36. U.S. Embassy in Tehran, "War History Report," 13.

37. Bullard to Eden, 10 April 1942, FO371 EP31385, as cited in Azimi, *Iran: The Crisis of Democracy*, 64.

38. Bullard to FO, 29 July 1942, FO 371 EP31385, as cited in Azimi, *Iran: The Crisis of Democracy*, 64.

39. U.S. Embassy in Tehran, "War History Report," 10.

40. U.S. Embassy in Tehran, "War History Report," 10.

41. U.S. Embassy in Tehran, "War History Report," 12–13.

42. U.S. Embassy in Tehran, "War History Report," 18–19.

43. U.S. Embassy in Tehran, "War History Report," 19.

44. U.S. Embassy in Tehran, "War History Report," 20.

45. United States, Department of State, *Foreign Relations of the United States, 1943*, Diplomatic Papers, vol. 4, *The Near East and Africa* (Washington, D.C.: Government Printing Office, 1964), 363–70 (hereafter cited as *Foreign Relations of the United States*); Kuniholm, *The Origins of the Cold War in the Near East*, 149.

46. *Foreign Relations of the United States, 1943*, 4: 431–33.

47. *Foreign Relations of the United States, 1943*, 4: 435.

48. *Foreign Relations of the United States*, Diplomatic Papers, *The Conferences at Cairo and Tehran, 1943* (Washington, D.C.: Government Printing Office, 1961), 840–41; Ramazani, *Iran's Foreign Policy, 1941–1973*, 62–63.

49. Nasrollah S. Fatemi, *Oil Diplomacy: Powderkeg in Iran* (New York: Whittier, 1954), 228–29.

50. Fatemi, *Oil Diplomacy*, 235–36.

51. Zabih, *The Communist Movement in Iran*, 78–79.

52. Fatemi, *Oil Diplomacy*, 231.

53. Kianuri, *Khatirat-i Nur al-Din Kianuri* (The Memoirs of Nur al-Din Kianuri), 102–103.

54. Fatemi, *Oil Diplomacy*, 248–51; Sicker, *The Bear and the Lion* (New York: Praeger, 1988), 63–64.

55. *Foreign Relations of the United States*, Diplomatic Papers. *The Conferences at Malta and Yalta, 1945* (Washington, D.C.: Government Printing Office, 1955), 336–37.

56. *Foreign Relations of the United States, 1945*, Diplomatic Papers, vol. 8, *The Near East and Africa* (Washington, D.C.: Government Printing Office, 1969), 360.

57. *Foreign Relations of the United States*, Diplomatic Papers, *The Conferences at Malta and Yalta, 1945*, 738–40.

58. Lenczowski, *Russia and the West in Iran*, 233.

59. U.S. Department of State, RG 59, Decimal File 891.00/3-245, 20 March 1945, Ebling to Secretary of State, National Archives, College Park, Md.

60. *Foreign Relations of the United States, 1945*, 8: 371.
61. *Foreign Relations of the United States, 1945*, 8: 375–79.
62. Azimi, *Iran: The Crisis of Democracy*, 121–23.
63. *Foreign Relations of the United States, 1945*, 8: 383.
64. *Foreign Relations of the United States, 1945*, 8: 386–88.
65. *Foreign Relations of the United States, 1945*, Diplomatic Papers, vol. 2, *The Conference of Berlin (Potsdam)* (Washington, D.C.: Government Printing Office, 1960), 590–94.
66. *Foreign Relations of the United States, 1945*, 8: 402–403.

Chapter Two

The Iranian Crisis of 1945–46 and Its Role in Initiating the Cold War

The Iranian Crisis of 1945–46 played a significant role in the development of the Cold War between the United States and the Soviet Union. This crisis began in 1945 with the rebellion of the Azeris and the Kurds against the Iranian government to establish their own autonomous regimes in the Iranian province of Azerbaijan. The Azeris and the Kurds had long standing grievances against the Iranian government for neglecting to take measures to improve their living conditions, and disregarding their civil liberties. The Soviets were supportive of the Azeri and Kurdish aspirations and played a major role in organizing their separatist movements. The Iranian government dispatched its troops to restore control over the Azerbaijan province. Soviet troops stationed in northern Iran, however, prevented Iranian troops from entering Azerbaijan.

In 1946, Iran filed a complaint at the United Nations Security Council against the Soviet Union for its interference in the Azerbaijan crisis. The Soviet Union eventually withdrew its troops from northern Iran in the spring of 1946 due to U.N. and U.S. pressure, as well as negotiations with the Iranian government, who had agreed to grant the Soviets an oil concession and the establishment of a joint Iranian-Soviet oil company. The Iranian crisis was not settled until December 1946, when Iranian troops finally gained control of the Azerbaijan province. The effects of this crisis, however, lingered throughout 1947, as the Soviets were expecting the Majlis to approve the Iranian-Soviet agreement for the establishment of a joint oil company. The Majlis, however, refused. The Soviets, in turn, subjected Iran to a period of intense hostile propaganda. At the same time, U.S.-Soviet rivalry escalated in Iran, with repercussions to follow.

REBELLION IN AZERBAIJAN

The Azeris and the Kurds, two minority groups in Iran, had several grievances against the Iranian government. Many of these people lived in poverty and wanted the Iranian government to meet their basic human needs. For years, the Iranian government had disregarded the rights of these people, as evidenced by their inadequate representation in the Majlis. The Soviet Union decided to support the Azeris and the Kurds in establishing their own autonomous regimes in the Iranian province of Azerbaijan. The Soviet Union used its influence through the Tudeh Party and its troops stationed in northern Iran to aid the Azeri and Kurdish separatist movements.

The Tudeh Party's loyalty to the Soviet Union was evident by the publication of a special article in one of its newspapers in Azerbaijan. The article emphasized the importance of Iran maintaining good relations with the Soviet Union, since it would help strengthen movements within the country striving for liberty and justice.[1] The Iranian government became alarmed at the activities of the Tudeh Party and ordered a crackdown. General Hasan Arfa, the Iranian chief of staff, began to carry out plans to destroy the party. General Arfa punished army officers suspected of being Tudeh members and reassigned many to distant parts of the country, such as Zahedan.[2] The Iranian government then declared martial law on August 23, 1945. Shortly thereafter, the police raided the offices of the Tudeh Party in Tehran, and its publications were shut down.[3] The news of the government's crackdown on the Tudeh Party, led to an uprising by groups of armed workers and peasants in Mazandaran province in northern Iran. The Iranian government sent its forces to restore order, but they were prevented to enter Mazandaran by Soviet forces stationed in northern Iran. The Soviets stated that they did not want the Iranian forces to disrupt peace nor jeopardize their forces.[4]

The founding of two pro-Soviet political parties in September 1945, would make the Azeri and Kurdish dreams of establishing their own autonomous regimes in northern Iran a reality: the Democratic Party of Azerbaijan and the Democratic Party of Kurdistan. Ja'far Pishihvari founded the Firqah-i Dimukrat-i Azerbaijan or the Democratic Party of Azerbaijan. While Pishihvari was born in Tabriz, he had migrated to Baku at a young age. Pishihvari was exposed to communist ideology through his membership in the Adalat Committee, which was a branch of the Bolshevik Party in the Caucasus. Upon his return to Iran, and a visit to Tehran in 1930, Pishihvari was jailed by Reza Shah's orders on charges of being a communist. Following his release from jail in 1941, Pishihvari joined the Tudeh Party.[5] He left the party soon thereafter due to ideological differences.

In May 1943, Pishihvari founded the newspaper *Azhir* (Alarm), which often published articles critical of the Tudeh Party.[6] In his memoirs, Pishihvari noted that the Tudeh Party had weakened due to years of strife among its members and their not knowing what direction to take within the framework of Iranian politics.[7] Pishihvari ran as a candidate from Azerbaijan for the Majlis elections in 1943–44 and won. At the opening of the Majlis session, Pishihvari delivered a speech, which condemned the dictatorship and corruption that had plagued Iran's political system, and how the country was being exploited by foreign powers. Because of this speech, many Majlis deputies became suspicious of Pishihvari's intentions and his credentials were ultimately rejected in July 1945.[8]

Pishihvari was upset by his experience with the Majlis and the Tudeh Party. He returned to Azerbaijan and declared the founding of the Democratic Party of Azerbaijan on September 3, 1945. The goals of this party were to achieve Azerbaijan's autonomy, the permanent use of the Azeri dialect as the official language of Azerbaijan, and advancing economic growth and social justice.[9] In order to increase membership, Pishihvari allowed members of the Tudeh Party in Azerbaijan to join his party. The Tudeh Party leaders in Tehran were displeased with Pishihvari's actions, since they favored the maintenance of a unified Iranian state. While the Tudeh Party agreed with Pishihvari that the Iranian government had to respect the rights of its minority groups, it did not support secessionism.[10]

The Tudeh Party leaders in Tehran held a special meeting to discuss the founding of Pishihvari's party. Khalil Maleki, a well-known Tudeh leader, stated that Pishihvari's actions had weakened any chances of a socialist future in Iran. Maleki and other Tudeh leaders issued a resolution refusing to acknowledge Pishihvari's party. The Soviet embassy, however, asked the Tudeh Party to refrain from publishing and distributing this resolution among the public. The Soviets argued that the resolution would be harmful to the future of socialism in Iran. As a result, the Tudeh Party refrained from publishing its resolution and instead sent its warm wishes to Pishihvari on the founding of his party.[11]

On September 14, 1945, George Kennan, the American chargé d'affaires in Moscow, reported to the State Department that the Soviet press had provided special coverage regarding the founding of Pishihvari's Democratic Party. The Soviet government agreed with Pishihvari that there was no freedom under the Shah's rule and that people's lives would not improve. Furthermore, the Azeris had the right to make their own decisions regarding the question of autonomy.[12] Kennan thought that there were certain similarities between what was happening in Azerbaijan and other parts of the world, such as Armenia and Sinkiang. He believed that the Soviets were taking advantage of minority groups and nationality problems to divide and conquer the world.[13]

Using Pishihvari as a role model, Qazi Muhammad, a Kurdish leader, founded the Democratic Party of Kurdistan in September 1945. The Soviets had arranged for Qazi Muhammad to visit Baku beforehand in order to guide and help him set up his party.[14] Qazi Muhammad was from Mahabad, located in southwest Azerbaijan. Mahabad's population consisted mainly of Kurds. The Kurds initially had a small party known as Komala (Committee), founded in 1943 to represent their interests. The Komala, however, was an ineffectual party due to organizational problems and small membership. As a result, it was replaced by the Democratic Party of Kurdistan.

There were certain differences between the Democratic Party of Kurdistan and Pishihvari's Democratic Party of Azerbaijan. The members of Pishihvari's party consisted mainly of Iranians, who had previously resided in the Soviet Union and become acquainted with communist ideology as well as former members of the Tudeh Party. The members of the Democratic Party of Kurdistan comprised of Kurdish leaders, who had hardly any education or knowledge of communism for that matter. For these reasons, the Soviets found it more difficult to interact with the Kurds. Nonetheless, Soviet agents managed to secure the cooperation of the Kurds by providing cash and guns to them.[15]

Meanwhile, the U.S. government had been observing the developments in Iran with concern. On September 25, 1945, Ambassador Murray wrote to James Byrnes, the American Secretary of State, that the Soviet goal was not only to take control over the Iranian province of Azerbaijan, but eventually to establish a pro-Soviet regime in Iran. These developments, in turn, would harm British oil interests in Iran and American oil interests in Saudi Arabia and other parts of the Middle East. Murray recommended for the United States to take a stronger stand, as the war had ended and there was no need for foreign troops to remain in Iran.[16] This memorandum shows that the Truman administration, unlike its predecessor, had a clear conception of its interests in the Middle East and saw Iran as a buffer state to its oil interests in Saudi Arabia and the Persian Gulf region. However, the United States would develop a direct interest in Iranian oil by 1953, and Iran's strategic importance would become greater than ever.

Meanwhile, Mikhail Maximov, the Soviet ambassador to Iran, had met with Murray, to discuss political developments in Iran. Maximov argued that the Iranian government was persecuting individuals who were opposed to the Shah's dictatorship. Further, the Iranian government did not appreciate the efforts of Soviet troops to restore order in the north, nor the efforts of the American advisers in Iran. Maximov added that the Iranians were critical of the

United States for its Lend-Lease program. Earlier in 1945, the United States had notified the Iranian government that it could purchase surplus property from the U.S. Army. Iranian newspapers had reflected negatively on this issue, observing that Iran's purchase of U.S. military equipment would worsen its weak economy.[17] It was obvious from this conversation that the Soviets were not only displeased with Iran's plan to purchase U.S. military surplus property, but with the gradual warming of U.S.-Iranian relations.

In October 1945, the Democratic Party of Azerbaijan stepped up its efforts to establish an autonomous regime in Azerbaijan by organizing several demonstrations against the Iranian government. These demonstrations eventually led to the disruption of communication lines between Azerbaijan and Tehran. On November 16 and 17, 1945, militia groups loyal to the Democratic Party of Azerbaijan took control of a vast area in Azerbaijan from Sarab to Mianduab.[18]

By November 19, 1945, Iranian newspapers and radio reported that the Democratic Party had taken control of Azerbaijan. The Shah ordered Iranian forces to head to Azerbaijan, yet they were stopped at Qazvin by Soviet forces and threatened if they proceeded. On November 20, 1945, the Iranian attaché in Washington asked the State Department for advice about this issue. The Iranian government also sent letters to the Soviet Union on November 22 and 23, demanding to know why Iranian troops had been prevented from entering Azerbaijan.[19]

At the same time, Ambassador Murray met with Ahad Yakubov, the Soviet consul in Tehran, to discuss the crisis in Azerbaijan. Yakubov said that the activities of the Democratic Party in Azerbaijan were not unlawful, as reported by the Iranian press. Yakubov added that the Soviet forces had not interfered with Iran's public security and that the Soviet government would investigate the situation.[20]

On November 24, 1945, Averell Harriman, the American ambassador to the Soviet Union, delivered a letter from his government to the Soviet government regarding the situation in Iran. The letter stated that the Iranian government had notified the United States about several riots that had occurred in northern Iran, where Soviet troops were stationed. When Iranian troops were sent by the Shah to gain control over Azerbaijan, they were prevented by Soviet forces from proceeding. The United States reminded the Soviet Union of its pledge to respect the principles of the Tehran Declaration of 1943, and informed the Soviet government that all American forces would be withdrawn from Iran by January 1, 1946, suggesting that Soviet and British forces do the same.[21]

On November 24, 1945, the Soviet government responded to the United States, stating that the information about the uprisings in northern Iran was not accurate and that the people of Azerbaijan were only asking the Iranian government to respect their rights. Soviet troops had prevented Iranian troops from crossing into Azerbaijan to prevent further chaos. The Soviet Union would continue to respect the principles of the Tehran Declaration and saw no reason why it should remove its forces by January 1, 1946.[22] At the same time, Hussein Ala, the new Iranian ambassador to the United States, met with President Truman to discuss the political situation in Iran. President Truman sympathized with Ala and the problems that Iran was experiencing.[23]

Meanwhile, the Central Committee of the Democratic Party sent a statement of its policies to the American, British, and Soviet consuls. It emphasized that the people of Azerbaijan had the right to a democratic government and to this end would elect and send their own representatives to the Majlis. On December 12, 1945, the Democratic Party held its First National Assembly in Tabriz, where it declared the establishment of the Autonomous Republic of Azerbaijan and Pishihvari as its prime minister.[24]

Following these developments, Qazi Muhammad sent five Kurdish delegates to represent the Democratic Party of Kurdistan at the National Assembly in Tabriz.[25] The Kurdish delegates, however, could make no sense of the Assembly's activities and returned to Mahabad. This was followed by a Kurdish uprising in Mahabad and western Azerbaijan. On December 15, 1945, members of the Kurdish Democratic Party proclaimed the founding of the Kurdish People's Republic and Qazi Muhammad became its president.[26]

On December 18, 1945, Prime Minister Hakimi went before the Majlis and discussed the crisis in Azerbaijan. He noted how the Soviets were behind these events, and that the Iranian government had to remain strong in order to defeat Pishihvari and his party.[27] At the same time, the Iranian government was aware of the developments taking place next door, in Turkey. The Iranian press provided full coverage of the problems that existed between the Soviet Union and Turkey. Turkish-Soviet relations had become strained due to Soviet claims on the Turkish provinces of Ardahan and Kars, as well as the Soviet intention to gain control of the Turkish Straits.[28] Iran and Turkey were in no position to take any action against the Soviet Union and instead focused on the Moscow Conference of Foreign Ministers, which was scheduled for December 16–26, 1945.

On December 19, 1945, Secretary of State Byrnes and Stalin met to discuss the crisis in Azerbaijan. Byrnes reminded Stalin of the Allied pledge to respect Iran's sovereignty and warned that the Iranian government would file a complaint against the Soviet Union at the United Nations. Stalin, in turn, discussed issues that were of concern to the Soviet Union. Among these was that Iranians could cross over into Soviet Azerbaijan and sabotage the Baku oil fields. Stalin argued that the Soviet troops were not interfering in Iranian affairs. He said that the Russo-Persian Treaty of 1921 gave the Soviet Union the right to send its troops into Iran if its security was ever threatened. Furthermore, it was up to the Soviet Union to decide when it would withdraw its forces from Iran.[29]

On December 20, 1945, the Iranian government decided that it would file a complaint against the Soviet Union for interfering in the Azerbaijan crisis, and informed the American, British, and Soviet governments accordingly.[30] Following the Iranian government's announcement, Ernest Bevin, the British foreign minister, proposed that the three Allied powers put together a commission that would visit Iran and report on the Azerbaijan crisis. The U.S. and Soviet governments agreed to this plan.[31] On January 1, 1946, Sir Reader Bullard, the British ambassador in Iran, informed the Iranian government of Bevin's proposal, which was discussed by the Majlis. The Iranian government worried that the commission's activities would lead to more foreign intrigues in the country.[32] Therefore, it rejected Bevin's proposal and said that an Iranian negotiating team led by Sayyid Hasan Taqizadeh would place Iran's complaint against the Soviet Union before the Security Council meeting, which was scheduled to meet in London. On January 19, 1946, Taqizadeh asked the Security Council to review Iran's case and recommend measures to settle it.

Andrei Vyshinsky, the head of the Soviet negotiating team, rejected Iran's accusations and said that the Soviets had a right to maintain their troops on Iranian soil according to the terms of the Russo-Persian Treaty of 1921, and the Tripartite Treaty of 1942. He argued that the Soviet troops were not involved with the crisis in Azerbaijan and that the Soviets were facing negative propaganda from the Iranian government.[33] Having heard from both sides, the Security Council announced that Iran and the Soviet Union had to negotiate and keep the council informed of the result.[34]

THE SETTLEMENT OF THE IRANIAN CRISIS

While the Iranian case was being reviewed at the Security Council, Prime Minister Hakimi resigned and was succeeded by Ahmad Qavam. Qavam thought that the best way to solve the Azerbaijan crisis was to pursue policies that were conciliatory to the Soviets. He dismissed Hasan Arfa, the Iranian chief of staff, who had previously carried out campaigns against the Tudeh Party, along with other government officials opposed to the Soviet Union.[35] Qavam then contacted Stalin and asked if he could visit the Soviet Union to negotiate and settle the Azerbaijan crisis. Stalin agreed, and Qavam left for Moscow on February 19, 1946. Qavam met with Stalin and requested that the Soviet troops withdraw from northern Iran. Stalin argued that the Soviets had the right to maintain their troops in Iran according to the Russo-Persian Treaty of 1921. At the same time, Stalin indicated his government's interest in negotiating an oil concession with Iran and the establishment of an Iranian-Soviet oil company, which Qavam refused at the time.[36]

Following his meeting with Qavam, Stalin gave a speech about the differences between communism and capitalism, which received much coverage across the world. On February 22, 1946, George Kennan, the American chargé in Moscow, sent a long telegram to the State Department, which would provide the groundwork for the U.S. strategy of containment.[37] Kennan had provided an analysis of the Soviet Union's objectives and its shortcomings following the end of the Second World War, and by doing so had shed light on Soviet behavior toward countries such as Iran and Turkey. Kennan stated that the only way for the West to triumph was to remain strong in face of Soviet challenge.[38] The State Department provided copies of Kennan's telegram to the president and other governmental departments. Republican politicians used this telegram as well as Stalin's speech to criticize the Truman administration's policy and soft stance toward the Soviet Union. These comments would indeed lead the Truman administration to take a tougher stance toward the Soviet Union. In a speech on February 28, 1946, Secretary of State Byrnes, reaffirmed the U.S. government's intention to defend the values stated in the United Nations Charter.[39]

The deadline for the evacuation of the Allied troops from Iran was March 2, 1946. The American and British forces had left but the Soviet forces remained. The Iranian government sent a letter protesting to the Soviet Union, and Hussein Ala, the Iranian ambassador to the United States, notified Secretary of State Byrnes about this issue.[40] At the same time, Robert Rossow, the American vice consul in Tabriz, reported that Soviet troops had begun to move toward Tehran and the Turkish border. The Soviets wanted Turkey to surrender its eastern provinces of Ardahan and Kars, and to grant them control of the Turkish Straits.[41]

On March 6, 1946, the State Department sent a letter to the Soviet government asking it to respect the terms of the Tripartite Treaty and withdraw its troops from Iran.[42] At the same time, Rossow sent telegrams from Tabriz noting the constant movement of Soviet troops throughout northern Iran. The United States delivered another letter to the Soviet Union on March 8 asking it for an explanation to which the Soviet Union never responded.[43]

Following his trip from Moscow and the meeting with Stalin, Qavam made arrangements to meet with Wallace Murray, the American ambassador in Iran. Murray asked Qavam to remain strong and promised U.S. support for Iran. The two men met again on March 14, 1946, and Murray supported

Iran's right to defend itself. Murray also asked Qavam to watch out for a possible Tudeh-inspired coup, which could subsequently lead to the occupation of Tehran by Soviet forces.[44]

On March 15, 1946, one of Qavam's advisers went to see Murray for advice. The Soviet chargé had met Qavam and warned him not to make any further complaints to the U.N. Security Council, as it would have serious consequences for Iran. Murray notified Secretary of State Byrnes and asked for advice. Byrnes replied that Qavam had to file an appeal with the Security Council, and that Murray should reassure Qavam of continuous U.S. support for Iran.[45]

On March 18, 1946, Ambassador Ala once again brought the Iranian issue before the United Nations and asked that it be placed on the Security Council's agenda scheduled for March 25. The next day, Andrei Gromyko, the Soviet representative to the United Nations, asked the council to postpone the meeting, as Iran and the Soviet Union were conducting negotiations.[46] Edward Stettinius, the American representative, told the Security Council that he would place Iran's complaint at the top of the agenda during the forthcoming meeting and would expect both sides to report the results of their talks. President Truman was displeased with Gromyko's attitude and reaffirmed U.S. support for Iran.[47]

In the meantime, Ivan Sadchikov, the new Soviet ambassador to Iran, was pressuring Qavam to reach an agreement. On March 24, 1946, Sadchikov gave Qavam three official letters from his government. The first letter said that the Soviet troops would be evacuated from Iran within six weeks. The second letter proposed the establishment of an Iranian-Soviet oil company, with the majority of the shares going to the Soviet Union. The third letter offered Soviet Union's help in settling the Azerbaijan crisis through negotiations with Pishihvari.[48] Qavam accepted the contents of the first two letters but rejected the third on the basis that the Azerbaijan crisis was a domestic issue and had to be settled by the Iranian government.

The Azerbaijan crisis was discussed once again at the Security Council meeting on March 25, 1946. Gromyko argued that since Iran and the Soviet Union had reached an agreement regarding the removal of the Soviet troops, Ala's letter of 18 March should not be included on the Security Council's agenda. Secretary of State Byrnes replied that he knew nothing about this agreement and that the issue would have to be placed on the agenda. The following day, Gromyko proposed that the discussion of the Iranian issue be postponed until April 10, or else his government would not participate in the negotiations. The Security Council refused, and on March 27 placed Iran's case on its agenda. Gromyko rejected this decision and left in anger.[49] When the Security Council met on March 29, the Soviet negotiating team was absent. The Security Council announced that it would meet on April 3, 1946, and expected both sides to report the results of their talks. Negotiations between the two sides, however, took longer than expected therefore the Security Council decided that it would review the case on May 6.[50]

On April 4, 1946, Qavam informed Ambassador Murray that the Iranian and Soviet governments had reached an agreement on the following points: Soviet troops would withdraw from Iran by May 6, 1946; the proposal for the establishment of a joint Iranian-Soviet oil company would be submitted to the Majlis; and the Azerbaijan crisis was recognized as a domestic problem that was to be resolved by the Iranian government.[51] At the same time, Walter Bedell Smith, the new American ambassador to the Soviet Union, met with Stalin to discuss the Azerbaijan crisis. Stalin was upset by Iran's complaint to the U.N. and the slow pace of negotiations with the Iranian government over obtaining an oil concession. Smith replied that while the United States would not interfere with Soviet interests, the idea of obtaining an oil concession seemed unfair. Smith then asked about Turkish-Soviet relations. Stalin replied that the Soviets wanted to patrol the Turkish Straits because the Turks were in no position to control the Straits effectively.[52]

The United States had provided diplomatic support for Iran at the Security Council and decided to do the same for Turkey to ward off any Soviet intimidation. The death of Mehmet Ertegun, the Turkish ambassador to the United States provided such opportunity for the United States. The Turkish embassy had asked the United States if it could return Ertegun's body to Turkey on a battleship. This measure was taken as a courtesy for diplomats who had died during service. The United States agreed and chose the U.S.S. *Missouri*. On April 6, 1946, the *Missouri* arrived at Istanbul with Ertegun's body. This gesture was to highlight U.S. support for Turkey especially in light of constant Soviet harassment of the Turks.[53]

On April 6, 1946, Gromyko wrote a letter to the Security Council asking it to remove the Iranian case from its agenda. Secretary of State Byrnes refused.[54] Qavam told Murray that he was ready to withdraw the Iranian complaint from the Security Council due to continuous Soviet pressure. Murray advised Qavam not to do so, as it would further weaken Iran. Qavam, however, instructed Ala to withdraw Iran's complaint from the Security Council.[55] Edward Stettinius, stated that while it appeared that an agreement had been reached between the Iranians and the Soviets, the Security Council had no concrete proof that all Soviet troops had withdrawn from northern Iran. The Security Council would remove this case from its agenda on May 6, 1946, if it knew for sure that the Soviet troops were gone.[56]

The Security Council met on May 6, 1946 as planned. On that day, Gerald Dooher, the American vice consul in Tabriz, reported that Soviet troops had withdrawn from northern Iran. But Ambassador Ala told the council that there was not enough proof to verify the Soviet troop withdrawal from northern Iran. Since the Soviet representative was absent, the Security Council postponed its hearings until May 20, 1946, when the Iranian representative was to submit an official report regarding the complete withdrawal of Soviet troops from northern Iran.[57]

In the meantime, Qavam and Ala argued over the settlement of the Iranian crisis. While Qavam wanted to placate the Soviets, Ala wanted U.N. involvement in the matter. On May 20, 1946, Ala wrote to the Security Council that the Iranian government could not verify complete Soviet troop withdrawal from northern Iran. The following day, however, Qavam asked Ala to inform the Security Council that the Soviet troops had withdrawn from Azerbaijan. Both Ala and Stettinius refused Qavam's report, which upset Qavam and the Soviets.[58]

On May 28, 1946, the American embassy in Iran asked Qavam not to pressure Ala to withdraw the Iranian complaint from the Security Council, as it would weaken Iran's arguments against the Soviet Union. On the same day, the Security Council announced that it expected an official report from the Iranian government regarding the complete Soviet troop withdrawal from northern Iran and made June 4 the deadline for the submission of this report. There was no further word from the Iranian government. The Security Council therefore did not hold a meeting that week, nor for the remainder of 1946 regarding the Iranian issue.[59] Eventually it became known that the Soviets had withdrawn their troops from northern Iran by the end of May 1946.

An important question here is whether President Truman ever sent an ultimatum to the Soviet Union to withdraw its troops from northern Iran. The only evidence that might hint at such ultimatum is found in a press conference and radio broadcast. On April 24, 1952, Truman made the following statements, "In 1945 I had to send an ultimatum to the head of the Soviet Union to get out of Iran. They got out because we were in a position to meet a situation of that kind."[60] Later that day, a representative from the White House told the press, "The President had used the term ultimatum in a non-technical layman sense. The President was referring to the United States leadership in the United Nations and finding a solution through diplomatic channels, in the spring of 1946, which became the major factors in Soviet withdrawal from Iran."[61] There is no doubt that U.S. support for Iran was one of the key reasons why the Soviets decided to withdraw their troops from northern Iran. But there was another critical reason. The Soviet departure carried a certain price for the Iranian government, which was the granting of an oil concession and establishment of an Iranian-Soviet oil company with the majority of the benefits going to the Soviet Union.

Meanwhile, Ambassador Wallace Murray had been replaced by George V. Allen, who had previously served as the deputy director of Near Eastern and African Affairs at the State Department. Compared to his three predecessors and his successors, Allen was one of the most influential American ambassadors ever assigned to Iran. In fact, he became the first American ambassador to get directly involved in Iranian affairs.

In a report to the State Department on June 8, 1946, Allen observed that Qavam was trying too hard to appease the Soviet Union and the Tudeh Party. Allen was critical of Qavam for removing Ala from his post as the Iranian representative to the Security Council, and the arrest of Hasan Arfa, the Iranian chief of staff, without any specific reasons. Allen thought that the United States had to advise Qavam about the direction of his policies, which could prove harmful in the long run.[62] While Allen's speculation with regard to Qavam's policies were accurate, he seemed unaware that Qavam was trying to placate the Soviets through negotiations and compromise with the Tudeh Party until the Azerbaijan crisis was settled. In fact, Qavam would approach the U.S. government time and time again to ask for financial and military aid and even sought U.S. support in his decision to end the Azerbaijan crisis in 1946.

Qavam tried to negotiate with Pishihvari to end the Azerbaijan crisis. On June 13, 1946, the Iranian government concluded a special agreement with Pishihvari. As part of this agreement, the Iranian government would recognize the National Assembly of Azerbaijan as the Provincial Council. The Provincial Council would nominate a group of candidates for the position of governor of Azerbaijan. The Iranian government would then choose the governor of Azerbaijan from this list. In addition, seventy-five per cent of the revenues generated from tax collection in Azerbaijan would be set aside for the province, with the remainder going to the Iranian government.[63] Following his negotiations with Pishihveri, Qavam announced the founding of a new party called the Democratic Party of Iran, which would be led by him. Qavam had created this party to undermine Pishihvari's party and help prevent the spread of communism in Iran.[64]

Following their humiliation in the Security Council, the Soviets decided to retaliate against Iran. The Soviets used their influence through the Tudeh Party and the Workers' and Toilers' Union, whose members were Iranian workers at the Anglo-Iranian Oil Company (AIOC), to create problems in the Khuzistan province, which was part of the British sphere of influence. The Tudeh Party led strikes against the AIOC in May and June of 1946 asking for a raise for the workers. In addition the Tudeh Party wanted the AIOC to pay its workers more for work done on Friday (which is the Iranian day off).[65] The AIOC refused to pay extra for work done on Friday as it was expecting the

Iranian government to submit information about its new labor law and issues pertaining to minimum wage.[66]

The Tudeh Party and the workers then organized a general strike, which took place on July 14, 1946, in Khuzistan. The Iranian government considered this strike illegal, since the participants had not notified nor asked for the government's permission. On that day, workers, who were Tudeh supporters, clashed with a group of Arabs living in the area. The Arabs were against the Tudeh Party and favored maintaining the status quo. The Tudeh Party thought that the British were arming the Arabs in the area in order to protect their oil investments in southern Iran. To restore order, the Iranian government declared martial law in Khuzistan.[67] Qavam sent Mozafar Firuz as one of his representatives to Abadan to negotiate with the workers. Sir Claremont Skrine, a consul at the British embassy also went to Abadan to negotiate with the workers. The issue of minimum wage and payments for work done on Friday was settled, but the AIOC refused to give any payment to workers during the period of the strikes.[68]

Meanwhile, the State Department had issued a report regarding U.S. policy toward Iran. It stated that the U.S. policy was to maintain Iran's sovereignty and help its people improve their standard of living through democratic reforms.[69] In a meeting with Ambassador Allen on July 31, 1946, the Shah said that he wanted to obtain a financial loan from the United States to help improve the economy and his people's standard of living, which would serve as a shield against the spread of communism and negative Soviet propaganda. The Shah knew that his government had to come up with a specific plan for economic development before the United States would consider any loans to Iran. Ambassador Allen replied that Iran could receive financial aid for certain purposes, such as an airline project under the supervision of TWA or an electric power project under the supervision Westinghouse.[70] Allen then informed the State Department about the Shah's request for U.S. financial aid.

Meanwhile, Qavam had changed his cabinet and appointed three Tudeh Party members as ministers. Prior to these appointments, the Tudeh Party had pressured Qavam to take certain key issues into consideration. Among these were for Qavam to make changes within his cabinet to include Tudeh Party members and for Qavam's Democratic Party to unite with other parties such as the Tudeh Party, and the Democratic Party of Azerbaijan and Kurdistan.[71] Iraj Iskandari, was one of the Tudeh members, who joined Qavam's cabinet. He later wrote in his memoirs that the reason why the Tudeh Party wanted its members to join Qavam's cabinet was to strengthen the party's position within the Iranian political system and bring an end to the Shah's oppressive rule.[72]

On August 13, 1946, Qavam told Ambassador Allen about his dissatisfaction with the Tudeh ministers and the political stalemate in Azerbaijan. Qavam said that he had thought about using military force to bring Azerbaijan under the Iranian government's control. Qavam then asked Allen whether Iran could expect any help from the United States if the Soviet Union were to get involved. Allen advised Qavam not to use force and instead suggested continuous negotiations with Pishihvari. Allen had initially been wary of Qavam's interaction with the Tudeh Party but he later observed in a memorandum to the State Department that Qavam wanted to maintain good relations with the United States. Furthermore, Qavam's request to extend the terms of the GENMISH for an additional two years, as well as support for a U.S. oil concession in southeastern Iran, proved that he wanted to maintain good relations with the United States.[73]

On September 9, 1946, the Iranian government asked the United States for a loan in the amount of $50 million to help carry out economic development projects.[74] The United States said that it would consider this request. In a meeting with Allen, Qavam emphasized that Iran was experiencing critical domestic problems and asked for U.S. financial and military aid in the amount of $250 million. Allen replied that Iran could expect no more than $10 million in credit from the Export-Import Bank. The United States would not sell any military equipment at this time, since it had refused to sell to other countries. Allen nonetheless told Qavam that he would report his request for financial and military to the U.S. government.[75]

Meanwhile, the Soviets were pressuring the Iranian government to hold elections for a new Majlis that would ratify the Iranian-Soviet oil agreement. In addition, the Soviets wanted the Iranian government to agree to the creation of an Iranian-Soviet aviation company that would operate in northern Iran. The Soviets got so impatient that they sent a representative from the Soviet embassy in Tehran to ask Iraj Iskandari, one of the Tudeh ministers, why the Iranian government was stalling to approve the agreements.[76] Allen discussed these matters with the Shah, observing that Qavam's cabinet had to be changed for the sake of political stability. Allen advised the Shah to order Qavam to remove the Tudeh ministers from his cabinet or resign.[77] The Shah presented Qavam with the two choices. Qavam, in turn, dismissed the Tudeh ministers and formed a new cabinet.

On October 18, 1946, the State Department issued a report regarding U.S. policy toward Iran. It said that the key objective of U.S. policy was to maintain Iran's sovereignty free from Soviet control. At the same time, it was important for the United States to promote its military and economic interests in the Middle East. To prevent Iran from falling to communism, it was necessary for the United States to provide diplomatic support as well as financial and military aid.[78] The memorandum then recommended a series of steps for the U.S. government to take into consideration: Ambassador Allen should convince the Shah of U.S. support for Iran's sovereignty; the Exim Bank should provide a loan to Iran so that it could pursue development projects; the United States should provide military aid to Iran to help strengthen its domestic security; and cultural ties between United States and Iran should be promoted by means of special programs.[79]

On October 22, 1946, Allen notified Secretary of State Byrnes about a meeting with Abul Hasan Ibtihaj, the director of Iran's National Bank, who had asked for U.S. financial aid to carry out economic development projects. Ibtihaj said that the Iranian government would prepare the necessary details for each project and submit them to the Exim Bank and the World Bank accordingly. Ibtihaj said that the Iranian government needed nearly $250 million in foreign credits.[80] Allen informed the State Department that the United States could help by supervising an economic and engineering survey, which was estimated to cost $225,000.[81] This survey was needed before the Iranian government could provide details for each project and submit its application for financial credits.

Meanwhile, in a radio address on October 27, 1946, Qavam said that the Iranian government was planning to hold elections for the Majlis and that it would announce the date shortly thereafter. Qavam had made this announcement to placate the Soviets, who were upset that it had taken so long for the Iranian government to hold elections for the Majlis, which in turn was supposed to ratify the Iranian-Soviet agreement.[82] The following day, Secretary Byrnes announced that the United States had agreed to sell a limited amount of weaponry, not exceeding $10 million, to Iran.[83] Encouraged by this news, Qavam announced that elections for Majlis would be held on December 7, 1946. Qavam added that Iranian forces would be sent to the provinces to maintain order during the elections.[84]

The Soviet embassy in Tehran contacted Qavam and the Shah asking whether the Iranian government was planning to regain control over Azerbaijan. The Shah and Qavam, who had previously discussed the issue, said that the Iranian forces were being sent to Azerbaijan to maintain order during the elections.[85] On November 27, 1946, the Iranian newspaper *Ittila'at* published an interview with Ambassador Allen asking for his opinion about the Iranian government's decision to send its forces throughout the country, to maintain order during the elections. Allen had replied that Iran had made the right choice and the United States supported Iran's sovereignty.[86]

While Qavam and the Iranian government were preparing to send security forces throughout the country in connection with the elections, the Soviet embassy warned that the movement of the Iranian forces in the northern provinces would be considered a threat to Soviet security. Qavam told Allen about the Soviet warning. Allen advised Qavam to carry on as planned and that the Iranian government could always notify the Security Council if the Soviets were to interfere.[87] Iranian forces entered Tabriz on December 11, 1946, and took control of Azerbaijan. Pishihvari's supporters had tried to resist the Iranian forces but to no avail. Pishihveri fled across the border to the Soviet Union, where he was granted refuge.[88]

The Shah told Allen that the crisis in Azerbaijan had ended due to the efficient conduct of the Iranian forces and U.S. support for the maintenance of Iran's sovereignty.[89] There was no immediate reaction from the Soviets, as much remained at stake. The Soviets were still waiting for the day when the Iranian Majlis would ratify the Iranian-Soviet oil agreement.

The United States was pleased with the return of Azerbaijan to the Iranian government's control and believed that it was time for the Iranian government to put its house in order through necessary social and economic reforms. The Iranian government took a significant step on December 17, 1946, when it signed a contract with Morrison-Knudsen International Engineering Company. This was an American firm, which was to study Iran's infrastructure and prepare a report pertaining to issues such as agriculture and irrigation methods, industries, and transportation so that Iran could apply for loans from the Export-Import Bank and the World Bank to pursue its economic development projects.[90]

Even though the Iranian government had previously said that it would hold elections on December 6 and had sent its forces to the provinces as part of the deal, elections had not been conducted as planned. It became obvious that the Iranian objective had been to take effective control over Azerbaijan, which had been successfully achieved. Throughout the remainder of December 1946, the Soviets pressured the Iranian government to hold elections for a new Majlis that would ratify the Iranian-Soviet oil agreement. Elections for the Fifteenth Majlis took place on January 12, 1947. The Majlis, however, announced that it would not meet right away, as it had to go over the credentials of its deputies. For the time being, the Iranian government was able to stall the ratification of the oil agreement.

During this period, unexpected developments in international affairs led the United States to launch its first major crusade against communism. The principles of the crusade were embodied in the Truman Doctrine. On February 21, 1947, the British government had sent two important letters to Loy Henderson, the director of the Office of Near Eastern and African Affairs. These letters indicated that the British government could no longer provide financial aid to Greece and Turkey after March 31, 1947. The British government wanted the United States to take over this role.[91]

Loy Henderson notified George C. Marshall, the new U.S. secretary of state, about these letters. Secretary Marshall, however, was overseas at the time, therefore Dean Acheson, the under secretary of state, took action. Acheson set up a committee to study the issue and recommended that the United States take over the British role in providing aid to Greece and Turkey. President Truman and other governmental departments agreed to this recommendation. Both Acheson and Henderson played an important role in preparing a speech that would persuade the U.S. Congress and the people of a new U.S. policy that was needed to protect the country's interests overseas from the threat of international communism.[92]

Acheson had met with several congressional members beforehand to prepare them for Truman's speech. Acheson discussed the problems endured by Iran and Turkey, which had resulted from Soviet interference in their affairs. He added that Greece would fall to communism, if it did not receive U.S. financial and military aid.[93] Acheson believed that if the Soviets gained control of Greece and Turkey, it would pave the way for the spread of communism in other countries such as Iran. The United States was the only power that could save those countries. Henderson and Acheson had initially thought about placing Iran in the same category of Greece and Turkey, but they decided not to so as it would interfere with British interests. The British government had not mentioned Iran as part of its request to the United States, because it wanted to protect its oil investments.[94]

On March 12, 1947, President Truman went before the Congress and presented the Truman Doctrine. He asked Congress to authorize U.S. military and financial assistance for Greece and Turkey in the amount of $400 million. Truman discussed the fight between the forces of democracy and totalitarian rule that was taking place around the world. Congress discussed the issue for several weeks, and eventually passed a law whereby the United States would provide military and financial assistance to Greece and Turkey.[95]

The Truman Doctrine was greeted with mixed results in Iran. The Shah told Ambassador Allen that he was pleased with the fact that the United States would provide assistance to Greece and Turkey. The Shah said that even though Iran did not seem to be a target for Soviet attack, the weakness of the Iranian Army would eventually encourage a renewal of Soviet activities in the country. The Shah said that while he understood the reasons behind U.S. aid to Greece, given the activities of the communist guerrillas, he could not understand why Turkey was receiving more aid than Iran. The Shah added that the Soviet claim on the Turkish Straits was nothing but rhetoric, and if the Soviets took any measures, Turkey could always file a complaint with the United Nations.[96] The Shah was upset that Iran was not mentioned as part of the Truman Doctrine and said that he expected better treatment from the United States.

In March 1947, Qavam gave a New Year's speech to the Majlis and said that the Iranian government wanted to carry out a seven-year economic plan for the country. Qavam emphasized that the major source of financing for Iran's development plans was the AIOC. This, in turn, alarmed the British government, because it knew that the Iranian government expected the AIOC to raise Iran's share of oil revenues. In an attempt to divert the Iranian government's attention from the AIOC, the British embassy told Qavam that the British Middle East Office (BMEO) in Cairo would help the Iranian government with its economic development plans. Qavam agreed to meet with a group of BMEO advisers who specialized in agriculture, forestry, and animal husbandry. The BMEO, however, lost to an American competitor, the Overseas Consultants Incorporated (OCI), who in 1948 managed to sign contracts with the Iranian government.[97]

On April 10, 1947, an Iranian negotiating team visited the United States to discuss the purchase of U.S. surplus military equipment. The U.S. government had agreed to sell Iran a limited amount of military supplies to help strengthen the Iranian Army and Gendarmerie in providing better security in the country.[98] The United States granted Iran a credit in the amount of $25 million for the purpose of purchasing U.S. surplus military equipment.[99]

The Iranian government still had to deal with the Iranian-Soviet agreement of 1946 and its ratification by the Majlis. Even though the Majlis met on July 17, 1947, it did not resume its legislative activities until August 26. On August 30, the new Majlis voted for Qavam to continue as prime minister, and he was reappointed by the Shah.[100] The Soviets continued to pressure the Iranian government to have the Majlis ratify the oil agreement. The United States was aware of these pressures and continued its support for Iran. On September 11, 1947, in a gathering at the Iranian-American Cultural Society, Ambassador Allen said that the United States respected Iran's sovereignty and that Iran was in charge of its own natural resources.[101] Shortly thereafter, the United States extended the services of its military and gendarmerie agreements with Iran until May 20, 1949. The U.S. Army Mission (ARMISH) became the official military mission to the Iranian Army and succeeded the small advisory mission that had been sent to Iran during the Second World War. ARMISH would coordinate its efforts with the Iranian Ministry of War and the Iranian Army Command to organize and strengthen the Iranian Army.[102]

The Majlis met on October 22, 1947, to discuss the Iranian-Soviet agreement. Qavam met with Majlis deputies and discussed his previous negotiations with the Soviet Union. Several Majlis deputies reminded Qavam of the December 2, 1944 law, which forbid the Iranian government to negotiate any oil concessions with foreign powers. As a result, the Majlis rejected the Iranian-Soviet oil agreement.[103] Qavam notified the Soviet ambassador in Iran of the decision made by Majlis. The Soviet ambassador replied that the Iranian-Soviet agreement was not a concession and that the Iranian government had gone against its word. The Soviets then began to increase their negative propaganda against the Iranian government. As a result, Qavam resigned and was replaced by Ebrahim Hakimi.[104]

Following the settlement of the Iranian crisis, the United States became more directly involved in Iranian affairs. During the years 1948–50, the United States had to contend with several key issues: the continuous negative Soviet propaganda against both Iran and the United States; the Shah's preoccupation with constitutional reform in Iran, which took effect following an assassination attempt on his life; and the question of the level of U.S. military and economic assistance to Iran.

HOSTILE SOVIET PROPAGANDA AGAINST IRAN

During 1948, the Soviet Union stepped up its hostile propaganda against the Iranian government and the United States. These attacks became evident in the Soviet press as well as in radio broadcasts. The Iranian government and Majlis were criticized for not ratifying the Iranian-Soviet oil agreement in 1947 and for maintaining strong ties with the United States. On January 31, 1948, the Soviet government delivered an official letter to the Iranian government criticizing the October 1947 military agreement between Iran and the United States. It stated that by allowing ARMISH to function in Iran, the country was being transformed into a base for U.S. military activities against the Soviet Union.[105] The U.S. State Department and the Iranian government denied the Soviet charges. The Iranian government said that the information provided by the Soviet government was false and that the American advisers would not intervene in Iranian military activities. Rather, they provided advice regarding the Iranian Army's administrative affairs.[106]

Secretary of State Marshall thought that the Soviet letter was meant to frighten the Iranian Majlis not to ratify the agreement for Iran's purchase of U.S. surplus military equipment and to prevent the Iranian government from establishing close ties with the United States.[107] On February 17, 1948, the Majlis nonetheless passed the arms credit bill, which authorized the Iranian government to purchase U.S. surplus military supplies worth $10 million. Shortly thereafter, Fatollah Nouri-Esfandiary, the Iranian Foreign Minister, contacted the State Department asking for additional credit to cover charges for the delivery of the military items and a revision of the ARMISH agreement. The Iranian government wanted the deletion of certain articles pertaining to the duties of ARMISH. The Iranian government was told that these articles could not be revised and they were the same for other countries that had received U.S. military missions.[108]

Coincident with these developments, John Wiley replaced Allen as the new American ambassador to Iran. Wiley had no experience in Middle Eastern affairs but had previously served at the U.S. embassies in the Soviet Union and in Vienna. Wiley encouraged the Iranian government to take a strong stand in the face of continuous hostile Soviet propaganda and to find a way to rid itself of Article VI of the Russo-Persian Treaty of 1921, which authorized the Soviets to send their troops into Iran if they ever felt that their borders were threatened.

On March 17, 1948, the Shah met with representatives from the State Department to discuss economic development projects in Iran. The Shah said that economic development in Iran was the best shield against the spread of communism. John D. Jernegan, acting chief of the Division of Greek-Turkish-Iranian Affairs, said that Iran could apply for financial aid from the World Bank. He cautioned, however, that the bank would not approve a large sum in the amount of $250 million as requested by Iran. The bank would provide loans based on the value of the projects.[109]

The Shah said that aside from economic development, Iran also needed a strong army to defend itself from the Soviet Union. The Shah noted that the United States had supported Greece and Turkey in the face of constant Soviet threats, and he saw no reason why Iran should not be treated accordingly. Jernegan convinced the Shah that the Soviet Union would not attack Iran because it would lead to U.S. and U.N. intervention in the conflict.[110]

On March 24, 1948, the Soviet government delivered another letter to the Iranian government stating, that it was not satisfied by Iran's reply regarding the activities of the American military advisers, and that Iran's actions contradicted the principles of the Russo-Persian Treaty of 1921. The Iranian government replied that Iran was free to adopt any policy that was in its best interests. In response, the Soviets increased their negative propaganda against the Iranian government through the press and radio broadcasts.[111]

On May 13, 1948, the United States announced that it had signed a new surplus credit agreement with Iran. This agreement was negotiated and signed by Fred Ramsey, the U.S. Foreign Liquidation Commissioner, and Fatollah Nouri-Esfandiary, the Iranian foreign minister. According to this agreement, Iran would receive a credit in the amount of $10 million to purchase U.S. surplus military equipment, as well as credit in the amount of $16 to cover the cost of shipping and handling from the United States to Europe and subsequently Iran.[112]

Despite this agreement, the Shah and his new prime minister, Abdul Hussein Hazir, remained concerned about the lack of U.S. military aid to Iran. In a meeting with Ambassador Wiley on September 1, 1948, the Shah criticized the level of the U.S. arms credit program for Iran, and noted that Turkey was receiving more military and economic aid from the United States. The Shah thought that the United States did not seem to be aware of Iran's strategic importance.[113]

The Shah's worries were allayed to a certain extent when, on October 7, 1948, the Overseas Consultants Incorporated (OCI) signed a contract with the Iranian government to carry out a survey regarding Iran's economy as well as social conditions. The OCI was chaired by Max Thornburg, the former vice president of California Texas Oil Company. The OCI, which was affiliated with a group of U.S. oil companies, became involved with Iran's economic development between 1945 and 1955. In 1946, Thornburg had initially advised the Iranian government to hire Morrison-Knudsen. This time, however, he recommended the Iranian government to use the services of the OCI.[114]

THE SHAH'S PLANS FOR CONSTITUTIONAL REFORM

The State Department was concerned about the Shah's plans for constitutional reform, which it thought would lead to dictatorship. In a telegram from Secretary Marshall to Ambassador Allen on January 8, 1948, Marshall said that he did not believe that constitutional reform would have any affect on economic development. Marshall thought that granting the Shah the power to dissolve the Majlis would lead to further disorder, since the Majlis was a national forum that tried to protect Iran against any foreign intrigues.[115]

Allen agreed with Marshall's comments and said that a constitutional amendment that would give the Shah the authority to dissolve the Majlis would lead to an abuse of power. Allen said that he had discussed this situation with Sir John Le Rougetel, the British ambassador in Tehran. The British were also worried that a strong government in Iran could threaten their interests. Allen concluded that the United States should exert its influence to prevent the rise of dictatorship in Iran.[116] But while Allen and Marshall were contemplating these thoughts, they were in for a surprise.

In an unexpected move, the Shah had ordered General Sadiq Kupal, to replace Norman Schwarzkopf as the new chief of the Military Mission for the Reorganization of the Gendarmerie (GENMISH), which violated one of the articles of the 1943 agreement between the United States and Iran. According to Article 20 of the 1943 agreement, the chief of the mission was also the head of the Gendarmerie. Kupal told Schwarzkopf that while he was taking control, he would still cooperate with him and other American advisers. Schwarzkopf told Allen that the mission would fall apart unless the U.S. government insisted on the Iranian government's full observance of Article 20.[117]

In a telegram to Allen, Secretary Marshall regretted the fact that the Iranian government had taken matters into its hands without notifying the United States and told Allen to ask the Iranian government whether it wanted to end the agreement. At the same time, he told Allen that the United States was willing to modify the contents of Article 20.[118] Allen met with Prime Minister Hakimi and Farajollah Aqelvi, Minister of the Interior. Both men said that the Iranian government did not want to end nor amend the agreement. The Shah, however, told Allen that the Iranian government wanted an amendment of Article 20.[119] Negotiations between the two sides continued throughout the summer of 1948. In June 1948, Colonel James Pierce replaced Schwarzkopf. Iran and the United States eventually agreed that the head of GENMISH would only serve as an adviser and provide his recommendations to an Iranian commander of the Gendarmerie. The Gendarmerie eventually became part of the Iranian Army in 1949 and GENMISH continued as a small advisory mission.

The Shah's success in changing the GENMISH contract led him to take similar measures with the ARMISH contract. The Shah asked the U.S. government to modify Article 24 of the ARMISH contract. According to this article, a foreign country could not send military advisers to Iran without U.S. approval.[120] The purpose of this article was for the Iranian government to only utilize the services of American advisers so that communist countries such as the Soviet Union would not force Iran into hiring their advisers. The U.S. government told the Iranian government that this article was included in all U.S. military mission agreements with other countries. If the Iranian government insisted on removing this article, the United States would terminate its mission.[121] The Shah did not push the matter any further and backed down.

Meanwhile, the Soviet government continued its negative propaganda against the Shah and his relations with the United States. These attacks caused the Shah concern, and he continued to ask the United States for more financial and military aid. In late September 1948, Ibtihaj, the director of the National Bank, was sent to the United States to ask for U.S. financial and military aid and at the same time to discuss the Shah's plans for constitutional reform. The Shah in particular wanted to create a Senate, and be given the right to dissolve the Majlis.[122]

At the same time, the State Department asked Ambassador Wiley to meet with the Shah to discuss the issue of constitutional reform. Wiley told the Shah that there was no need for constitutional reform given that the Shah was in charge of foreign policy and defense issues. Wiley also asked the Shah not to intimidate the Majlis by threatening to abdicate.[123] Ambassador Le Rougetel and the British foreign office also agreed with the U.S. view that the Shah had to be careful about the issue of constitutional reform.[124]

While the State Department remained concerned over the Shah's plans for constitutional reform, it counted on the Shah to maintain stability in Iran. In a report prepared on January 13, 1949, the State Department took the position that the primary objective of U.S. policy toward Iran was to prevent the domination of the country by the Soviet Union. It noted that the Shah was the only reliable individual in Iran to promote U.S. interests. Therefore the United States had to provide continuous support to the Shah so that he could withstand any Soviet pressures, which could in the long run threaten U.S. interests in the region.[125] For these reasons, the U.S. government decided to invite the Shah for his first state visit.

On February 4, 1949, there was an assassination attempt on the Shah's life. The Shah was shot during a visit to Tehran University. The government announced that the sniper was a member of the Tudeh Party with ties to a radical Muslim group, Parcham-i Islam (Flag of Islam). As a result, the Iranian government declared martial law in Tehran, outlawed the Tudeh Party, and made several arrests. On the same day, President Truman sent a telegram to the Shah conveying his best wishes for a speedy recovery.[126]

Following the assassination attempt, the Shah issued a decree for the convening of a Constituent Assembly that would deal with the issue of constitutional reform. The Constituent Assembly met from April 21 to May 11, 1949, and amended the Constitution to grant special powers to the Shah, including the power to dissolve the Majlis.[127]

THE QUESTION OF U.S. AID TO IRAN

There had been growing discontent among the Iranian people over the state of the economy, which was not improving. As a result, the Majlis passed a law in March 1949 that required the revenues from the sale of oil to be devoted to economic development rather than unnecessary government expenditures. This law was based on a survey previously conducted by Morrison-Knudsen, and reviewed by Overseas Consultants Inc. (OCI), which put together an economic development plan for Iran to be carried out within seven years. This plan came to be known as the First Seven-Year Plan. It included programs to improve agriculture, education and public health. The Majlis, in turn, authorized the creation of the Plan Organization, a government agency to carry out the First Seven-Year Plan. Iran's oil revenues were to be utilized by the Plan Organization to finance the development projects.[128]

It is important to note that except for the recommendations put forth by Morrison-Knudsen and OCI that Iran's oil income be devoted to the development of the country, the U.S. government voiced no further opinions on this matter.

The United States had already made it clear to the Iranian government that it could not expect large sums of U.S. aid to finance its development projects. In other words, the Iranians had to make use of their oil revenues to finance those projects. Despite the low levels of economic aid, the United States would nevertheless provide technical aid to Iran under the auspices of the Point IV program in order to help the country with its development projects.

The Iranian government continued to ask the United States for financial aid to help fund its seven-year plan. In a letter to Ambassador Wiley on April 26, 1949, Prime Minister Saed, who had replaced Hajir, outlined a series of projects that needed financing. Among these were the improvement of agriculture and the construction of new roads, highways, and airports.[129] Ambassador Wiley passed on Iran's request for financial aid to Secretary of State Acheson, who had replaced George Marshall. Wiley said that it was in the interests of the United States to respond to Iran's request, since it proved that the United States was adamant about maintaining Iran's sovereignty.[130]

In the aftermath of the Truman Doctrine and the Marshall Plan, the United States had also thought about establishing a collective defense arrangement that would provide security to its allies in Western Europe. When Czechoslovakia fell to the communists and the Soviets imposed the Berlin blockade in 1948, a number of Western European states decided to take action. In 1948, Belgium, Britain, France, Luxembourg, and Holland signed the Treaty of Brussels to promote collective defense. The United States supported this treaty and at the same time began to plan for a special military alliance that led to the establishment of the North Atlantic Treaty Organization (NATO) in 1949.[131] NATO membership was initially limited to the United States and its Western European allies. However, it came to include countries such as Greece and Turkey, due to their strategic location. Turkey's membership in NATO upset the Shah, since Turkey was receiving more assistance from the United States. Since the Shah and his government were not receiving much financial aid from the United States, they turned their attention to the Iranian oil industry and its revenues.

In the aftermath of the Second World War, it became obvious to both the Iranian government and the Anglo-Iranian Oil Company that certain changes had to be made to the 1933 oil agreement, given the economic problems in Iran. In early 1948, the AIOC said that it would negotiate a new agreement that would pay higher oil revenues to Iran. Discussions continued in the spring of 1949, and on May 14, it was announced that the two sides had reached an agreement. As a result, in July 1949, a Supplemental Agreement to the 1933 concession was signed that would raise Iran's oil revenues. The Iranian government submitted this agreement to the Majlis to be ratified.[132] The British and the Iranian governments, however, did not know they were in for a long wait. The agreement was never ratified by the Majlis and led instead to the oil nationalization dispute of 1951.

The Iranian government continued to ask the United States for financial aid throughout the spring of 1949. On May 27 1949, Hussein Ala, the Iranian Foreign Minister asked the United States for financial aid in the amount of $500 million to help strengthen the economy. Ala's request was followed by Prime Minister Saed's request for U.S. military aid that included such items as weapons and uniforms as needed by the Iranian Army.[133] The Iranian government obviously failed to understand that the United States would not grant or loan large sums of money to any country.

On July 21, 1949, the National Security Council produced a report regarding U.S. policy toward Iran. It stated that the primary objectives of this policy were to prevent Soviet control of the country and to strengthen Iran's relations with the West.[134] To this end, the United States announced that its Mutual Assistance Program (MAP) had set aside $27 million for Iran, Korea, and the Philippines. Iran was placed in this category instead of the one that included Greece and Turkey, which received a higher share. The Shah was upset at this news and even thought of canceling his November trip to the United States. Ambassador Wiley asked the State Department to reconsider Iran's share in MAP.[135]

The Shah nonetheless began to prepare for his state visit to the United States and arrived on November 16, 1949. He met with Secretary of State Acheson and President Truman to discuss the issue of U.S. financial and military aid to Iran. While the Shah was excited about carrying out economic reforms using the income from Iran's oil royalties, he observed that there were not enough resources left to improve the Iranian Army. For these reasons, he was asking the United States for military aid.[136] The Iranian press provided full coverage of the Shah's visit to the United States and noted that relations between the two countries had grown stronger.[137] In the end, however, the Shah failed to secure additional U.S. financial and military aid, and it became evident that Iran had to rely on its oil revenues for its development plans.

Despite his disappointment, the Shah and the Iranian government continued to pressure the United States with their demands. On January 26, 1950, Ambassador Ala met with George McGhee, the assistant secretary for Near Eastern Affairs, to discuss Iran's need for more financial and military aid. McGhee told Ala that U.S. aid was not granted on the basis of a country's specific needs, rather it was in accordance with U.S. policies. McGhee told Ala that these continuous requests for U.S. aid would create an unfavorable image of Iran.[138]

In February 1950, the Bureau of Near Eastern Affairs prepared a report on political and economic factors that would affect the status of U.S. military aid to Iran. The report began by stating that the key objectives of U.S. policy toward Iran were to prevent Soviet control of the country and to strengthen Iran's relations with the West. U.S. policy was intent on promoting economic and social reforms in Iran to prevent the spread of communism. U.S. aid to be utilized in the above capacities would come from sources such as the Point IV, Smith-Mundt, and Fulbright programs.[139] The report also outlined the objectives of Soviet policy in Iran, which included overthrowing the monarchy and replacing it with a communist regime. This would provide the Soviets access to the Persian Gulf region, and threaten Western oil interests in Middle East. Therefore, the United States had to do its best to prevent these developments from taking place.[140] In another discussion regarding Iran, the State Department also identified certain factors that left the Shah's regime on shaky grounds. Among these were economic problems, the activities of the outlawed Tudeh Party, and political strife among government officials. The State Department then discussed the reasons it was important for the United States to consider providing financial aid to Iran[141]

Meanwhile, Prime Minister Saed resigned and was succeeded by Hasan Ali Mansur. Ambassador John Le Rougetel's term had also come to an end and he was succeeded by Sir Francis Shepherd. Shepherd asked the Shah and Mansur to submit the Supplemental Agreement of 1949 once again to the Majlis. Shepherd had told the Shah that this agreement was the best the AIOC could offer to help raise Iran's oil revenues.[142] Mansur submitted the agreement to the Majlis but the deputies refused to consider it. The British and the Shah, upset over Mansur's weakness and his inability to deal with the Majlis deputies, agreed that it was best if he were removed from his post.[143]

The United States was also concerned about developments that were taking place in East Asia. In 1949, Mao Zedong and the communists had taken over China. In addition, the Soviets and the Chinese were supporting North Korea in its quest to take over South Korea. These developments led the Truman administration to accept the recommendations of a report prepared by the State Department, known as NSC-68. The report said that the Soviet Union's intention was to dominate countries around the world. To prevent this from happening, the United States had to give up its frugality when it came to defense spending so that it could meet its foreign policy objectives. Given the circumstances, the NSC-68 led to the Truman administration's pursuance of the rearmament program.[144] These concerns also led the United States to negotiate an agreement for Mutual Defense Assistance to Iran and to establish a Military Assistance Advisory Group (MAAG) on May 23, 1950.[145] As a result of this agreement, the United States would arrange for the manufacture and shipment of military equipment to Iran.

In June 1950, John Wiley was replaced by Henry Grady, who became the new American ambassador to Iran. Grady had previously served as American ambassador to India and Greece. As far as political developments in Iran were concerned, both the U.S. State Department and the British Foreign Office wanted the Shah to dismiss Mansur and appoint General Ali Razmara as the next prime minister.[146] The United States favored this appointment based on what they had heard about Razmara. Gerry Dooher from the American embassy had met with Razmara. It appeared that Razmara wanted to carry out several reforms and even pursue an anticorruption campaign. In addition, he wanted the Majlis to approve the Oil Supplemental Agreement of 1949.[147]

Upon assuming office, Razmara pledged to undertake a reform program that would lead to improvements in health care, education, and the people's standard of living, especially in rural areas. Razmara then submitted a request for financial aid from the Exim Bank to help finance a number of projects including the construction of roads and highways and improving irrigation methods.[148] The United States sent an economic advisory group to Iran in June 1950 to report on the implementation of projects listed under the Point IV program. The projects were meant to strengthen Iran's economy and improve the people's standard of living.[149]

Meanwhile, the Soviets had decided to change their tactics in dealing with the Iranian government and take a more conciliatory approach. On July 25, 1950, the Soviet ambassador met with Razmara and said that his government was willing to offer any kind of assistance to Iran. This came as a surprise to the Iranian government, which had endured two years of negative Soviet propaganda. Razmara said that his government expected the release of Iranian officers being held by the Soviets as a result of border skirmishes between the two countries, and the return of gold belonging to Iran that was being held in the Soviet Union. The Soviet ambassador said that these issues would be discussed by his government.[150]

Razmara's negotiations with the Soviets became a major point of concern for the United States. On September 14, 1950, Alan Kirk, the American ambassador to the Soviet Union, observed that if Iran and the Soviet Union were to reach an agreement, it could strengthen procommunist groups in Iran and destabilize the Shah's rule. Therefore, a U.S. loan or grant would be crucial in strengthening the Iranian economy and at the same time would hinder Soviet efforts to draw Iran into their orbit.[151]

On October 6, 1950, the Exim Bank announced that it would provide $25 million in credit to the Iranian government so that it could finance the purchase of U.S. equipment and technical services to improve agriculture, construct roads and highways, and engage in other economic development projects.[152] On October 19, 1950, Iran signed its first technical cooperation project with the United States under the auspices of the new Point IV program, which was designed to improve among other things agriculture, education, health, and living conditions in rural areas. The United States provided $500,000 for technical cooperation in Iran from the Point IV program for that fiscal year.[153]

The Truman administration had successfully carried out its strategy of containment in Iran by providing strong diplomatic support to the country during the Iranian crisis of 1945–46, encouraging the Iranian government to carry out reforms, and providing a limited amount of technical and military aid. The limited aid is understandable, given the fact that at the time, Iran was not a top priority in U.S. interests. At the same time, the Iranian government had to put its own house in order before it could expect any substantial aid. Since the U.S. aid was insufficient, the Iranian government turned to its oil revenues, pressing the AIOC and the British government to increase Iran's share. This in itself precipitated the Iranian oil nationalization dispute of 1951 and drew the United States more deeply into Iranian affairs.

NOTES

1. *Khavar-i Now*, 2 August 1945.
2. Nur al-Din Kianuri, *Khatirat-i Nur al-Din Kianuri* (The Memoirs of Nur al-Din Kianuri). (Tehran: Ittila'at Press, 1371/1992), 105.
3. Abdul Samad Kambaksh, *Nazari bi Junbish-i Kargari va Komunisti dar Iran* (A view of the Labor and Communist Movement in Iran) (Stockholm: Salzland Press, 1975), 103 as cited in Zabih, *The Communist Movement in Iran* (Berkeley: University of California Press, 1966), 97.
4. Sepehr Zabih, *The Communist Movement in Iran*, 97–98.
5. *Rahbar*, 8 August 1944, as cited in Ervand Abrahamian, "Communism and Communalism in Iran: The Tudeh and the Firqah-i Dimukrat," *International Journal of Middle Eastern Studies* 1 (1970): 306.
6. Abrahamian, "Communism and Communalism in Iran," 306.
7. Najafgholi Pesyan, *Marg Bud Bazgasht Ham Bud* (There was Death and Return) (Tehran: Sherkat-i Sahami-yi Chap, 1326/1947), 21.
8. Nasrollah S. Fatemi, *Oil Diplomacy: Powderkeg in Iran* (New York: Whittier, 1954), 265.
9. For a discussion of the Soviet connection to the Democratic Party of Azerbaijan see Fernande Raine, "Stalin and the Creation of the Azerbaijan Democratic Party in Iran, 1945," *Cold War History* 2 (October 2001): 1–38; Maziar Behrooz, *Rebels with a Cause: The Failure of the Left in Iran* (London: I.B. Tauris, 2000), 26.
10. Abrahamian, "Communism and Communalism in Iran," 298, 302–305.
11. Society of Iranian Socialists, "Text of Khalil Maleki's Defense Trial," 2 (October 1966): 46, as cited in Abrahamian, "Communism and Communalism in Iran," 311.

12. *Foreign Relations of the United States, 1945*, 8: 407.
13. *Foreign Relations of the United States, 1945*, 8: 400, 424.
14. William Eagleton, *The Kurdish Republic of 1946* (Oxford: Oxford University Press, 1963), 56–57; Ramazani, *Iran's Foreign Policy, 1941–1973*, 113.
15. U.S. Embassy in Tehran,"Political Developments Among the Azerbaijani Kurds in 1946," 15 January 1947, Record Group 84, Box 12, File 800, National Archives, College Park, Md.
16. *Foreign Relations of the United States, 1945*, 8: 417–19.
17. *Foreign Relations of the United States, 1945*, 8: 420–22.
18. U.S. Department of State, RG 59, Decimal File 891.00/3-2346, 23 March 1946, "Report on Conditions in Northern Iran Between 3 August and 31 December 1945 from the British Consulate General in Tabriz to the American Embassy in Tehran," National Archives, College Park, Md.
19. *Foreign Relations of the United States, 1945*, 8: 431–37.
20. *Foreign Relations of the United States*, 445–47.
21. United States, Department of State *Bulletin* 8, no. 336 (2 December 1945): 884 (hereafter cited as Department of State *Bulletin*).
22. Department of State *Bulletin* 8, no. 337 (9 December 1945): 934–35.
23. Kuniholm, *The Origins of the Cold War in the Near East*, 281.
24. Jody Ememi-Yeganeh, "Iran vs. Azerbaijan (1945–46): Divorce, Separation or Reconciliation?" *Central Asian Survey* 3, no. 2, 14–17; Fatemi, *The U.S.S.R. in Iran*, 85–89; *Foreign Relations of the United States, 1945*, 8: 455–65; Pesyan, *Marg Bud Bazgasht Ham Bud* (There was Death and Return), 30–31.
25. Eagleton, *The Kurdish Republic of 1946*, 61.
26. Eagleton, *The Kurdish Republic of 1946*, 61; Archie Roosevelt, "The Kurdish Republic of Mahabad," *The Middle East Journal* 1, no. 3 (July 1947): 257.
27. *Ittila'at* and *Kayhan*, 19 December 1945.
28. *Kayhan*, 22 December 1945.
29. James F. Byrnes, *All in One Lifetime* (New York: Harper & Brothers, 1958), 333–34.
30. *Foreign Relations of the United States, 1945*, 8: 500–501.
31. *Foreign Relations of the United States, 1945*, Diplomatic Papers, vol. 2, *General Political and Economic Matters* (Washington, D.C.: Government Printing Office, 1967): 750–52.
32. *Foreign Relations of the United States, 1946*, vol. 7, *The Near East and Africa* (Washington, D.C.: Government Printing Office, 1969), 293–97.
33. *Foreign Relations of the United States,1946*, 7: 309–11.
34. *Foreign Relations of the United States,1946*, 7: 311.
35. Hasan Arfa, *Under Five Shahs* (Edinburgh: R. and R. Clark, 1964), 314; *Foreign Relations of the United States, 1946*, 7: 304.
36. *Foreign Relations of the United States, 1946*, 7: 315.
37. For a discussion of the U.S. strategy of containment during the Cold War see George F. Kennan, "The Sources of Soviet Conduct," *Foreign Affairs* 25 (July 1947): 566–82; George F. Kennan, *Memoirs: 1925–1950* (Boston: Bantam, 1967), 304; George F. Kennan and John Lukacs, *George F. Kennan and the Origins of Contain-*

ment, 1944–1946 (Columbia, Mo: University of Missouri Press, 1997); John L. Gaddis, *Strategies of Containment* (New York: Oxford University Press, 1982); Richard S. Kirkendall, ed., *The Truman Period as a Research Field, A Reappraisal, 1972* (Columbia, Mo.: University of Missouri Press, 1974); Barton J. Bernstein, *Politics and Policies of the Truman Administration* (Chicago: Quadrangle, 1970); Efstathios Fakiolas, "Kennan's Long Telegram and NSC-68: A Comparative Theoretical Analysis," *East European Quarterly* 31 (Winter 1997): 415–34; and Elizabeth Edwards Spalding, *The First Cold Warrior: Harry Truman, Containment, and the Remaking of Liberal Internationalism* (Lexington, Ky: University Press of Kentucky, 2006).

38. *Foreign Relations of the United States, 1946*, vol. 6, *Eastern Europe and the Soviet Union* (Washington, D.C.: 1969): 696–709.

39. Byrnes, *Speaking Frankly* (New York: Harper & Brothers, 1947), 254–56; Gary Hess, "The Iranian Crisis of 1945–46 and the Cold War." *Political Science Quarterly* 89 (March 1974): 133–34; Kuniholm, *The Origins of the Cold War in the Near East*, 311.

40. *Foreign Relations of the United States, 1946*, 7: 339.

41. Robert Rossow, "The Battle of Azerbaijan, 1946." *Middle East Journal* 10 (Winter 1956): 20–21.

42. *Foreign Relations of the United States, 1946*, 7: 340–42.

43. *Foreign Relations of the United States, 1946*, 7: 348.

44. *Foreign Relations of the United States, 1946*, 7: 350–56.

45. *Foreign Relations of the United States, 1946*, 7: 356–60.

46. *Foreign Relations of the United States, 1946*, 7: 365–67.

47. *Foreign Relations of the United States, 1946*, 7: 367.

48. *Foreign Relations of the United States, 1946*, 7: 379–80.

49. *Foreign Relations of the United States, 1946*, 7: 381–83.

50. *Foreign Relations of the United States, 1946*, 7: 396–97.

51. *Foreign Relations of the United States, 1946*, 7: 405–407.

52. *Foreign Relations of the United States, 1946*, 6: 732–36.

53. David Alvarez, "The *Missouri* Visit to Turkey: An Alternative Perspective to Cold War Diplomacy," *Balkan Studies* 15 (2 November 1974): 225–36; Kuniholm, *The Origins of the Cold War in the Near East*, 335–36.

54. *Foreign Relations of the United States, 1946*, 7: 410–11.

55. *Foreign Relations of the United States, 1946*, 7: 417–23.

56. *Foreign Relations of the United States, 1946*, 7: 424–26.

57. *Foreign Relations of the United States, 1946*, 7: 452–53.

58. *Foreign Relations of the United States, 1946*, 7: 469–72.

59. *Foreign Relations of the United States, 1946*, 7: 489–93.

60. *Foreign Relations of the United States, 1946*, 7: 348–49; Harry S. Truman, *Memoirs*, vol. 2, 94–95.

61. *Foreign Relations of the United States, 1946*, 7: 349.

62. U.S. Department of State, RG 59, Decimal File 891.00/6-846, 8 June 1946, Allen to Secretary of State, National Archives, College Park, Md.

63. *Foreign Relations of the United States, 1946*, 7: 497–98.

64. *Foreign Relations of the United States, 1946*, 7: 505.

65. U.S. Embassy in Tehran, "Disturbances in Khuzistan," 17 July 1946, RG 84, Box 10, Confidential Files 1940–1952, National Archives, College Park, Md.

66. U.S. Embassy in Tehran, "Report on Tudeh by Colonel Underwood, AIOC Security Officer," 19 July 1946, RG 84, Box 10, Confidential File 1940–1952, National Archives, College Park, Md.

67. U.S. Embassy in Tehran, "Disturbances in Khuzistan."

68. U.S. Embassy in Tehran, "Disturbances in Khuzistan"; Habib Ladjevardi, *Labor Unions and Autocracy in Iran* (Syracuse, N.Y.: Syracuse University Press, 1985), 136.

69. *Foreign Relations of the United States, 1946*, 7: 507–509.

70. *Foreign Relations of the United States, 1946*, 7: 509.

71. Ja'far Mahdi-Nia, *Zindigi -yi Siyasi Qavam al-Saltaneh* (The Political Life of Qavam al-Saltaneh) (Tehran: Panus and Pasgard, 1370/1991), 317–20.

72. Iraj Iskandari, *Khatirat-i Siyasi Iraj Iskandari* (Political Memoirs of Iraj Iskandari) (Tehran: Ilmi, 1368/1989), 132.

73. U.S. Embassy in Tehran, "Political Position of Prime Minister Qavam Os-Saltaneh," 12 September 1946, RG 84, Box 10, Confidential Files 1940–1952, National Archives, College Park, Md.

74. *Foreign Relations of the United States, 1946*, 7: 520.

75. *Foreign Relations of the United States, 1946*, 7: 518–20.

76. Kuniholm, *The Origins of the Cold War in the Near East*, 387.

77. Kuniholm, *The Origins of the Cold War in the Near East*, 388–91.

78. *Foreign Relations of the United States, 1946*, 7: 535–36.

79. *Foreign Relations of the United States, 1946*, 7: 536–37.

80. *Foreign Relations of the United States, 1946*, 7: 539–40.

81. *Foreign Relations of the United States, 1946*, 7: 540.

82. U.S. Department of State, RG 59, Decimal File 891.00/10-2846, 28 November 1946, Allen to Secretary of State, National Archives, College Park, Md.

83. *Foreign Relations of the United States, 1946*, 7: 554.

84. *Ittila'at* and *Kayhan*, 24 November 1946.

85. U.S. Department of State, RG 59, Decimal File 891.00/11–2846, 28 November 1946, Allen to Secretary of State, National Archives, College Park, Md.

86. *Ittila'at*, 27 November 1946; *Foreign Relations of the United States, 1946*, 7: 548–49.

87. *Foreign Relations of the United States, 1946*, 7: 551–52.

88. *Foreign Relations of the United States, 1946*, 7: 560–61.

89. U.S. Department of State, RG 59, Decimal File, 891.00/12-1746, 17 December 1946, Allen to Secretary of State, National Archives, College Park, Md.

90. International Engineering Company for Morrison-Knudsen International, *Report on Program for the Development of Iran*, vol. 1 (San Francisco: MKI, 1947), 3–4, 21.

91. *Foreign Relations of the United States, 1947*, 5: 32–37.

92. Bruce Kuniholm, "Loy Henderson, Dean Acheson, and the Origins of the Truman Doctrine," in Douglas Brinkley, ed., *Acheson and the Making of U.S. Foreign Policy* (New York: St. Martin's Press, 1993), 73.

93. Dean Acheson, *Present at the Creation* (New York: W. W. Norton, 1969), 219.

94. Kuniholm, "Loy Henderson, Dean Acheson, and the Origins of the Truman Doctrine," 98; Bruce Kuniholm, "Rings and Flanks: The Defense of the Middle East in the Early Cold War," in Keith Neilson and Ronald Haycock, eds., *The Cold War and Defense* (New York: Praeger, 1990), 115.

95. United States Congress, Senate, *Legislative Origins of the Truman Doctrine: Hearings Held in Executive Session before the Committee on Foreign Relations*. 80th Congress, First Session on S. 938 (Washington, D.C.: Government Printing Office, 1973).

96. U.S. Department of State, RG 59, Decimal File 891.00/3-2747, 27 March 1947, Allen to Secretary of State, National Archives, College Park, Md.

97. Paul W. T. Kingston, *Britain and the Politics of Modernization in the Middle East, 1945–1958* (Cambridge: Cambridge University Press, 1996), 72–78.

98. Department of State *Bulletin* 16, no. 407 (20 April 1947): 720.

99. *Ittila'at*, 20 June 1947.

100. Ramazani, *Iran's Foreign Policy, 1941–1973*, 168.

101. "U.S. Bids Iran Resist Threats as Debate on Soviet Oil Nears," *New York Times*, 12 September 1947, 1.

102. Thomas Ricks, "U.S. Military Missions to Iran, 1943–1978: The Political Economy of Military Assistance," *Iranian Studies*, 12 (Summer–Autumn 1979): 173; United States Department of State, *Treaties and Other International Acts*, Series 1650–99 (Washington, D.C.: Government Printing Office, 1947), 3–4.

103. Fatemi, *Oil Diplomacy*, 326; Ramazani, *Iran's Foreign Policy, 1941–1973*, 169.

104. Ramazani, *Iran's Foreign Policy, 1941–1973*, 169.

105. *Foreign Relations of the United States*, 1948, vol. 5, *The Near East, South Asia and Africa* (Washington, D.C.: Government Printing Office, 1975), 99–101.

106. *Foreign Relations of the United States*, 1948, 5: 101–105.

107. *Foreign Relations of the United States*, 1948, 5: 107–108.

108. *Foreign Relations of the United States*, 1948, 5: 114.

109. *Foreign Relations of the United States*, 1948, 5: 117–18.

110. *Foreign Relations of the United States*, 1948, 5: 119–21.

111. *Foreign Relations of the United States*, 1948, 5: 125–29.

112. Department of State *Bulletin* 19, no. 476 (15 August 1948): 211; *Foreign Relations of the United States, 1948*, 5: 145.

113. *Foreign Relations of the United States, 1948*, 5: 175.

114. Frances Bostock and Geoffrey Jones, *Planning and Power in Iran: Ebtehaj and the Economic Development under the Shah* (London: Frank Cass, 1989), 98–99; Thomas Ricks, "U.S. Military Missions to Iran, 1943–1978," 175–76.

115. *Foreign Relations of the United States, 1948*, 5: 88–90.

116. *Foreign Relations of the United States, 1948*, 5: 95–97.

117. *Foreign Relations of the United States, 1948*, 5: 97.

118. *Foreign Relations of the United States, 1948*, 5: 106.

119. *Foreign Relations of the United States, 1948*, 5: 107, n. 1.

120. *Foreign Relations of the United States, 1948*, 5: 132, 134–37; James F. Goode, *The United States and Iran, 1946–51* (London: Macmillan Press, 1989), 29.

121. *Foreign Relations of the United States, 1948*, 5: 136–37; Goode, *The United States and Iran, 1946–51*, 29–30.

122. U.S. Department of State, RG 59, Decimal File 891.00/10-748, 6 October 1948, Lovett to Wiley, National Archives, College Park, Md.

123. U.S. Department of State, RG 59, Confidential Files, 891.00/11–148, 1 November 1948, Wiley to Secretary of State, National Archives, College Park, Md.

124. Le Rougetel to FO, 25 January 1949, FO371 EP754664, as cited in Azimi, *Iran: The Crisis of Democracy, 1941–1953*, 201.

125. U.S. Department of State, RG 59, Decimal File 891.00/1349, 13 January 1949, "Invitation to the Shah of Iran to Visit the United States," National Archives, College Park, Md.

126. *Foreign Relations of the United States, 1949*, vol. 6, *The Near East, South Asia, and Africa* (Washington, D.C.: Government Printing Office, 1977), 478.

127. Azimi, *Iran: The Crisis of Democracy, 1914–1953*, 205; *Ittila'at*, 23 April 1949; *Foreign Relations of the United States, 1949*, 6: 486.

128. George Baldwin, *Planning and Development in Iran* (Baltimore: Johns Hopkins Press, 1967), 24–31; Julian Bharier, *Economic Development in Iran, 1900–1970* (London: Oxford University Press, 1971), 88–89.

129. *Foreign Relations of the United States, 1949*, 6: 510–13.

130. *Foreign Relations of the United States, 1949*, 6: 514–16.

131. *Foreign Relations of the United States, 1949*, vol. 4, *Western Europe* (Washington, D.C.: Government Printing Office, 1975): 271–85; George Harris, *Troubled Alliance: Turkish American Problems in Historical Perspective, 1945–1971* (Washington, D.C.: American Enterprise Institute, 1972), 35–38.

132. J. H. Bamberg, *The History of the British Petroleum Company*, vol. 2 (Cambridge: Cambridge University Press, 1982), 385–99; Benjamin Shwadran, *The Middle East, Oil, and the Great Powers* (New York: Praeger, 1955), 104–105.

133. *Foreign Relations of the United States, 1949*, 6: 528–29.

134. *Foreign Relations of the United States, 1949*, 6: 545–51.

135. *Foreign Relations of the United States, 1949*, 6: 552–55.

136. *Foreign Relations of the United States, 1949*, 6: 572–78.

137. *Ittila'at* and *Kayhan*, 16 November 1949.

138. *Foreign Relations of the United States, 1950*, vol. 5, *The Near East, South Asia, and Africa* (Washington, D.C.: Government Printing Office, 1978), 448–51.

139. *Foreign Relations of the United States, 1950*, 5: 465–70.

140. *Foreign Relations of the United States, 1950*, 5: 470–72.

141. *Foreign Relations of the United States, 1950*, 5: 491–99.

142. Shepherd to Bevin, 8 April 1950, FO 371 EP82310, as cited in Azimi, *Iran: The Crisis of Democracy, 1941–1953*, 223.

143. Shepherd to Bevin, 8 April 1950, FO 371 EP82310, as cited in Azimi, *Iran: The Crisis of Democracy, 1941–1953*, 223.

144. Steven L. Rearden, "Frustrating the Kremlin: Acheson and NSC 68," in Douglas Brinkley, ed., *Dean Acheson and the Making of U.S. Foreign Policy*, 159–72; John

L. Gaddis, *Strategies of Containment: A Critical Appraisal of Postwar American National Security Policy (New York: Oxford University Press, 1982)*, 89–126.

145. United States Department of State, *Bulletin* 22, no. 570 (5 June 1950): 922–23.

146. *Foreign Relations of the United States, 1950*, 5: 549–50.

147. *Foreign Relations of the United States, 1950*, 5: 558–59.

148. Department of State, *Current Economic Developments*, no. 264, 24 July 1950.

149. Jahangir Amuzegar, *Technical Assistance in Theory and Practice: The Case of Iran* (New York: Praeger, 1966), 44, 46; U.S. Department of State, RG 59, Decimal File 888.00TA/6-1050, 10 June 1950, "Suggestions for Point IV Program," National Archives, College Park, Md.

150. *Foreign Relations of the United States, 1950*, 5: 574–75.

151. *Foreign Relations of the United States, 1950*, 5: 588–89.

152. *Foreign Relations of the United States, 1950*, 5: 604–605.

153. U.S. Department of State, United States Treaties and Other International Agreements1,*TIAS* no. 2139 (19 October 1950): 721–31; U.S. Department of State, RG 59, Decimal File 888.00-TA/10-1950, 19 October 1950, National Archives, College Park, Md.

Chapter Three

The Oil Nationalization Dispute and Its Ramifications

The nationalization of the Iranian oil industry by prime minister Muhammad Musaddiq in 1951 and the subsequent oil dispute changed the course of superpower rivalry in Iran. Certain factors set the oil nationalization dispute in motion. Among these were: Iran's grievances against the AIOC for its control over Iranian oil and the inadequate amount of revenues allotted to Iran, which had led to new agreements between the two sides in 1933 and 1949; Musaddiq's policy of Negative Equilibrium, which advocated Iran's maintenance of a neutral stance in international affairs and sought to curtail foreign control of Iranian resources; and the effects of the Saudi-Aramco 50/50 oil agreement on the Iranian government.

The Anglo-American and Soviet response to the oil nationalization crisis is divided into two distinct periods. The first period is March 1951–July 1952, during which the Truman administration encouraged the Iranian and the British governments to solve their problems through diplomatic negotiations. The U.S. government sent envoys to both countries to mediate the dispute, but to no avail. The British also sent their own negotiating teams to Iran to settle the dispute, but had no success. The Soviet Union was pleased with Musaddiq's decision to nationalize the oil industry, as it would curtail British influence in Iran. Yet the Soviet Union was not sure where it would fit within the confines of Musaddiq's policy of Negative Equilibrium. The Soviets and their protégé, the Tudeh Party, became aggravated, when the United States mediated in the oil dispute and even accused Musaddiq of being an American puppet.

The second period of Anglo-American and Soviet response to the oil nationalization crisis is August 1952 to August 1953. During this period, the Truman administration realized that Musaddiq's unwillingness to accept any solution to the oil crisis was plunging Iran further into chaos. Truman's presidential term, however, came to an end in 1953, when he was succeeded by General Dwight D. Eisenhower, a Republican. Truman's policy toward Iran took a different turn under his successor. The British were able to convince the Eisenhower administration of the communist threat in Iran, if Musaddiq were to remain in power. The fear of losing Iran to the communists led the Eisenhower administration to side with the British government in a covert operation to overthrow Musaddiq's government and for the Shah to consolidate his rule. During this time, the Soviets tried to improve their relations with Iran, and the Tudeh Party even warned Musaddiq of an impending coup to overthrow his government. Musaddiq, however, took no heed, and his government was overthrown in 1953 by a coup engineered by the CIA and MI6.

PRELUDE TO THE OIL NATIONALIZATION DISPUTE

Iran had longtime grievances against Great Britain for its control over Iranian oil. In 1901, the Qajar dynasty had granted William Knox D'Arcy an oil concession, which gave him the right to search for and process Iranian oil for sixty years. The only areas restricted to D'Arcy were Iran's northern provinces, which were considered part of the Russian zone of influence. In 1908, oil was discovered in Masjid-i Sulaiman, located in the Khuzistan province. In 1909, the Anglo-Persian Oil Company (APOC) was founded with D'Arcy as its director.[1] The Anglo-Persian Oil Company was later renamed the Anglo-Iranian Oil Company (AIOC) in 1935.

In 1913, the British Admiralty decided for the British Navy to use oil instead of coal and began to negotiate with the APOC to buy shares in the company. On May 20, 1914, the British government signed an agreement with the APOC, which led to the British government's control over the company. Winston Churchill, First Lord of the Admiralty, asked the British parliament to approve the agreement as it was in the best interests of the British government. As a result, the British parliament approved the agreement.[2]

Relations between the Iranian government and the APOC were strained from the beginning. In 1932, Reza Shah cancelled the D'Arcy concession, demanding higher oil revenues and better social services for the Iranian workers. The dispute was settled by the League of Nations in 1933 and Iran signed a new agreement that would increase its oil revenues. The terms of the new concession was extended for another sixty years until December 31, 1993. The concession could come to an end sooner if the company were to relinquish the concession or if the Court of Arbitration were to nullify it.[3]

Following the Second World War, the Iranian government and the AIOC realized that certain changes had to be made to the 1933 agreement. This was because the AIOC wanted to build its general reserves and had to limit the distribution of its dividends. These measures, in turn, affected the Iranian government, as its revenues depended on those dividends. In 1948, the AIOC announced that it would negotiate the issue of adjusting the oil revenues with the Iranian government. The Iranian government replied that while it wanted an increase in Iran's oil revenues, it favored a reduction in the number of foreign workers employed by the AIOC.[4] Negotiations over these issues continued between the two sides throughout 1948 and the early months of 1949.

On July 17, 1949, the Iranian government and the AIOC signed a supplemental agreement to the 1933 agreement, which led among other things to an increase in Iran's revenues from four to six shillings a ton.[5] The Iranian Majlis did not ratify this agreement and instead set up an oil committee to review the matter. This committee was supervised by Dr. Muhammad Musaddiq, who would nationalize the Iranian oil industry in 1951.

Musaddiq was born into a well-known family in Iran. He had studied in Switzerland and obtained a law degree. When he returned to Iran in 1914, Musaddiq began to work at the Ministry of Finance. In 1924, Musaddiq was elected to the Majlis. He played an important part in the events that led to the cancellation of the D'Arcy concession in 1932 and the negotiations that led to a more profitable oil agreement for Iran in 1933. In 1944, Musaddiq became critical of the Soviets for pressuring the Iranian government to grant them an oil concession. He delivered a special speech before the Majlis on October 24, 1944, in which he announced his doctrine of Negative Equilibrium (Siyast-i Movazaneh-yi Manfi) and its place within the framework of Iran's foreign policy.[6] This doctrine was directed toward Iran pursuing a neutral stance in international affairs and ending foreign control over Iran's natural resources. Musaddiq was affected in particular by Iran's historical experience in relations with Britain and the Soviet Union. He wanted to strengthen the Majlis and its activities so that it could better resist foreign influence and pressures that could prove detrimental to Iran's interests.[7]

On December 12, 1944, in response to constant Soviet pressure to obtain an oil concession in northern Iran, Musaddiq had introduced a bill to the Majlis that forbid the Iranian government to negotiate any oil concessions during the war.[8] In 1947, Musaddiq's opposition to the Iranian-Soviet agreement of 1946, which had promised the Soviets an oil concession and the establishment of a joint Iranian-Soviet oil company should they withdraw their troops from Azerbaijan and northern Iran, led to its defeat.

The Iranian people respected Musaddiq's views regarding the nationalization of the Iranian oil industry. In October 1949, Musaddiq created his own political party, called the National Front. The National Front was composed of different political groups and its members came from different ideological backgrounds. Conservative members of the National Front included religious clergy, such as Ayatollah Abul Qassim Kashani, and bazaar merchants. Those at the center included intellectuals such as Allahyar Saleh and Karim Sanjabi. Those with a leftist ideology included university students and workers. The National Front's objectives were to uphold the Iranian constitution, conduct fair elections, and nationalize the Iranian oil industry. Throughout 1949 and 1950, the National Front organized several demonstrations against the Shah, demanding that fair elections take place. Its efforts bore fruit, as eight of its candidates were elected to the Sixteenth Majlis.[9]

On December 12, 1950, the oil committee supervised by Musaddiq announced that it was not in Iran's best interest to accept the Supplemental Agreement of 1949. The committee then asked Prime Minister Razmara to withdraw the agreement from the Majlis. Razmara agreed and withdrew the agreement. On January 11, 1951, the Majlis passed a resolution that rejected the bill containing the Supplemental Agreement of 1949.

These developments could be understood in light of the events that were taking place in other oil-producing countries. In 1949, it became known that an American oil company in Venezuela had agreed to evenly split the profits with Venezuela's government. In 1950, the Arabian-American Oil Company (Aramco) announced that it had concluded a 50/50 agreement with the Saudi government.[10] Following these announcements, the AIOC knew that it had to reach a new agreement with the Iranian government.

To prepare for negotiations with the AIOC, Prime Minister Razmara proposed the formation of an advisory committee composed of nine representatives chosen from among government officials, the Majlis, and the Senate. The Majlis, however, wanted to appoint its own committee.[11] On February 10, 1951, Razmara asked the AIOC to consider a new agreement with the Iranian government similar to the Saudi-Aramco 50/50 agreement. The AIOC said that it would consider the proposal. At the same time, the AIOC offered to help the Iranian government by providing £5 million as well as monthly payments in the amount of £2 million for the remainder of the year.[12]

Razmara tried to persuade the Majlis not to rush to nationalize the Iranian oil industry. At the same time, he tried to convince the Majlis deputies that it was in Iran's best interest to negotiate a 50/50 agreement with the AIOC. Razmara then met with Sir Francis Shepherd, the British ambassador in Iran, and told him that the British had to appear to agree with the idea of nationalization if the Majlis deputies were to vote on the 50/50 agreement with the AIOC. Shepherd rejected Razmara's plan and said that the British government would not accept the idea of nationalization. The AIOC, however, was willing to negotiate a 50/50 agreement if the terms of the concession were not changed.[13]

THE PUSH FOR NATIONALIZATION OF
THE IRANIAN OIL INDUSTRY

On February 19, 1951, Musaddiq presented a resolution to the Majlis oil committee for the Iranian oil industry to be nationalized. The oil committee asked Prime Minister Razmara to consider the issue of nationalization. Razmara responded by appointing a group of Iranian advisers from the Ministry of Finance and the Ministry of Foreign Affairs to prepare a report regarding the pros and cons of nationalizing the Iranian oil industry. Once the report was prepared, Razmara presented it to the Majlis oil committee. The report advised the Iranian government not to nationalize the oil industry. It warned that if Iran canceled the concession, it would have to pay substantial damages to the AIOC. Since Iran did not have enough financial resources to compensate the AIOC, it would lose its credibility among the international community.[14] The contents of this report were broadcast on the Iranian radio and printed in newspapers.

Musaddiq disagreed with the report and remained adamant about nationalizing the oil industry. The Majlis oil committee supported Musaddiq on this issue and drafted a resolution to this effect. Razmara had risked his life by trying to negotiate with the British. On March 7, 1951, he was assassinated by a member of the Fedaiyan Islam, a radical group that supported the nationalization of the oil industry. The Fedaiyan believed that Razmara was pro-British as evident from his speech to the Majlis arguing against nationalization of the oil industry. Following Razmara's assassination, the oil committee adopted Musaddiq's resolution to nationalize the Iranian oil industry.[15] The Shah nominated Hussein Ala, as the next prime minister.

On March 14, 1951, Ambassador Shepherd gave a letter to the Iranian government written by the British government indicating its dismay regarding the oil commission's decision to nationalize the oil industry even before the AIOC's concession had expired. The letter added that the Majlis had no legal rights to end the AIOC's operations. The letter concluded that the AIOC was willing to negotiate the equal distribution of profits with the Iranian government if it was allowed to keep its concession.[16] The Majlis disregarded Shepherd's letter. Instead, it approved the oil committee's resolution to nationalize the oil industry.[17] Shortly thereafter, the Iranian Senate also approved the committee's resolution for nationalizing the oil industry.[18]

Prime Minister Ala now had to deal with two critical problems: the beginning of strikes by oil industry workers in southern Iran and British anger regarding the nationalization of the oil industry. The oil industry strike began in Khuzistan on March 22 and continued until April 27, 1951. As a result, Prime Minister Ala declared martial law in Khuzistan.[19] Iranian forces managed to restore order. The British government reacted to the strikes in Khuzistan by announcing that its warships were being sent to the region to safeguard the oil industry in southern Iran. Ambassador Shepherd asked Prime Minister Ala whether the Iranian government had done anything to make sure the British employees residing in the area were safe.[20]

On April 8, 1951, Prime Minister Ala replied to the British letter of March 14, stating that the AIOC did not seem to be aware of the changes that were happening in Iran. There was nothing the Iranian government could do except to wait for the Majlis oil committee's decision regarding the implementation of plans associated with nationalization.[21] The British government replied that it had a right to protect its interests in Iran. At the same time, the British government was willing to negotiate a new agreement with the Iranian government. As part of this new agreement, the AIOC's legal concession and assets in Iran would be transferred to a new British company, whose board would also have Iranian members. Furthermore, the new agreement would allocate the profits to Iran on an equal basis. While the British government had not said a word about nationalization, it did mention that as part of the new agreement, foreign technicians would gradually be replaced with Iranians.[22]

The British letter and the arrival of British warships in the Persian Gulf had no effect on the Majlis oil committee. On April 29, 1951, the oil committee formulated a nine-point resolution to implement the nationalization law. It called for the removal of the AIOC and the establishment of a joint committee set up by the Senate and Majlis to run the oil industry. Prime Minister Ala resigned while this debate was taking place.[23]

Ala's resignation was no surprise to anyone, given his inability to prevent the Majlis from passing the resolution to nationalize the Iranian oil industry. Ambassador Shepherd favored Sayyid Zia al-Din Tabataba'i as the next prime minister, since he was pro-British. Sayyid Zia had helped Reza Khan carry out his coup and had become prime minister in 1921. Following Ala's resignation, Sayyid Zia had indicated his interest in becoming prime minister. There were, however, two problems associated with Sayyid Zia's appointment. First, the U.S. State Department disapproved of British attempts to have Sayyid Zia appointed as prime minister, since he intended to dissolve the Majlis.[24] Second, the Majlis wanted Musaddiq to be appointed prime minister, to which the Shah acquiesced. The nine-point law was passed by the Majlis and the Senate and was officially declared by the Shah on May 1, 1951.[25]

Prime Minister Musaddiq not only had to deal with British wrath in response to the nationalization law but also with threats from political groups such as the Fedaiyan Islam and the Tudeh Party. On May 1, 1951, Herbert Morrison, the British foreign secretary, told the British Parliament that the British government would not accept Iran's confiscation of the AIOC. Morrison then notified

Ambassador Shepherd that the British government did not recognize the law passed by the Iranian Majlis and the Senate to nationalize the oil industry. The British ambassador relayed this message to Musaddiq. On May 8, 1951, Musaddiq replied that the Iranian government had acted appropriately and it was ready to sell its oil and compensate the AIOC for any losses. The AIOC informed Musaddiq that it was turning the matter over to the International Court of Justice to determine whether the Iranian government's actions were legal.[26]

Musaddiq also had to deal with threats from the outlawed Tudeh Party. On May 7, 1951, the Tudeh Party addressed a letter to Musaddiq, which was published in a leftist newspaper. The letter asked Musaddiq to give freedom to all political parties, release political prisoners, and rescind anticommunist laws.[27] The Tudeh Party and other radical groups, such as the Fedaiyan Islam, had become impatient with Musaddiq and his attempts to negotiate with the AIOC. Musaddiq declared that he was being threatened by the Fedaiyan Islam, and sought refuge in the Majlis. Musaddiq's fears were understandable, given Razmara's assassination by a member of the Fedaiyan Islam. As a result, the police raided the headquarters of Fedaiyan Islam and arrested many of its members.[28]

On May 29, 1951, Herbert Morrison, the British foreign secretary, told the British Parliament that the British government had decided to consider the idea of the nationalization of the Iranian oil industry and would send its representatives to Iran to negotiate.[29] The Iranian government replied that it was ready to meet with the British negotiating team. The change in the British government's attitude can be attributed to American diplomatic efforts to settle the dispute.

THE ANGLO-AMERICAN AND SOVIET RESPONSE TO THE OIL NATIONALIZATION CRISIS: PHASE I, MARCH 1951–JULY 1952

Following the Majlis oil committee's announcement that the Iranian oil industry would be nationalized, the United States knew that there would be a change in the status of the AIOC, given that the Iranians were aware of the Saudi-Aramco 50/50 oil agreement. The United States was prepared to help both the Iranian and British governments to reach a new agreement that would satisfy the Iranian government and at the same time ensure the steady flow of oil to the West.

On March 14, 1951, the National Security Council prepared a report regarding U.S. policy in Iran. It stated that the primary objective of the United States was to prevent Soviet control of Iran, which could either result from an invasion or the spread of communism in the country. To this end, the United States would continue its diplomatic support and its military and financial aid to Iran, and at the same time advise the British government to reach a fair settlement with the Iranian government.[30]

Meanwhile, George McGhee, the U.S. Assistant Secretary of State, had paid a state visit to Pakistan. It was during that visit when he heard of Razmara's assassination. The State Department asked McGhee to visit Iran and observe not only the political situation following Razmara's death but also attempts by the National Front to nationalize the Iranian oil industry. A year earlier, McGhee had informed the AIOC that Aramco was offering a 50/50 profit-sharing deal to Saudi Arabia and advised the AIOC to take similar steps in Iran. The AIOC had refused to listen. McGhee believed that the nationalization dispute could have been avoided if the AIOC had listened and acted wisely. During his short visit to Iran on March 17, 1951, McGhee met with the Shah as well as Ambassador Shepherd and the American ambassador, Henry F. Grady. McGhee wanted to know whether there were any chances for the two sides to negotiate a 50/50 agreement but realized that the Iranian government intended to nationalize the AIOC.[31]

Meanwhile, U.S. State Department officials were preparing to meet with officials from the British Foreign Office to discuss the Iranian nationalization issue. The meeting was scheduled for April 9, 1951, and was to take place in Washington.[32] George McGhee, who was part of the U.S. delegation, told the British officials that they had to accept nationalization otherwise it would hurt any chances of future negotiations. McGhee thought that the British seemed unaware of the gravity of the security aspects of the nationalization crisis, as it could be emulated by other countries and lead to the disruption of peace around the world. McGhee stated that the United States supported Iran's sovereignty and asked the British to accept the nationalization of the oil industry.[33] The Anglo-American talks, however, ended at an impasse. Shortly thereafter, the Majlis oil committee adopted the nine-point resolution to implement the nationalization law, which was approved by the Majlis and Senate and promulgated as law on May 1, 1951.

The British government refused to acknowledge the nationalization law. While the U.S. government privately supported the idea of nationalization, it did not want the Iranian government to take any unilateral actions and confiscate the AIOC. At the same time, the United States advised the British government to accept the nationalization law and enter into negotiations with Iran. The Soviet Union supported Iran's nationalization of its oil industry, yet it chose not to get directly involved in this dispute in fear of losing its foothold in Iran.[34] The Soviets continued to support the Tudeh Party quietly behind the scenes.

On May 2, 1951, Ambassador Grady met with Prime Minister Musaddiq. Grady said that if the Iranian government were to confiscate the AIOC, it would be considered a unilateral act. It was best for the Iranian government to negotiate with its British counterpart. Musaddiq replied that the Majlis had made its decision and there was nothing else that could be done. Grady then met with the Shah, who was not only upset about the nationalization law but the appointment of Musaddiq as prime minister. The Shah said that he was helpless to do anything about these developments.[35]

On May 14, George McGhee held a meeting with a group of U.S. oil companies operating in the Middle East to discuss the nationalization issue in Iran. McGhee said that the U.S. objectives in Iran were to maintain security in the country, the continuance of Iran's relations with the West, and its steady flow of oil to international markets. McGhee noted that while the United States supported the idea of nationalization, it could not let its views be known, as it would weaken the British position. In addition, it could lead to negative developments in other oil-producing countries. If the United States were to oppose nationalization, the Iranian government would terminate its relations with the West. Therefore the United States had to convince the British government to offer a new agreement to Iran. McGhee and the representatives of the U.S. oil companies observed that while Iran could use the help of American technicians to run the oil industry, it was not wise to get involved, as it would interfere with British interests.[36]

Meanwhile, the British government announced that its forces were ready to occupy southern Iran if necessary. The United States was against this plan. President Truman and Secretary of State Acheson thought that the British occupation of southern Iran would lead to a military conflict with the Soviet Union. The Soviets would use this as an excuse to occupy northern Iran based on Article VI of the Russo-Persian Treaty of 1921.[37] The United States managed to convince the British government to back away from its military option.

On May 18, 1951, the U.S. government made a significant statement to the press regarding the Iranian oil nationalization crisis. The United States was concerned over the growing dispute between Iran and Great Britain and advised the two sides to negotiate. While, the United States understood Iran's desire to control its resources, it advised the Iranian government not to confiscate the AIOC, but to negotiate instead with the British government.[38] The Iranian government was disappointed by these comments and even accused the United States of unwanted interference in its domestic affairs. The U.S. government replied that it had no intention of meddling in Iranian affairs. It added that the only way for the Iranian government to get control over its resources was through negotiations with the British government.[39]

On May 25, 1951, Ambassador Shepherd notified Musaddiq that the British government was willing to discuss the nationalization issue by sending its team of negotiators to Iran. The British government also asked the International Court of Justice to mediate. President Truman contacted Prime Minister Clement Atlee of Britain and Prime Minister Musaddiq encouraging them to settle the dispute through negotiations. As a result, on June 11, 1951, Basil Jackson, the vice chairman of the AIOC Board of Directors, and his negotiating team, arrived in Tehran.[40]

The Iranian negotiating team wanted the AIOC to pay the Iranian government 75 percent of the oil revenues that it had held back since March 20, 1951, and place the remaining 25 percent in the bank to cover any future charges that the company may have.[41] Jackson proposed a new agreement that acknowledged Iran's nationalization law, offered a one time payment of £10 million, a monthly payment of £3 million, and for Iran to take its portion of assets in the AIOC and place them in a new Iranian National Oil Company that would grant the use of those assets to a company to be established by the AIOC.[42] The British plan was for the AIOC to maintain control over the new operating company in Iran and continue marketing Iranian oil.

The Iranian negotiating team rejected Jackson's proposal, arguing that it violated Iran's nationalization law. As a result, the British government asked the International Court of Justice to issue an order that would stop the Iranian government from confiscating the AIOC. The Iranian government notified the court that it did not have jurisdiction and that Iran would not send any representatives to the court.[43]

Meanwhile, in a statement to the press, Secretary of State Acheson voiced his concern about the Iranian government's decision to shut down the oil refinery in Abadan. Despite the Iranian government's rejection of Jackson's proposals, Acheson hoped that the oil dispute would be resolved and the operation of the oil refinery would continue uninterrupted.[44] Musaddiq wrote to President Truman stating that the Iranian government would do its best to ensure the steady flow of oil even if the British technicians were to resign or if the British government was to delay the shipment of oil products. Musaddiq added that his government would hire foreign technicians to help run the oil industry.[45]

On July 5, 1951, the International Court of Justice announced that the management and daily operation of the AIOC had to continue as it had prior to the nationalization law. The court then recommended the formation of a supervisory board that would make sure that the AIOC's operations continued without any disruption.[46] The Iranian government rejected the court's recommendations. Meanwhile, President Truman had written to Musaddiq encouraging the Iranian government to reach an agreement with its British counterpart. Truman emphasized the importance of the court's recommendations and offered to send a negotiating team headed by Averell Harriman to Iran.[47]

The Tudeh Party organized several demonstrations against Harriman in front of the American embassy. The demonstrators shouted slogans against the AIOC and the U.S. government's interference in Iranian affairs.[48] From the time the nationalization law went into effect until July 1952, the Tudeh Party suspected Musaddiq of collaborating with the United States. The Tudeh Party believed that the United States supported the nationalization issue in order to undermine and replace Britain's position in Iran.[49]

In a meeting with Harriman, Musaddiq said that he wanted to end decades of British control over Iranian oil. Harriman replied that the Iranian government had to find a solution that would not only help Iran gain control over its oil but could also benefit from British technical aid. From July 17 to 27, Harriman's team met with Ambassador Grady to discuss possible solutions to the oil dispute. Musaddiq told Harriman that the British government had to publicly acknowledge the acceptance of the nationalization of the Iranian oil industry prior to the resumption of talks between the two sides.[50]

Harriman and his staff then left for London to negotiate with the British government. The British agreed to send a new negotiating team to Tehran, led by Richard Stokes, which arrived on August 4, 1951. The Harriman mission had also returned to Tehran to mediate between the two sides. At the conclusion of the talks, Stokes presented an eight-point proposal to the Iranian government, which was rejected.[51]

Harriman reported to the State Department that while the Stokes mission had offered to accept the nationalization law, it had upset the Iranian government by indicating joint efforts in running the oil industry, implying that the Iranians could not function without British help. The Iranian government had its own reasons behind its refusal of Stokes's proposals. Among these were that the proposals did not address: Iran's need for an equitable division of oil revenues; the employment of non-British foreign technicians by the Iranian government; and the purchase of Iranian oil by various customers other than the British.[52] The Stokes mission left Iran on August 23, followed by the Harriman mission.

Prime Minister Attlee wrote to President Truman about the Stokes mission and the deteriorating political situation in Iran, which could pave the way for a communist takeover. Attlee wanted the United States to support the British government on the fact that the stalemate in the negotiations had resulted from the Iranian government's refusal to cooperate. Truman and Acheson discussed this issue and decided that Truman would not reply to Attlee just yet. Later when Acheson attended a conference in San Francisco, he told a group of British diplomats that the United States could not publicly support the British government with every decision, as the Iranian government would think that the United States was conspiring with the AIOC.[53]

On September 10, 1951, the British government not only imposed a blockade on the sale of Iranian oil but also stopped payments to any accounts held by the Iranian government. Musaddiq paid no attention and instead sent a letter to Harriman with new proposals to resume negotiations with the British government. Musaddiq stated that the British had only two weeks to consider his offer, after which the Iranian government would ask the British employees to leave Iran.[54]

Harriman replied that the Iranian government should not upset the British government any further, and he refused to discuss Musaddiq's proposals. On September 19, 1951, the Iranian government gave Ambassador Shepherd a list of proposals similar to the ones sent by Musaddiq to Harriman. The ultimatum had been taken out and instead the Iranian government had indicated that it would resume negotiations. The British government rejected the Iranian government's proposals.[55]

Meanwhile, Loy Henderson had succeeded Henry Grady as the next American ambassador to Iran. Henderson had been the director of the State Department's division of Near Eastern Affairs from 1945 to 1948. He had also served as American ambassador to India until 1951, when he was given the post in Iran. Henderson was more experienced in Middle Eastern affairs than any other American ambassadors assigned to Iran. Henderson later played an important role in overthrowing Musaddiq's government.

On September 27, 1951, Iranian forces took control of the Abadan oil refinery. The British government decided not to retaliate and, instead, asked the United Nations Security Council to review this issue. The Security Council stated that the review of this issue did not mean that the council was qualified to solve the problem. Rather, it was necessary to hear both sides of the dispute before the question of the council's qualifications could be determined. Dr. Ali Qoli Ardalan, the Iranian representative, asked the council to wait until the Iranian negotiating team arrived in New York. Therefore the council scheduled its next meeting for October 15, 1951.[56]

During this time, the U.S. government came up with a plan for U.S. oil companies to help provide oil to allies that had been affected by the British blockade on the sale of Iranian oil. The United States delivered nearly 46 million barrels of oil to its allies during the first year of the blockade.[57] The United States also thought about the formation of a consortium that would purchase and sell Iranian oil to other customers. This plan was not implemented at the time because of the anti-trust litigation that had been previously brought against the U.S. oil companies.[58] The idea of a consortium that would purchase and market Iranian oil was later revived and put into practice in 1954.

An Iranian negotiating team headed by Musaddiq arrived in New York on October 8, 1951. Musaddiq appeared before the U.N. Security Council and said that Iran was ready to negotiate for the sale of its oil and compensate the AIOC. He added that the British resolution to get the U.N. Security Council involved made no sense, as the council was not qualified to settle the dispute. On October 19, the council ended its meetings and announced that it would wait to hear from the International Court of Justice regarding its decision.[59] Musaddiq then went to Washington to discuss the oil dispute with Truman, Acheson, and McGhee.[60] Truman told Musaddiq that the United States had no interest in Iranian oil and only wanted to help the two sides solve the dispute.[61] Musadddiq met with Acheson and McGhee throughout the remaining part of October, to discuss a new proposal that would lead to the resumption of negotiations with the British government. The State Department reviewed the new proposal and sent it to Winston Churchill, who had become the new British prime minister following the elections of October of 1951. Churchill rejected the new proposal, which centered on the issues of management, marketing, and prices.[62]

The British government was dismayed that the U.S. government was still negotiating with Musaddiq. Anthony Eden, the British foreign secretary, discussed these concerns this in his memoirs. Eden did not agree with the U.S. view that if Musaddiq were removed from power, Iran would experience further chaos. Eden suspected that the United States was supportive of Musaddiq's policy of Negative Equilibrium. What added to those suspicions was that the Iranian government had announced that the United States was supportive of its efforts to settle the oil dispute.[63] Eden then set up a meeting with Secretary Acheson to discuss the British government's concerns. The two men met in Paris in early November 1951.

Musaddiq was still in the United States when the meeting between Eden and Acheson took place. The U.S. government wanted to reach an agreement with Musaddiq before he left. The United States had to decide whether to provide financial aid to Musaddiq to keep his government in tact or let the country go down in chaos. The British did not agree with this view, arguing that there were other alternatives to Musaddiq's government. Musaddiq's government could be replaced by one that would cooperate with the British government. While the Anglo-American debate over Musaddiq continued, the two sides eventually decided to ask the International Bank for Reconstruction and Development (IBRD), or the World Bank, to mediate as a third party in the oil dispute.[64]

Robert Garner, vice president of the World Bank, arranged a meeting with Musaddiq. Garner told Musaddiq that Iranian government had to consider certain suggestions before the bank could mediate in the conflict. Among these were: if the bank were to invest in the Iranian oil industry, it expected a return on its investment; and British technicians would continue with their jobs as before.[65] Musaddiq agreed to the bank's first suggestion but refused to have British technicians operating the Iranian oil industry. He also agreed to have the bank's negotiating team visit Iran to help settle the dispute. Prior to his departure from the United States, Musaddiq asked the U.S. government for a loan in the amount of $120 million to help keep the Iranian economy afloat. President Truman told Musaddiq that his request would be taken into consideration.[66]

On December 31, 1951, Hector Prudhomme, director of the World Bank's loan department, and Torkild Rieber, petroleum adviser to the World Bank, arrived in Tehran. They gave Musaddiq a memorandum from Garner, which outlined the information that Garner had discussed with Musaddiq. The World Bank intended to put together a board of management and employ technicians to run the Iranian oil industry. The profits from the sale of Iranian oil were to be divided among the Iranian government, the World Bank, and the purchaser. It was not clear from Garner's memorandum who the purchaser was. Therefore Musaddiq wrote Garner asking about this issue. Musaddiq made it clear that if Britain were the main purchaser, he would reject the bank's proposals.[67]

Musaddiq was told that his letter could not be answered until the bank had had time to study his question. Prudhomme then asked Musaddiq if the bank's negotiating team could visit the refinery in Abadan to prepare a report for the bank, to which Musaddiq agreed.[68] In the meantime, Musaddiq found himself in a controversy with the U.S. government. On January 8, 1952, the United States had asked the Iranian government to allow for the continuation of its military aid to Iran according to section 511(a) of the Mutual Security Act, known as the Battle Act.[69] The controversy associated with the Mutual Security or the Battle Act was that countries receiving U.S. military aid had to pledge their commitment to the defense of the West. Musaddiq refused to answer in fear of a backlash from the Soviet Union, if he were to pledge the assurances to the United States. He believed that Iran needed financial aid instead of military aid. The Shah, however, favored the continuation of U.S. military aid. The question of U.S. military aid to Iran remained unknown at the time.

The U.S. government nonetheless decided to continue its technical aid to Iran. If the United States were to end its technical and military aid to Iran, the country could further plunge into chaos.[70] While the United States had no intention of giving any substantial aid to Iran, it did not want Iran to fall to communism. Loy Henderson was able to get Musaddiq's approval for the continuation of U.S. technical aid to Iran.

Meanwhile, Prime Minister Churchill visited the United States and met with President Truman to discuss the developments in Iran. Truman and Churchill discussed the issue of U.S. military and technical aid to Iran. The United States had set aside $23 million for technical aid to Iran to be utilized in 1952, and indicated the possibility of Iran obtaining a loan in the amount of $25 million from the Export-Import Bank. Churchill was upset with the issue of U.S. aid to Iran. At the same time, he reviewed the World Bank's reports regarding its recent negotiations with Iran. Churchill and Truman both hoped that the World Bank could settle the dispute.[71]

On January 13, 1952, Musaddiq met with Henderson and asked for U.S. financial aid to alleviate Iran's budget deficit. Musaddiq said that without any aid, the Iranian government would not survive and the Tudeh Party would take over. This was the first time that Musaddiq had brought up the threat of communism.[72] The United States did not respond to Musaddiq's request for financial aid. Instead, it announced that it would halt its military aid to Iran, as the Iranian government had not given the United States any response regarding its continuation nor the required assurances. The Iranian press provided much coverage of this story pondering whether this meant the United States would also cut its technical aid to Iran.[73]

The World Bank organized its second visit to Iran on February 11, 1952. The bank argued that the Iranian government had to agree to the employment of British technicians if the oil industry were to function effectively. Musaddiq refused to accept the employment of British technicians. Another problem was that the Iranian government wanted a higher price for its oil. Since the bank was unable to reach an agreement, Garner and his team left Iran. Shortly thereafter the bank announced that the talks would no longer continue given the lack of progress.[74]

On March 20, 1952, the State Department announced that it could not provide financial aid to Iran in the sum of $120 million, as requested by Musaddiq. The State Department said that the Iranian government could still settle its dispute with the AIOC and receive higher oil revenues.[75] Despite this announcement, the U.S. government would continue with its technical aid to Iran. On April 15, 1952, the United States announced that it had reached an agreement with the Iranian government to provide technical aid designed to improve agriculture, education, and public health.[76]

At the same time, the United States came up with a solution that was meant to change Musaddiq's mind into accepting the continuation of U.S. military aid to Iran. The U.S. government would insert a clause in its agreement that would specify Iran's commitment to the United Nations Charter instead of the Battle Act. Musaddiq agreed and on April 24, 1952, signed an agreement with Henderson to resume the continuation of U.S. military aid to Iran.[77]

The Soviet government sent a letter to the Iranian government criticizing its acceptance of U.S. military aid. The Iranian government replied that Iran's acceptance of U.S. military aid did not mean that Iran had let go of its neutral stance. Iran had accepted U.S. military aid in order to strengthen the country's security.[78]

The International Court of Justice held its hearings regarding the dispute between the Iranian government and the AIOC. On June 9, 1952, Musaddiq put forth his arguments in support of the nationalization of the Iranian oil industry. Professor Henry Rolin of Brussels University presented legal arguments in favor of Iran's questioning the court's jurisdiction and asked the court to dismiss the case. Sir Eric Beckett, legal adviser to the British Foreign Office, and his assistant, Sir Lionel Heald, represented the British government. They asked the court to state that it had jurisdiction to review the case and that it was illegal for Iran to nationalize the oil industry. The court was to reach a decision within a month.[79]

Meanwhile, the Iranian Majlis and the senate voted in favor of Musaddiq's second term as prime minister. Musaddiq asked the Majlis for special powers with regard to economic and administrative decisions, and asked the Shah to grant him full control over the Ministry of Defense and the Iranian Army. Musaddiq's objective was to secure his position as prime minister, but the Shah and the Majlis did not favor granting Musaddiq the special powers. As a result, Musaddiq resigned.[80]

The Shah appointed Ahmad Qavam as prime minister. In the past, Qavam had established good relations with the British and the U.S. governments. He was critical of Musaddiq's choices and his inability to settle the dispute. The National Front and other political parties were upset at Qavam's appointment, as they thought he would side with the British and jeopardize the nationalization process. Qavam tried to negotiate with the National Front and other political parties, such as the Tudeh Party, but they refused to cooperate.

On July 19, 1952, Ambassador Henderson met with Qavam to discuss political developments in Iran. Qavam later told Hasan Arsanjani, one of his advisers, that Henderson had told him that the U.S. government would help Iran overcome its budget deficit.[81] Even if the U.S. government favored Qavam over Musaddiq, it did not say anything publicly, fearing that it would stir anti-American sentiments and lead to further demonstrations in Iran. This issue was discussed in a memorandum from Henderson to the state department observing that the Tudeh Party and members of the National Front were of the opinion that Qavam and Henderson's collaboration had led to Musaddiq's resignation.[82]

Meanwhile, Ayatollah Kashani announced a day of national protest against Qavam's government. On July 21, 1952, there were several clashes between demonstrators and the police, which led to several deaths and injuries. This incident became known as the National Revolt of July 21. While Ayatollah Kashani and the National Front had helped organize the demonstration, the clashes with police were blamed on the activities of the Tudeh Party. Prominent Tudeh leaders and members have discussed in their memoirs that following Musaddiq's resignation, the Tudeh Party realized that Qavam's appointment as prime minister would lead to an end to their activities. If the Tudeh Party had been suspicious about Musaddiq being pro-American, they knew for a fact that Qavam was on friendly terms with the British and would do anything in his power to settle the oil nationalization dispute. The Tudeh Party therefore decided to support the National Front in bringing Musaddiq back to power.[83] Aside from its objection to Iran's decision to resume the acceptance of U.S. military aid, the Soviet Union had remained unusually quiet during this period. It nonetheless continued its support of the Tudeh Party, hoping that it would emerge victorious and gain control of political power in Iran.

On July 22, 1952, two important events led to Musaddiq's return to power: the International Court of Justice announced that it did not have jurisdiction over the Iranian oil dispute case; and Qavam resigned due to his inability to settle the oil dispute.[84] Musaddiq was confirmed prime minister by the Majlis for a second term. The Shah reluctantly agreed to Musaddiq's appointment as prime minister to prevent the country from falling into chaos. The Majlis then granted Musaddiq special powers for six months as well as control over the Ministry of Defense.[85]

THE ANGLO-AMERICAN AND SOVIET RESPONSE TO THE OIL NATIONALIZATION CRISIS: PHASE II: AUGUST 1952 TO AUGUST 1953

The U.S. government was concerned about the changes in the Tudeh Party's activities and its sudden decision to support Musaddiq and the National Front. Henderson sent several reports to the State Department about the Tudeh Party's activities, including its clashes with the Iranian police, shouting anti-Shah and anti-American slogans during demonstrations, and even disfiguring the Shah's statues.[86] By early August 1952, the National Front had begun to weaken due to internal strife among its members. Hussein Maki, a Majlis deputy and member of the National Front, told Henderson that he had been against granting special powers to Musaddiq. Ayatollah Kashani, the Speaker of the Majlis, was also upset with Musaddiq because he had appointed three Tudeh Party members to his cabinet.[87]

To keep the public contented, Musaddiq's government announced that it would undertake a reform program that would benefit the society. Among these were: reform of the Iranian economy; reform of the judiciary; reform of the electoral law; and passing a bill that would help increase the farmers' share of crops and income.[88] Musaddiq, however, faced certain problems in carrying out the reforms. First, the majority of the Majlis deputies were wealthy landowners, who wanted to protect their interests and maintain the status quo. They were therefore against Musaddiq's reforms. Second, Musaddiq needed financial resources to overcome the budget deficit while he was carrying out the reforms. To this end, he once again turned his attention to the oil dispute, hoping to find a solution that would provide much needed revenues.

On August 7, 1952, Musaddiq sent a letter to the British embassy in Tehran asking the AIOC to pay Iran's share of oil revenues, which the company had withheld, and for the British government to lift its boycott on the sale of Iranian oil. He added that if the British government accepted these terms, the Iranian government would resume negotiations.[89] Since there was no reply, Musaddiq contacted the British embassy, reiterating his proposals and emphasizing that he needed financial aid to carry out his reforms. Musaddiq even suggested that the two governments ask the International Court of Justice to settle the issue of Iran's compensation to the AIOC. He then asked the British government to consider providing financial aid to Iran, and even went so far to suggest that he was willing to sell Iranian oil to the AIOC if a fair agreement could be worked out.[90]

The British government, meanwhile, had been discussing Musaddiq's request with the U.S. government, and suggested a joint Anglo-American proposal to the Iranian government to settle the oil dispute.[91] On August 25, 1952, Ambassador Henderson was told by the State Department that President Truman and Prime Minister Churchill had agreed on a joint proposal to the Iranian government. Ambassador Henderson and George Middleton from the British embassy were to discuss the joint proposal with Musaddiq.[92] Among the points discussed in the proposal were: the International Court of Justice would determine the amount of the Iranian government's compensation to the AIOC; the Iranian government and the AIOC would have their own special representatives to discuss the sale of Iranian oil on the world market; the British government would resume the export of its products to Iran; and the U.S. government would provide a grant in the amount of $10 million to help Iran with its budget deficit.[93]

The Iranian government rejected the joint Anglo-American proposal and threatened to end its diplomatic relations with Britain if it did not make a payment in the amount of £49 million, and turn over the issue of the AIOC's to the International Court of Justice. The £49 million was the estimated share of Iran's oil revenues being held by the AIOC. Musaddiq also indicated his displeasure over the AIOC's monopoly of the purchase of Iranian oil as indicated in the proposal, and referred to the British boycott on the sale of Iranian oil, which had led to the deterioration of the Iranian economy.[94]

The British and the U.S. governments replied separately to Musaddiq. Anthony Eden, the British foreign secretary, said that the British government had no intention to monopolize the purchase of Iranian oil. Rather, the proposal had suggested a fair method of settling the dispute. Secretary of State Acheson was upset about the Iranian government's lack of understanding, since the proposal acknowledged the nationalization of the Iranian oil industry and the Iranian government was free to sell its oil to any customer it wanted.[95]

Musaddiq replied to both Acheson and Eden that he was willing to settle the dispute with the British government, but he wanted the AIOC to pay £20 million to his government prior to the resumption of negotiations. This payment would be considered the first installment toward the £ 49 million that Musaddiq had mentioned earlier.[96] The British government refused to pay the sum indicated by Musaddiq. On October 22, 1952, Musaddiq informed the British embassy that he was ending diplomatic relations with Britain. As a result, the staff of the British embassy left.[97]

Meanwhile, the American political scene was dominated by the presidential elections. On November 6, 1952, the Republicans, led by General Dwight D. Eisenhower, defeated the Democrats. Eisenhower had chosen Richard Nixon as his running mate and appointed John Foster Dulles secretary of state. The Truman administration had relied extensively on the State Department in conducting U.S. foreign policy. During the Eisenhower administration, however, the CIA worked more closely with the White House and was able to influence U.S. foreign policy effectively. The CIA was to be headed by Allen Dulles, the brother of the secretary of state. In Iran, Ambassador Henderson maintained his position until 1954.

During this time, the British government had devised a plan to overthrow Musaddiq's government. The British government sent Christopher Montague Woodhouse, the chief MI6 officer in Iran to the United States to obtain support for its plan called Operation Boot. The plan was for two Iranian agents known as the Rashidian brothers and a number of Bakhtiari tribal leaders to organize riots against Musaddiq's government. These activities were to be carried out under General Fazlollah Zahedi's supervision. General Zahedi had actually served as Musaddiq's minister of the interior and was a member of the National Front. Woodhouse met with CIA and State Department officials. Instead of addressing the oil crisis, Woodhouse emphasized the communist threat to Iran. He argued that Musaddiq's government could be easily overthrown by a coup organized by the Tudeh Party, which would be supported by the Soviet Union. For these reasons, Musaddiq's government had to come to an end.[98] The Truman administration rejected the Woodhouse plan. Yet the new Eisenhower administration would take these ideas into consideration.

Despite the unsettled oil dispute, the U.S. government continued to provide technical aid to Iran in order to strengthen its economy and prevent it from falling to communism. William Warne, the U.S. director of technical cooperation, signed an agreement with Musaddiq on the establishment of a Joint U.S.-Iranian Economic and Social Development Commission on January 1, 1953. As part of this agreement, the U.S. government would provide $20 million in technical aid to Iran.[99]

On January 8, 1953, Musaddiq sent a letter to the Majlis asking for an extension of his special powers for another year. He said that these powers would help rehabilitate Iran's economy and for his government to resist foreign pressures. The Majlis deputies were once again uncertain about granting Musaddiq these powers. Ayatollah Kashani, the Speaker of the Majlis, was against granting these powers to Musaddiq. Deputies, such as Hussein Maki, who were also opposed to the granting of these powers, resigned in protest. Deputies, who supported Musaddiq on this issue, took sanctuary in the Majlis until he was given these powers. Despite their disagreement, the majority of the National Front's members supported Musaddiq. As a result, the Majlis extended Musaddiq's special powers.[100]

Musaddiq now had to decide whether to renew a twenty-five-year-old agreement between the Soviet Union and Iran regarding the Caspian Fishery. The Soviet government wanted to renew the agreement. Musaddiq refused to renew the agreement and also refused the Soviet proposal for the purchase and management of the Caspian Fishery.[101] The Soviet government backed down for the moment, but it approached the Iranian government in the following months with offers that the latter could not refuse.

Meanwhile, Sir Patrick Dean from the British Foreign Office had got in touch with the CIA to discuss a plan to overthrow Musaddiq's government, and replace him with General Zahedi. On February 3, 1953, there was a meeting between British and U.S. officials. Allen Dulles, the Director of the CIA, and Kermit Roosevelt, chief of the CIA's Middle East division were also present. The British then asked Roosevelt to be in charge of this operation, which became known as Operation AJAX. The two sides said that they would continue their negotiations shortly regarding the details of the operation.[102]

Meanwhile, General Zahedi had also been planning a military coup against Musaddiq and had sought the help of several army officers. Zahedi's son, Ardeshir, informed the American embassy in Tehran that his father was ready to carry out a coup. At the same time, a group of Bakhtiari tribal chiefs, who had agreed to help Zahedi, attacked a unit of Iranian security forces in Khuzistan. Musaddiq ordered Zahedi to be taken in for questioning and told the Majlis that he would resign because of the plots against his government.[103]

On February 24, 1953, a number of Majlis deputies affiliated with the National Front, visited the Shah. They conveyed a message from Musaddiq to the Shah. Musaddiq wanted the Shah to announce that the Iranian Army had to follow Musaddiq's orders, and for the Shah to stop the distribution of royal estates to the peasants and let Musaddiq take care of it. The Shah agreed with the first request but he wanted to continue with the distribution of lands to the peasants, as it would strengthen his base of support.[104]

On February 25, 1953, Hussein Ala, the minister of court, met with Henderson and told him about a recent conversation between the Shah and Musaddiq. Apparently Musaddiq had asked the Shah to leave Iran and remain overseas until the political situation had stabilized. Musaddiq believed that the Shah's departure from Iran would end any plans to overthrow his government. The Shah had agreed to go overseas for the time being.[105] Ala told Henderson that the Shah intended to visit the holy Shiite shrines in Iraq and to then visit Europe. Both Ala and Henderson believed that the Shah's departure would jeopardize the monarchy. Ala asked Henderson not to discuss this conversation with either the Shah or Musaddiq, for the time being.[106]

On February 28, 1953, thousands of demonstrators asked the Shah not to leave Iran. The demonstrators gathered on Kakh Street, near the Shah's palace and Musaddiq's home. They shouted slogans against Musaddiq and gathered in front of his home. Musaddiq escaped over a rear wall and took sanctuary in the Majlis. The Shah announced that for the time being he would remain in Iran.[107]

While the United States was pleased with the Shah's announcement that he would remain in Iran, it remained concerned about the activities of the Tudeh Party. On March 1, 1953, the CIA prepared a memorandum about Iran, observing that Western influence had weakened and that the possibility of a communist takeover had increased. The Tudeh Party was ready to overthrow Musaddiq's weak government.[108] In a report to the State Department, Henderson discussed the activities of the Tudeh Party, noting its attempts to maintain good relations with the National Front. Henderson observed that the Tudeh Party had organized several demonstrations in support of Musaddiq due to his decision to release many Tudeh members from prison.[109]

On March 5, 1953, Stalin died and was succeeded by Nikita Khrushchev. Henderson reported to the State Department that thousands of Tudeh Party members had demonstrated in Stalin's honor and the Tudeh Party had published eulogies glorifying Stalin.[110] At the same time, Musaddiq met with

Henderson and asked whether the United States could provide financial aid to Iran. Henderson replied that the United States would not provide any financial aid to Iran, as it had rejected the Anglo-American proposal for the settlement of the oil dispute.[111] This rejection did not deter Musaddiq, whose attention was momentarily diverted by an internal crisis.

On April 21, 1953, Mahmud Afshartus, the Iranian chief of police, was kidnapped and murdered. It later became known that the kidnapping had been organized by General Zahedi to obtain confidential information about Musaddiq's government. Zahedi and Mozaffar Baqai, a Majlis deputy, were charged in connection to this murder, and Musaddiq ordered the two men to be arrested. Ayatollah Kashani, the Speaker of the Majlis, who was a friend of Zahedi, granted him sanctuary in the Majlis. Baqai also avoided arrest because he had immunity from the Majlis.[112] Musaddiq therefore could take no actions against Zahedi or Baqai, and he once again turned his attention to asking Eisenhower for financial aid.

On May 28, 1953, Musaddiq wrote a letter to Eisenhower. Musaddiq asked Henderson, who was to visit the United States, to deliver the letter. Musaddiq wanted the contents of this letter to remain private fearing a reprisal from his enemies in Iran. Musaddiq had discussed the problems Iran was experiencing, especially the deteriorating economy. He emphasized that these problems could be solved by either the British removing their blockade on the sale of Iranian oil or by Iran receiving U.S. financial aid. Musaddiq also highlighted the danger of Iran falling to communism if did not receive any financial aid.[113]

Meanwhile, the Soviet government decided to take advantage of the situation and offered the Iranian government a chance to settle their longtime dispute over two issues: the return of eleven tons of Iranian gold, which had been held by the Soviet Union since the Second World War; and a settlement of the disputed border between the two countries, along the Atrak river in northeast Iran. The Soviets also offered Iran a new trade agreement and to even change the terms of the Russo-Persian Treaty of 1921, which authorized the Soviets to move their troops into Iran if they ever felt their borders were threatened. On June 14, 1953, Musaddiq met with Ambassador Ivan Sadchikov to discuss these issues. Sadchikov said that a Soviet negotiating team would visit Iran shortly.[114] The U.S. government became alarmed at these developments and began to take countermeasures.

On June 25, 1953, the fate of Musaddiq's government was discussed once and for all at a State Department meeting. Among the officials present at this meeting were: Secretary of State John Foster Dulles; Allen Dulles, the director of the CIA; Kermit Roosevelt, chief of CIA's Middle East division; Loy Henderson, the American ambassador to Iran; Under Secretary of State

General Walter Bedell Smith; and other officials.[115] Roosevelt then discussed the details of Operation AJAX to overthrow Musaddiq's government.

Roosevelt provided a brief history of the origins of this plan, which began with the British request to U.S. officials to coordinate their efforts into overthrowing Musaddiq's government. While the British were mainly concerned about preserving their oil interests in Iran, the United States was concerned about the Soviet threat and a communist takeover of Iran. Roosevelt then stated that based on intelligence reports, two facts had to be taken into consideration. First, the Soviet threat to Iran was real. Second, the Iranian Army's loyalty remained with the Shah and not Musaddiq. Therefore, it was important to have the Shah and his army's cooperation in overthrowing Musaddiq's government. The U.S. and the British governments favored General Zahedi to be appointed as the next prime minister. To this end, the Shah would be advised to dismiss Musaddiq and nominate Zahedi as the next prime minister. Roosevelt said that a sum of $100,000 was needed to carry out Operation AJAX. This sum would be used to pay the Iranian Army and people to demonstrate in support of the Shah.[116] Operation AJAX was approved by the Eisenhower administration and would be carried out over the next two months.

On June 29, 1953, Eisenhower replied to Musaddiq's letter of May 28, stating that the United States had done its best to help both the British and the Iranian governments to settle their dispute. Even though the United States understood Iran's problems, it was not fair to give any financial aid to Iran as long as it could generate revenues from the sale of its oil if an agreement were made. In the meantime, the United States would continue to provide technical and military aid to Iran.[117] Eisenhower released the contents of Musaddiq's letter and his reply to the American press, despite Musaddiq's request to keep the contents of the letter private. Eisenhower's reply to Musaddiq received special coverage in Iran, with the Iranian press reporting that the United States would not provide any financial aid to Iran until the oil dispute was resolved.[118]

The Tudeh Party took advantage of this situation and attacked Musaddiq for his dialogue with the United States. On July 20, 1953, the Tudeh Party addressed a letter to Musaddiq criticizing him for asking the United States for financial aid, which was humiliating for Iran. Musaddiq was also criticized for agreeing to the renew U.S. military and technical aid to Iran. The Tudeh Party specifically asked Musaddiq to end Iran's military and technical agreements with the United States and to close the American embassy in Tehran.[119] On July 21 1953, Tudeh Party members engaged in demonstrations in remembrance of the previous year, which had led to the end of Qavam's government and Musaddiq's return as prime minister. The Tudeh supporters shouted anti-American slogans and rejected U.S. technical and military aid to Iran. The demonstrators, which included women and children, were estimated at 40,000.[120]

Musaddiq decided that the only way to bring an end to the plots against his government was to dissolve the Majlis, whose deputies were opposed to him. In support of Musaddiq, some of the National Front deputies resigned, claiming that the opposition had rendered the Majlis ineffectual. Musaddiq then announced that a referendum would be held so that the people would determine whether the Majlis should continue. The referendum was scheduled to take place between August 3 and August 10, 1953.[121] The deputies who were opposed to Musaddiq tried to stop the referendum by taking sanctuary in the Majlis, and when that did not work, they decided to boycott it. These measures made no difference and Musaddiq obtained the vote to dissolve the Majlis. Musaddiq had thought that the referendum would end the plots against his government but, in fact, it hastened his downfall. Musaddiq'a act of holding referendum was contrary to the principles of the Constitution, since only the Shah had the power to dissolve the Majlis.

The U.S. government was becoming more concerned about the political activities of the Tudeh Party and the visit of the Soviet negotiating team to Iran, which was to discuss past border disputes and the return of eleven tons of gold, which the Soviets had kept from Iran since the Second World War. On July 28, Secretary of State Dulles said at a press conference that the United States was concerned over the activities of the Tudeh Party, which Musaddiq government's had done nothing to address. The United States would not provide any financial aid to Iran as long as its government did nothing about Tudeh's activities.[122] Shortly thereafter, on August 9, 1953, the Soviet government asked for the Iranian government's permission to send a Soviet negotiating team to Iran to conduct negotiations.[123]

Meanwhile, the CIA and MI6 officials had taken steps to prepare the Shah for Operation AJAX. Ashraf Pahlavi, the Shah's sister, who was in France at the time, was asked to return to Iran and encourage the Shah to remain strong in the face of the events that were to happen.[124] General Schwarzkopf, the former chief of GENMISH, was sent by the U.S. government to Iran to meet with the Shah. Kermit Roosevelt traveled from Iraq to Iran and met with General Zahedi and his supporters to carry out Operation AJAX. Roosevelt met with the Shah and asked him to dismiss Musaddiq and appoint General Zahedi as the next prime minister.[125]

The Shah issued a decree on August 13, 1953 that dismissed Musaddiq and appointed General Zahedi as prime minister. The Shah then asked Colonel

Nimatollah Nassiri to present the decree to Musaddiq.[126] The Tudeh Party warned Musaddiq of an impending military coup to overthrow his government and even published these warnings in two of its newspapers, stating that it was prepared to do anything to prevent the coup from happening.[127] Yet the Tudeh Party took no definite action due to strife among its leaders and lack of coordination with the Soviet Union, which had been too busy with its own domestic affairs since Stalin's death. The important question here is how did the Tudeh Party know about the proposed military coup? In their memoirs, prominent Tudeh members reveal that the party's intelligence network, which had infiltrated the Iranian Army, became aware of an Anglo-American plan to overthrow Musaddiq and replace him with Zahedi.[128]

Colonel Nassiri delivered the Shah's decree to Musaddiq, who then ordered Nassiri to be arrested and announced that the military coup against him had failed. Musaddiq also issued a warrant for the arrest of Zahedi, who went into hiding.[129] Following these developments, the Shah and his wife left Iran for a visit to Iraq and then to Italy. On August 17, 1953, Ambassador Henderson returned to Iran from his vacation. Henderson met with Musaddiq to discuss the political situation in Iran. Musaddiq was hostile to Henderson, since he suspected an Anglo-American conspiracy to overthrow his government.[130]

On August 18, 1953, Tudeh Party members as well as Musaddiq's supporters mutilated statues of Reza Shah in public places throughout Tehran. A statue of Muhammad Reza Shah was also destroyed. Photographs of Muhammad Reza Shah were torn and set on fire. Newspapers affiliated with the Tudeh Party published articles demanding the spread of democracy and claimed that the Shah was no longer fit to rule, as he had left Iran. The Tudeh Party also asked Musaddiq to sign a decree that spelled the end of the monarchy.[131] On August 19, 1953, thousands of men, who were previously paid by CIA agents, gathered on the streets to demonstrate in support of the Shah. These demonstrations began in southern Tehran and spread throughout the capital. The headquarters of political parties and offices of newspapers supportive of Musaddiq were vandalized. General Zahedi's supporters took over the radio station and a number of government ministries. By the evening of August 19, General Zahedi had emerged from hiding and taken control. Mussadiq was arrested.[132]

The Shah returned to Iran on August 22, 1953. In a meeting with Henderson, the Shah voiced his gratitude for the continuance of U.S. support during this difficult period. Henderson conveyed a message from Eisenhower that congratulated the Shah for his strength, which had kept Iran's sovereignty intact. The Shah thanked Henderson and asked him to tell the president that Iran was safe due to Western support, the loyalty of the Iranian people, and God's help.[133]

NOTES

1. Nasrollah S. Fatemi, *Oil Diplomacy, Powderkeg in Iran*, 6–20; Mustafa Fateh, *Panjah Sal Naft-i Iran* (Fifty Years of Iranian Oil) (Tehran: Shirkat-i Sahami-yi Chap, 1956), 250–54; Ronald W. Ferrier, *The History of the British Petroleum Company: The Developing Years, 1901–1932*, vol. 1 (Cambridge: Cambridge University Press, 1982), 102–40; Fereidun Fesharaki, *Development of the Iranian Oil Industry* (New York: Praeger, 1976), 5–7; Ghulam Reza Nejati, *Junbish-i Milli Shudan-i San'at Naft-i Irani va Kudeta-yi 28 Murdad* (The Movement for the Nationalization of the Iranian Oil Industry and the Coup of the 28 Murdad) (Tehran: Shikat-i Sahami-yi Intishar, 1364/1986), 15; Benjamin Shwadran, *The Middle East, Oil, and the Great Powers* (New York: Praeger, 1955), 16–19; George Stocking, *Middle East Oil: A Study in Political and Economic Controversy* (Nashville: Vanderbilt University Press, 1970).

2. Fateh, *Panjah Sal Naft-i Iran*, (Fifty Years of Iranian Oil), 262–67; Fatemi, *Oil Diplomacy*, 22–40; Ferrier, *The History of the British Petroleum Company*, vol. 1, 165–210; Fesharaki, *Development of the Iranian Oil Industry*, 8–10; Nejati, *Junbish-i Milli Shudan San'at Naft-i Irani va Kudeta-yi 28 Murdad* (The Movement for the Nationalization of the Iranian Oil Industry and the Coup of the 28 Murdad), 17; Shwadran, *The Middle East, Oil, and the Great Powers*, 22–24; Stocking, *Middle East Oil*, 12–19.

3. J. H. Bamberg, *The History of the British Petroleum Company*, vol. 2: *The Anglo-Iranian Years, 1928–1954*, 33–50; Fateh, *Panjah Sal Naft-i Iran* (Fifty Years of Iranian Oil), 290–303; Fesharaki, *Development of the Iranian Oil Industry*, 13–14; Nejati, *Junbish-i Milli Shudan-i San'at Naft-i Irani va Kudeta-yi 28 Murdad* (The Movement for the Nationalization of the Iranian Oil Industry and the Coup of 28 Murdad), 21–22; Shwadran, *The Middle East, Oil, and the Great Powers*, 50–55; Stocking; *Middle East Oil*, 19–37.

4. Fateh, *Panjah Sal Naft-i Iran* (Fifty Years of Iranian Oil), 388–91; Fatemi, *Oil Diplomacy*, 328–33; Shwadran, *The Middle East, Oil, and the Great Powers*, 104.

5. L. P. Elwell-Sutton, *Persian Oil: A Study in Power Politics* (London: Lawrence and Wishart), 176–80. Fatemi, *Oil Diplomacy*, 333–34; Shwadran, *The Middle East, Oil, and the Great Powers*, 104–105.

6. Nasser Najmi, *Musaddiq, Mubariz-i Buzurg* (Musaddiq, The Great Warrior) (Tehran: n.p., 1359/1980), 26.

7. Farhad Diba, *Mossadegh, A Political Biography* (London: Croom Helm, 1986), 84; Homayoun Katouzian, *Musaddiq va Nabard-i Qudrat dar Iran* (Musaddiq and the Struggle for Power in Iran) (Tehran: Rasa, 1371/1992), 121–22; or Homayoun Katouzian, *Musaddiq and the Struggle for Power in Iran* (London: Tauris, 1990), 56; Husein Kayustuvan, *Siyasat-i Movazeneh-yi Manfi dar Majlis-i Chardahom*, vol. 1 (The Policy of Negative Equilibrium in the Fourteenth Majlis) (Tehran: Mozaffar, 1327/1948), 193; Abd al-Reza Hushang Mahdavi, *Tarikh-i Ravabit-i Kharij-i Iran az Payan-i Jang-i Jahan-i Duvum ta Sughut-i Regim-i Pahlavi* (A History of Iran's Foreign Relations from the End of the Second World War to the Fall of the Pahlavi Regime) (Tehran: Pishgam, 1368/1989), 53–55.

88 Chapter Three

8. Homayoun Katouzian, ed., *Musaddiq's Memoirs* (London: Jebhe, 1988), 265–66.

9. Ervand Abrahamian, *Iran Between Two Revolutions* (Princeton, N.J.: Princeton University Press, 1982), 252–62; Muhammad Reza Ghods, *Iran in the Twentieth Century* (Boulder, Colo.: Lynne Rienner, 1989), 182–84; Ali Janzadeh, *Musaddiq* (Musaddiq) (Tehran: Hangam, 1358/1979), 113–18; Homayoun Katouzian, *Mussadiq va Nabard-i Qudrat dar Iran* (Musaddiq and the Struggle for Power in Iran), 171–77; Homayoun Katouzian, *Musaddiq and the Battle for Power in Iran*, 71–77; Khalil Maleki, *Tarikhche-yi Jibhi-yi Milli* (The History of the National Front) (Tehran: Taban, 1333/1954); Nejati, *Junbish-i Milli Shudan-i San'at-i Naft-i Irani va Kudeta-yi 28 Murdad* (The Movement for the Nationalization of the Iranian Oil Industry and the Coup of 28 Murdad), 83–86; Nasrollah Shifteh, *Zindigi-Nameh va Mubarizat-i Siyasi-yi Dr. Muhammad Musaddiq* (The Life and Political Struggle of Dr. Muhammad Musaddiq) (Tehran: Kumesh, 1370/1991), 59–67.

10. Ronald W. Ferrier, "The Anglo-Iranian Oil Dispute," in *Musaddiq: Iranian Nationalism and Oil*, James A. Bill and William Roger Louis, eds. (Austin: University of Texas, 1988), 178–79; Shwadran, *The Middle East, Oil, and the Great Powers*, 104–105.

11. U.S. Department of State, RG 59, Decimal File 888.00/2-351, 3 February 1951, National Archives, College Park, Md.

12. Elwell-Sutton, *Persian Oil*, 201; Shwadran, *The Middle East, Oil, and the Great Powers*, 106; Azimi, *Iran: The Crisis of Democracy*, 238.

13. Shepherd to FO, 21 February 1951, FO 371 EP 91522, as cited in Azimi, *Iran: The Crisis of Democracy*, 238–39.

14. Elwell-Sutton, *Persian Oil*, 206–207; Shwadran, *The Middle East, Oil and the Great Powers*, 106.

15. Azimi, *Iran: The Crisis of Democracy*, 239; Fatemi, *Oil Diplomac*, 339; Katouzian, *Musaddiq and the Struggle for Power in Iran*, 83; Shwadran, *The Middle East, Oil, and the Great Powers*, 106.

16. Fatemi, *Oil Diplomacy*, 339–40; Shwadran, *The Middle East, Oil, and the Great Powers*, 107.

17. Shepherd to FO 14 March 951, FO 371 EP91524, as cited in Azimi, *Iran: The Crisis of Democracy*, 248.

18. Azimi, *Iran: The Crisis of Democracy*, 248; Elwell-Sutton, *Persian Oil*, 208–209; Fatemi, *Oil Diplomacy*, 339; *Foreign Relations of the United States, 1952–1954*, vol. 10, *Iran, 1951–1954* (Washington, D.C.: Government Printing Office, 1989): 8–9; Ramazani, *Iran's Foreign Policy, 1941–1973*, 197; Shwadran, *The Middle East, Oil, and the Great Powers*, 106.

19. Azimi, *Iran: The Crisis of Democracy*, 249–50; U.S. Department of State, RG 59, Decimal File 788.00/10-2451, 24 October 1951, "Martial Law in Khuzistan," National Archives, College Park, Md.

20. Elwell-Sutton, *Persian Oil*, 210; Fatemi: *Oil Diplomacy*, 340.

21. Fatemi, *Oil Diplomacy*, 340–41; Shwadran, *The Middle East, Oil and the Great Powers*, 107.

22. Fatemi, *Oil Diplomacy*, 341–42.

23. Azimi, *Iran: The Crisis of Democracy*, 254; Fatemi, *Oil Diplomacy*, 342–43; Shwadran, *The Middle East, Oil, and the Great Powers*, 108.

24. Franks (Washington) to FO, 16 April 1951, FO 371 EP 91455, as cited in Azimi, *Iran: The Crisis of Democracy*, 252–53; Katouzian, *Musaddiq's Memoirs*, 264–65.

25. Elwell-Sutton, *Persian Oil: A Study in Power Politics*, 215–17; Fatemi, *Oil Diplomacy*, 342–43; *Foreign Relations of the United States, 1952–1954* 10: 44; Ramazani, *Iran's Foreign Policy, 1941–1973*, 197; Shwadran, *The Middle East, Oil, and the Great Powers*, 108.

26. Elwell-Sutton, *Persian Oil*, 218–19; Fatemi, *Oil Diplomacy*, 344.

27. U.S. Department of State, RG 59, Decimal File 788.00/5-951, 9 May 1951, "Open Letter From the Central Committee of the Tudeh Party," National Archives, College Park, Md. For a discussion of the Tudeh Party's problems and its interaction with Musaddiq prior to the 1953 coup see Maziar Behrooz, "Tudeh Factionalism and the 1953 Coup in Iran," *International Journal of Middle East Studies* 33 (August 2001), 363–82.

28. Azimi, *Iran: The Crisis of Democracy*, 259–60; Elwell-Sutton, *Persian Oil*, 221; Sepehr Zabih, *The Mossadegh Era* (Chicago: Lake View Press, 1982), 28–29.

29. Fatemi, *Persian Oil*, 345.

30. *Foreign Relations of the United States, 1952–54*, 10: 21–23.

31. George McGhee, *Envoy to the Middle World: Adventures in Diplomacy* (New York: Harper & Row, 1983), 318–27.

32. U.S. Department of State, RG 59, Decimal File 788.00/3-2951, 29 March 1951, "US-UK Talks on Iran," National Archives, College Park, Md.

33. U.S. Department of State, RG 59, Decimal File 788.00/4-2751, 27 April 1951, "Discussion of the Iranian Situation," National Archives, College Park, Md.

34. Sicker, *The Bear and the Lion*, 84. There is a lack of Russian, Western, and Iranian primary and secondary sources regarding the Soviet response to the Iranian oil nationalization crisis between 1951–1953. This is a subject, which could definitely use more research and analysis in the future. I have discussed the Soviet and Tudeh Party's reaction as well as involvement in this crisis throughout this chapter based on the availability of a small number of primary and secondary sources.

35. *Foreign Relations of the United States, 1952–1954*, 10: 45–47.

36. *Foreign Relations of the United States, 1952–1954*, 10: 309–315.

37. Dean Acheson, *Present at the Creation* (New York: W. W. Norton, 1969), 507.

38. Department of State *Bulletin* 24, no. 621 (28 May 1951): 851.

39. Department of State *Bulletin* 24, no. 622 (4 June 1951): 891–92.

40. Elwell-Sutton, *Persian Oil*, 227–28; *Foreign Relations of the United States, 1952–1954*, 10: 65.

41. Elwell-Sutton, *Persian Oil*, 230–31; *Foreign Relations of the United States, 1952–1954*, 10: 65–66.

42. *Foreign Relations of the United States, 1952–1954*, 10: 65–66.

43. *Kayhan*, 27 June 1951.

44. *Foreign Relations of the United States, 1952–1954*, 10: 76.

45. *Foreign Relations of the United States, 1952–1954*, 10: 77–79.

46. Department of State *Bulletin* 25, no. 647 (19 November 1951): 814; *Kayhan*, 6 July 1951.

47. Department of State *Bulletin* 25, no. 630 (23 July 1951): 129–31; *Foreign Relations of the United States, 1952–1954*, 10: 84–85.

48. *Foreign Relations of the United States, 1952–1954*, 10: 92.

49. Iskandari, *Khatirat-i Siyas-i Iraj Iskandari* (The Political Memoirs of Iraj Iskandari) (Tehran:Elmi, 1368/1989): 149–50; Kianuri, *Khatirat-i Nur al-Din Kianuri* (The Memoirs of Nur al-Din Kianuri), 217–19; Hasan Zia Zarifi, *Hizb-i Tudeh va Kudeta-yi 28 Murdad 1332* (The Tudeh Party and the Coup of 19 August 1953) (Tehran: n.p., 1358/1979), 6–8.

50. *Foreign Relations of the United States, 1952–1954*, 10: 92–95.

51. Elwell-Sutton, *Persian Oil*, 252–53; *Kayhan*, 14 August 1951; Shwadran, *The Middle East, Oil, and the Great Powers*, 121–23.

52. *Foreign Relations of the United States, 1952–1954*, 10: 134.

53. *Foreign Relations of the United States, 1952–1954*, 10: 154–55.

54. J. H. Bamberg, *The History of the British Petroleum Company*, vol. 2, 454.

55. Department of State *Bulletin* 25, no. 640 (1 October 1951): 547–50; *Foreign Relations of the United States, 1952–1954*, 10: 162–63.

56. Department of State *Bulletin* 25, no. 642 (15 October 1951): 638; *Kayhan*, 28 September–8 October 1951.

57. National Security Council, *National Security Problems Concerning Free World Petroleum Demands and Potential Supplies*, NSC 138, 8 December 1952, as cited in Mark Gasiorowski, "The 1953 Coup d'Etat in Iran," *International Journal of Middle Eastern Studies* 19 (1987): 267.

58. James Bill, "The Politics of Intervention," in J. Bill and W. Louis, eds., *Musaddiq, Iranian Nationalism, and Oil* (Austin: University of Texas Press, 1988), 276.

59. Department of State *Bulletin* 25, no. 645 (5 November 1951): 746–54; *Foreign Relations of the United States, 1952–1954*, 10: 230–31.

60. McGhee, *Envoy to the Middle World*, 398; Nejati, Ghulam Reza, *Dar Kenar-i Pedaram: Khatirat-i Dr. Ghulam Husein Musaddiq* (By My Father's Side: The Memoirs of Dr. Ghulam Husein Musaddiq) (Tehran: Rasa, 1369/1990), 77–79, 89–92.

61. McGhee, *Envoy to the Middle World*, 398.

62. *Foreign Relations of the United States, 1952–1954*, 10: 244–55.

63. Anthony Eden, *Full Circle* (Boston: Houghton Mifflin, 1960), 219.

64. Eden, *Full Circle*, 221–24.

65. U.S. Department of State, RG 59, Decimal File 788.00/1-0252, 2 January 1952, National Archives, College Park, Md.

66. *Foreign Relations of the United States, 1952v1954*, 10: 283.

67. *Foreign Relations of the United States, 1952–1954*, 10: 301.

68. *Foreign Relations of the United States, 1952–1954*, 10: 302–303.

69. Department of State *Bulletin* 26, no. 659 (11 February 1952): 238; *Foreign Relations of the United States, 1952–1954*, 10: 305–306.

70. *Foreign Relations of the United States, 1952–1954*, 10: 307.

71. Department of State *Bulletin* 27, no. 702 (8 December 1952): 893; *Foreign Relations of the United States, 1952–1954*, 10: 311–20.

72. *Foreign Relations of the United States, 1952–1954*, 10: 323–26.

73. *Ittila'at* and *Kayhan*, 14 and 15 January, 1952.

74. *Foreign Relations of the United States, 1952–1954*, 10: 359–61; *Kayhan*, 21–26 February 1952.

75. Department of State *Bulletin* 27, no. 702 (8 December 1952): 893.

76. Department of State *Bulletin* 26, no. 672 (28 April 1952): 658–59.

77. Department of State *Bulletin* 26, no. 672 (12 May 1952): 746.

78. *Kayhan*, 25 May 1952.

79. *Foreign Relations of the United States, 1952–1954*, 10: 392–93.

80. *Kayhan*, 17 July 1952; Azimi, *Iran: The Crisis of Democracy*, 285–87; Sepehr Zabih, *The Mosaddeq Era* (Chicago: Lake View Press, 1982), 38–40.

81. Hasan Arsanjani, *Yadashtha-yi Siyas-i dar Vaqayeh-i Siy-i Tir 1320* (Political Notes on the Events of 21 July 1952) (Tehran: Pejman, 1355/1976), 52–54.

82. U.S. Department of State, RG 59, Decimal File 788.00/7-2352, 23 July 1952, National Archives, College Park, Md.

83. Iskandari, *Khatirat-i Siyas-i Iraj Iskandari* (The Political Memoirs of Iraj Iskandari), 149–50; Zia Zarifi, *Hizb-i Tudeh va Kudita-yi 28 Murdad 1332* (The Tudeh Party and the Coup of 19 August 1953), 12–13.

84. *Ittila'at* and *Kayhan*, 22–23 July 1952.

85. U.S. Department of State, RG 59, Decimal File 788.00 (w)77-2952, 29 July 1952, National Archives, College Park, Md.

86. U.S. Department of State, RG 59, Decimal File, 788.00/7-2352, 23 July 1952, National Archives, College Park, Md.

87. U.S. Department of State, RG 59, Decimal File 788.00/8-952, 9 August 1952, National Archives, College Park, Md.

88. Azimi, *Iran: The Crisis of Democracy*, 294–95; U.S. Department of State, RG 59, Decimal File 788.00/9-952, 9 September 1952, National Archives, College Park, Md; Habib Ladjevardi, "Constitutional Government and Reform Under Musaddiq," in J. Bill and W. Louis, eds., *Musaddiq, Iranian Nationalism, and Oil*, 76–77.

89. *Foreign Relations of the United States, 1952–1954*, 10: 434.

90. *Foreign Relations of the United States, 1952–1954*, 10: 444–45.

91. *Foreign Relations of the United States, 1952–1954*, 10: 445–61.

92. *Foreign Relations of the United States, 1952–1954*, 10: 462–72.

93. Department of State *Bulletin* 27, no. 688 (8 September 1952): 360; Eden, *Full Circle*, 229; *Foreign Relations of the United States, 1952–1954*, 10: 473–74.

94. Department of State *Bulletin* 27, no. 693 (6 October 1952): 532–35; *Foreign Relations of the United States, 1952–1954*, 10: 476–79.

95. Department of State *Bulletin* 27, no. 702 (8 December 1952): 894; *Ittila'at*, 6 October 1952.

96. Department of State *Bulletin* 27, no. 695 (20 October 1952): 624–25.

97. Department of State *Bulletin* 27, no. 702 (8 December 1952): 894–95; *Foreign Relations of the United States, 1952–1954*, 10: 495–97.

92   *Chapter Three*

98. Christopher M. Woodhouse, *Something Ventured* (London: Granada, 1982), 111–18.
99. *Foreign Relations of the United States, 1952–1954*, 10: 564–65.
100. Azimi, *Iran: The Crisis of Democracy*, 311–13; U.S. Department of State, RG 59, Decimal File 788.00/1-853, 8 January 1953, National Archives, College Park, Md.
101. Zabih, *The Mosaddeq Era*, 90–92.
102. Kermit Roosevelt, *Countercoup: The Struggle for the Control of Iran* (New York: McGraw-Hill, 1979), 120–24.
103. U.S. Department of State, RG 59, Decimal File788.00/2-2553, 25 February 1953, National Archives, College Park, Md.; Gasiorowski, "The 1953 Coup d'Etat in Iran," *International Journal of Middle Eastern Studies*, 19 (1987): 270.
104. *Foreign Relations of the United States, 1952–1954*, 10: 680.
105. *Foreign Relations of the United States, 1952–1954*, 10: 681.
106. *Foreign Relations of the United States, 1952–1954*, 10: 681–82.
107. *Foreign Relations of the United States, 1952–1954*, 10: 688–89.
108. *Foreign Relations of the United States, 1952–1954*, 10: 689–90.
109. U.S. Department of State, RG 59 Decimal File 788.00/3-253, 2 March 1953, National Archives, College Park, Md.
110. U.S. Department of State, RG 59, Decimal File 788.00/3-1753, 17 March 1953, National Archives, College Park, Md.
111. *Foreign Relations of the United States, 1952–1954*, 10: 717.
112. Azimi, *Iran: The Crisis of Democracy*, 320–21; Gasiorowski, "The 1953 Coup d'Etat in Iran," *International Journal of Middle Eastern Studies*, 19 (1987): 270–71.
113. Department of State *Bulletin* 29, no. 734 (20 July 1953): 74–75; *Foreign Relations of the United States, 1952–1954*, 10: 732.
114. U.S. Department of State, RG 59, Decimal File 788.00/6-2053, 20 June 1953, National Archives, College Park, Md.
115. Roosevelt, *Countercoup*, 1–10.
116. Roosevelt, *Countercoup*, 11–19.
117. Department of State *Bulletin*, 29 no. 734 (20 July 1953): 74–75.
118. *Ittila'at* and *Kayhan*, 9 July 1953.
119. U.S. Department of State, RG 59, Decimal File, 788.00/7-2053, 20 July 1953, National Archives, College Park, Md.
120. U.S. Department of State, RG 59, Decimal File 788.00/7-2153, 21 July 1953, National Archives, College Park, Md.
121. *Ittila'at* and *Kayhan*, 27 July 1953.
122. *Foreign Relations of the United States, 1952–1954*, 10: 740; *Ittila'at* and *Kayhan*, 29 July 1953.
123. *Ittila'at*, 8 August 1953.
124. Ashraf Pahlavi, *Faces in a Mirror* (New Jersey: Prentice-Hall, 1980), 134–40; Roosevelt, *Countercoup*, 145–46.
125. Roosevelt, *Countercoup*, 139–49, 155–68.
126. *Foreign Relations of the United States, 1952–1954*, 10:745–46.

127. Kianuri, *Khatirat-i Nur al-Din Kianuri* (The Memoirs of Nur al-Din Kianuri), 264–66; Zarifi, *Hizb-i Tudeh va Kudeta-yi 28 Murdad 1332* (The Tudeh Party and the 19 August Coup of 1953), 15–16; Maziar Behrooz, *Rebels with a Cause: The Failure of the Left in Iran* (London: I.B. Tauris, 2000), 10.

128. Kianuri, *Khatirat-i Nur al-Din Kianuri* (The Memoirs of Nur al-Din Kianuri), 264–66; Zarifi, *Hizb-i Tudeh va Kudeta-yi 28 Murdad 1332* (The Tudeh Party and the 19 August Coup of 1953), 15–16.

129. *Ittila'at* and *Kayhan*, 16 August 1953.

130. *Foreign Relations of the United States, 1952–1954*, 10: 748–52.

131. *Foreign Relations of the United States, 1952–1954*, 10: 782–83; Kianuri, *Khatirat-i Nur al-Din Kianuri* (The Memoirs of Nur al-Din Kianuri), 267–68; Zarifi, *Hizb-i Tudeh va Kudeta-yi 28 Murdad 1332* (The Tudeh Party and the Coup of 19 August 1953), 16.

132. U.S. Department of State, RG 59, Decimal File 788.00/8-1953, 19 August 1953, National Archives, College Park, Md; *Foreign Relations of the United States, 1952–1954*, 10: 784–85; *Ittila'at* and *Kayhan*, 20 August 1953.

133. *Foreign Relations of the United States, 1952–1954*, 10: 762–65.

Chapter Four

Iran's New Pro-Western Stance

The first Eisenhower administration had sought to contain communism in Iran and bring an end to the oil crisis through a coup engineered by the CIA and MI6 to restore the Shah's regime. This measure was followed by the U.S. attempt to realign Iran so that it openly identified with the West by providing the Shah's regime with much needed financial aid and by encouraging Iran to join the Baghdad Pact. The Shah was happy to oblige and took a new pro-Western stance, as opposed to Musaddiq's policy of Negative Equilibrium, which had advocated Iran's neutrality and freedom from any foreign influence.

Even before the start of its second term in 1957, the Eisenhower administration came to realize that providing the Shah's government with continuous financial aid had produced few concrete results within Iran. The Iranian government was still struggling with a huge budget deficit that only seemed to get worse. Therefore, the second Eisenhower administration decided to reduce the level of its financial aid to Iran and insisted that the Shah and his government undertake economic stabilization measures in order to prevent the country from falling to communism.

The Shah's attempts at political stabilization occurred in the face of both internal and external threats to his regime. The internal threats stemmed from opposition groups within Iran, such as the outlawed Tudeh Party and the National Front, which were still carrying on their clandestine activities against the Shah's regime. The external threats came from the Soviet Union and its hostile propaganda against the Shah's regime. However, as will be discussed, countries such as Egypt and Iraq, soon joined this list, where the monarchy had been overthrown by a military coup and antimonarchy sentiments prevailed.

In response to internal threats, the Shah and his government took two very different and opposing measures. First, in 1957, they created SAVAK, the Iranian Intelligence and Security Agency, with the aid of the CIA and MOSSAD, to monitor and maintain internal order. Second, the Shah and the Iranian government decided to promote a two-party system throughout 1957–58 to calm opposition and at the same time convey the image of a democratic society. Both of these measures would have repercussions in due course. In response to the Soviet threat, the Iranian government took comfort in the Eisenhower Doctrine, which pledged U.S. military aid should certain countries in the region face a Soviet attack. In response to the antimonarchy propaganda emanating from Egypt and Iraq throughout 1958–59, the Shah began to promote his policy of Positive Nationalism as opposed to the policy of Negative Equilibrium that had previously been advocated by Musaddiq.

In late 1958, Iran found itself on the verge of a second Cold War crisis, which was in part precipitated by the Shah's actions. The Soviet government had approached the Iranian government about negotiating a nonaggression pact. The Shah, dissatisfied by the cutbacks in U.S. financial aid, indicated his willingness to negotiate, and used the question of a nonaggression pact with the Soviet Union to attract U.S. attention. The United States became worried about the Shah's actions and intervened by offering its own bilateral agreement with the Iranian government in 1959. The Shah decided to conclude the bilateral agreement with the United States and disregarded his negotiations with the Soviet government, which reacted by launching a hostile propaganda campaign against the Shah's regime. The Shah feared that Soviet propaganda would lead to an uprising against his regime and a communist takeover. The hostile propaganda got so out of control that the Iranian government considered filing a complaint at the U.N. Security Council.

THE UNITED STATES ATTEMPTS TO STABILIZE IRAN

The U.S. government was satisfied with the military coup that had ended Musaddiq's unstable government and the Shah's appointment of General Zahedi as the new prime minister. Zahedi had to deal with three critical problems: the Iranian economy, which had gone bankrupt; the clandestine activities of the Tudeh Party; and the settlement of the oil nationalization dispute. The Iranian government decided that the only way to bring an end to its economic problems was to turn to the United States for help.

In a letter to Eisenhower, on August 26, 1953, Zahedi thanked the United States for its support and assistance to Iran over the years. Zahedi said that even though U.S. assistance had helped Iran modernize and promote security in the country, it was not enough to help the Iranian government solve its economic problems. The Iranian treasury was empty and its foreign exchange reserve was depleted. Zahedi emphasized that his government needed immediate financial aid from the United States to overcome its economic problems. Eisenhower replied that Zahedi's request would be reviewed by his administration.[1]

On September 3, 1953, the U.S. Foreign Operations Administration (FOA), announced that it would provide Iran a grant in the amount of $23.4 million as part of its technical assistance.[2] Shortly thereafter, Eisenhower also announced that the United States would provide emergency financial aid in the amount of $45 million to the Iranian government.[3] The U.S. government knew that it had to provide emergency aid to Iran until Iran's oil dispute had been settled. Ambassador Henderson told the Iranian government that the United States would also send food, medicine, and clothing to Iran as donated by relief organizations.[4]

The Iranian government was pleased with the U.S. financial aid, which enabled the Iranian economy to function until the oil dispute was settled. The Iranian government now turned its attention to dealing with the Tudeh Party. In the aftermath of the military coup, Zahedi had declared martial law and ordered the military governor to dissolve the Tudeh Party. As a result, hundreds of Tudeh members had been arrested.[5] The Tudeh Party reacted by distributing leaflets to the public criticizing Zahedi's government. On September 22, 1953, three air force officers affiliated with the Tudeh Party, inflicted damage on military planes stationed at the Ghaleh Morghi Airport in southern Tehran.[6] Shortly thereafter, three navy officers, affiliated with the Tudeh Party, tried to set an Iranian ship on fire in Khoramshahr. Their attempt failed; they were caught and eventually executed.[7] With the problem of the Tudeh Party temporarily under control, the Iranian government turned its attention to the settlement of the oil dispute.

The United States was aware that Iran's economic reconstruction depended upon oil revenues. On October 15, 1953, the State Department announced that Secretary of State Dulles was sending Herbert Hoover Jr., his adviser on petroleum affairs, to Iran to report on problems regarding the oil dispute and its settlement. Hoover was to meet with Prime Minister Zahedi and the Iranian oil advisory committee.[8]

Meanwhile, Secretary of State Dulles had attended the foreign ministers' meetings October 16–18, 1953 in London. Secretary Dulles and Foreign Secretary Eden held a discussion regarding the political situation in the Middle East. Eden said that he would announce his support of Zahedi's government before the British Parliament. This gesture was to let the Iranian government know that the British government wanted to resume diplomatic relations, which was needed prior to the resumption of negotiations to settle the oil dispute.[9] The United States also wanted the British and the Iranian governments to resume diplomatic relations. In a press conference on November 3, 1953, Secretary Dulles reiterated these views, hoping that the British and Iranian governments would renew their diplomatic relations in the near future.[10] Following this announcement, negotiations between British and Iranian government officials took place.

On December 5, 1953, the British and Iranian governments announced that they had resumed diplomatic relations.[11] In a statement to the Iranian people and the press, Prime Minister Zahedi said that the Iranian government had resumed diplomatic relations with the British government because it had accepted Iran's oil nationalization law. There were mixed reactions to this announcement. On December 6, 1953, Tehran University students began to demonstrate against the resumption of diplomatic relations between Britain and Iran. These demonstrations led to clashes with the police that left several dead and injured. While the Iranian government expressed regret over these events, it nonetheless made it clear that it would do anything to maintain order.[12]

Meanwhile, the AIOC had invited representatives from seven oil companies to attend a meeting in London to discuss the settlement of the oil dispute. The oil companies represented at this meeting were: Royal Dutch-Shell; Compagnie Française des Pétroles the Standard Oil of New Jersey; Socony-Vacuum Oil Co.; Standard Oil of California; Gulf Oil; and Texas Oil.[13] These companies discussed the idea of establishing a consortium that would purchase and market Iranian oil as a settlement to the oil dispute. The five U.S. oil companies were worried about joining a consortium, given the issue of antitrust prosecution. They overcame this problem, however, with the help of the U.S. government.

On December 9, 1953, Vice President Richard Nixon visited Iran. Nixon met with Zahedi and the Shah. The Shah asked Nixon about the Iranian Army whether it should be used to maintain domestic security or to defend Iran if it were attacked by another country. The Shah said that the public would be dismayed if it found out that the army could only maintain domestic security and was not strong enough to defend Iran from an outside attack. Nixon asked whether the Shah was willing to cooperate with its neighbors on defense. The Shah said that he would cooperate if Iran had an army strong enough to defend itself from an outside attack. Nixon said that the United States would review these issues and inform the Shah accordingly.[14]

Following Nixon's visit, the Iranian government made two important announcements. First, on December 19, 1953, the Shah issued a decree that dissolved the Seventeenth Majlis and the Senate, and called for elections to take place for both houses.[15] Second, on December 21, 1953, Musaddiq's trial was held and he was sentenced to three years in solitary confinement. In a conversation with Ambassador Henderson, the Shah said that the length of Musaddiq's sentence was appropriate and that a longer sentence would have angered the public and led to chaos.[16]

On January 2, 1954, the National Security Council produced a report regarding U.S. policy toward Iran. The report emphasized the importance of maintaining Iran's sovereignty, free from Soviet control and communism. Iran's fall to communism would jeopardize U.S. interests and create a security problem in the Middle East.[17] The report also discussed the U.S. emergency financial aid given to Iran to keep its economy alive. The United States looked favorably upon the formation of a consortium where five U.S. oil companies would be involved in the purchasing and marketing of Iranian oil.[18]

The U.S. government paved the way for the five oil companies to participate in the consortium. Members of the National Security Council met with Herbert Brownell, the U.S. Attorney General, to argue that it was in the best interests of the United States for the U.S. oil companies to be part of the consortium that would purchase and market Iranian oil.[19] These arguments proved effective and Brownell granted the U.S. oil companies immunity from antitrust prosecution.[20]

On February 19, 1954, Secretary of State Dulles sent a telegram to Ambassador Henderson discussing the National Security Council's report on U.S. military aid to Iran. The report said that the purpose of such aid was to strengthen the Iranian Army in providing domestic security. The report also said that it was important for Iran to participate in a regional defense pact with its neighbors.[21] Henderson was instructed to discuss certain issues with the Shah. Among these were that the United States had agreed for the Iranian Army to strengthen its capabilities beyond what was needed for domestic security, and that the United States was willing to give Iran additional military aid in terms of weaponry and training. At the same time, these measures were not enough for Iran to ward off an attack from another country. That is why it was best for Iran to join a regional defense pact.[22] Henderson met with the Shah to discuss U.S. views regarding the future of the Iranian Army. Henderson said that it was in Iran's best interest to have an army that could not only provide domestic security, but engage in defense of the country. To this end, it was important for Iran to maintain an adequate size for its army, and that it possess the necessary military equipment and offer appropriate training.[23]

Meanwhile, the international oil companies that were part of the proposed consortium to settle the Iranian oil dispute had ended their talks and presented their proposals to the Iranian government. The proposals said that an international oil consortium had been formed to help start the operation of the Iranian oil industry. The consortium consisted of the following oil companies: Royal Dutch-Shell; Compagnie Française des Pétroles Standard Oil of New Jersey; Socony-Vacuum; Standard Oil of California; Gulf Oil; Texas Oil; and the AIOC.[24] Representatives of the consortium were ready to negotiate with the Iranian government as soon as it was ready to negotiate. Negotiations between representatives of the consortium and the Iranian government began on April 14 and continued through May 18, 1954.[25]

On August 5, 1954, the Iranian government and the consortium signed an agreement that would make Iranian oil available to international customers.[26] The consortium would establish two operating companies with their headquarters in Iran to operate the Iranian oil industry. These companies, in turn, would be given authority from the Iranian government to sell Iranian oil and oil products.[27] The Iranian government also agreed to pay £25 million over ten years to the AIOC as compensation.[28]

The oil agreement coincided with the Iranian government's crackdown on the Tudeh Party's network in the Iranian Army. In the aftermath of Musaddiq's removal from power, Zahedi had declared martial law in Iran. On July 31, 1954, Zahedi announced that martial law would continue for an additional three months. The Iranian government had taken these measures to maintain order in face of any riots that might take place during negotiations or after the oil agreement had been reached.[29]

On August 12, 1954, the Iranian government announced that it had arrested 600 army officers who were Tudeh Party members. Timur Bakhtiar, the military governor, provided a brief history of the Tudeh Party and its infiltration of the Iranian Army,[30] which could be traced back to the Iranian crisis of 1945–46. From that point, the Tudeh Party was able to strengthen its position, and by 1952 it had gained a strong foothold in the Iranian Army. This was during Musaddiq's rule, when the country was dealing with the oil dispute.[31] A prominent Tudeh Party leader, Kianuri, also stated in his memoirs that at least 466 Tudeh Party members had served in the Iranian Army. Four hundred twenty-nine of these officers had been arrested and thirty-seven had escaped.[32] On September 29, 1954, the Iranian government began to court-martial these officers. Some were given a lengthy prison sentence, but many more were executed.[33]

On October 21, 1954, the Iranian Majlis approved the government's oil bill, which was passed by the Iranian Senate. As a result, the agreement signed between the Iranian government and the International Oil Consortium was ratified.[34] Following the ratification of the International Oil Consortium Agreement, the United States announced that it would offer financial aid to Iran consisting of loans and grants in the amount of $127.3 million. The specified amount of aid consisted of $21.5 million for a technical cooperation program, $52.8 million for the purchase of imported goods, and $53 million for short-term developmental aid.[35] Of the indicated sum of $127.3 million, $85 million was to be used as loans, and the remaining amount as grants, of which $15 million had already been used as emergency aid.[36] The Iranian government would be able to use this aid to finance its operations and rehabilitate the economy.

Meanwhile, the Iranian government had also made progress in its negotiations with the Soviet government regarding financial and border disputes. The Soviets had planned to send a negotiating team in 1953, but Musaddiq's government was overthrown and Zahedi's government had taken its time to respond. On December 2, 1954, the two sides announced that they had reached an agreement. The Soviet government had agreed to return eleven tons of gold to the Iranian government, which the Soviet government had owed since the Second World War; deliver consumer goods worth $8.7 million; and settle border disputes in the area along the Caspian Sea.[37]

Having dealt with the oil dispute, the Shah began to prepare for a state visit to the United States, which was to take place from December 13, 1954, through February 11, 1955. Prior to the Shah's visit, John Jernegan, the assistant secretary of state for Near Eastern Affairs, had prepared a memorandum discussing questions that the Shah may have regarding Iran's role in a regional defense pact and whether the United States would help Iran strengthen the Iranian Army.[38] The memorandum advised that the United States should not only help improve the Iranian Army in providing defense in case of an external attack, but have it contribute to the defense of the region as well. To this end, the United States would welcome Iran's joining a regional defense pact with Turkey, Iraq, and Pakistan.[39]

IRAN JOINS THE BAGHDAD PACT

The United States began to think about the defense of the Middle East during the early years of the Cold War. In 1947, the United States had provided military aid to Greece and Turkey and encouraged their membership in the North Atlantic Treaty Organization (NATO) in 1952. During 1951 and 1952, the United States also tried to set up a Middle East defense organization known as the Middle East Command. This organization was to have the United States, Great Britain, Turkey, and Egypt, as its members, but the plan failed due to Egypt's dispute with the West. In the aftermath of the Middle East Command, the United States began to consider a defense pact that would have countries located in the Northern Tier[40] as its members.

In May 1953, Secretary of State Dulles pursued the idea of establishing a regional defense pact that would protect countries that had been facing a threat from the Soviet Union. Dulles thought that the United States had to strengthen the defense of those countries as part of its policy.[41] The United States believed that Turkey had to take the lead in setting up and becoming a member of this pact, since it was the most stable country in the region. The Turkish government agreed to this suggestion.[42]

At the time, the United States and Turkey thought that given Iran's political and economic problems, it was not yet ready to join a defense pact. Therefore the next two candidates for membership in the pact were Iraq and Pakistan. The United States began to negotiate with these two countries, announcing that it would provide them with military assistance. On April 21, 1954, the United States signed a mutual defense assistance agreement with Iraq and with Pakistan, who would join a regional defense pact.[43] Meanwhile, Turkey had also entered into negotiations with Iraq and Pakistan. On April 2, 1954, Turkey and Pakistan signed a treaty of friendship and cooperation to promote security. Although this was not a defense pact, the two sides said that they would discuss how to participate in a defense pact. Negotiations between Turkey and Iraq continued throughout 1954.[44] These agreements served as a foundation for a significant regional defense pact that was to emerge in 1955.

On January 11, 1955, the State Department prepared a memorandum about whether Iran could play a part in the defense of the Middle East. It stated that the United States was not sure about Iran's part in a regional defense pact. Nonetheless, the United States had to encourage Iran to help countries that were vulnerable to Soviet threat.[45] This in turn, would also help strengthen Iran's new pro-Western stance and prevent it from pursuing a neutral policy, as had been the case under Musaddiq's premiership.[46] The United States decided that for the time being, it would make no decision about Iran's part in the defense of the Middle East. This was because the United States had to address certain key issues with regard to Iran such as: the United States could not increase its military aid to Iran because of a shortage of funds and weaponry; and the Defense Department was changing its strategies as a whole regarding the defense of the Middle East.[47]

On January 12, 1955, the Turkish and Iraqi governments announced their agreement on a defense pact. The Iraqi government had been hesitant to sign a defense pact with Turkey, as it could weaken its position within the Arab League. At the same time, the Iraqi government was aware that Soviet military bases were only a short distance from the Iraqi border.[48] The Iraqi government decided to join the defense pact despite the Arab League's disapproval. On February 24, 1955, the governments of Turkey and Iraq signed a Pact of Mutual Defense Cooperation in Baghdad, and stated that this pact was open to other states concerned about their security.[49] This pact became known as the Baghdad Pact.

Meanwhile, the British government had been concerned about the maintenance of two of its military bases inside Iraq. These bases were kept according to a treaty that was to expire in 1956 and were not to be renewed due to the Iraqi government's refusal. The pact between Turkey and Iraq, however, offered Britain a chance to maintain good relations with Iraq and maintain its foothold in the Middle East. On April 4, 1955, Britain joined the Baghdad Pact and signed a bilateral agreement with Iraq, which specified that Iraq would be in charge of its own military bases and that the British would help train and equip the Iraqi air force.[50]

Meanwhile, Prime Minister Zahedi resigned and was replaced by Hussein Ala. The Shah believed that Zahedi and his cabinet had not been successful in carrying out economic and social reforms. Zahedi had opposed Abul Hasan Ibtihaj, the plan director, and supported officials who were not interested in carrying out reforms.[51] On April 25, 1955, the Iranian government received some positive news that would help ameliorate some of its economic problems. First, the United States announced that it would provide a loan in the amount of $32 million to help the Iranian government with its economic reform.[52] Second, the Soviet government announced that it had ratified the Soviet-Iranian agreement of December 2, 1954, regarding border disputes and the return of Iranian gold.[53] On June 2, 1955, the Soviet government returned eleven tons of gold to the Iranian government. Later that month, the Soviet ambassador in Tehran delivered a letter from his government inviting the Shah for a state visit. The Shah accepted the invitation.[54]

Meanwhile, Ambassador Henderson was replaced by Selden Chapin, who became the new American ambassador in Iran. Chapin had served as ambassador to Panama and had no experience in Middle Eastern affairs. In a conversation with Ambassador Chapin, Prime Minister Ala said that the Shah had no choice but to accept the Soviet invitation for a state visit. If the Shah had refused the invitation, the Soviet government would have seen it as a rejection of maintaining diplomatic relations between the two countries.[55]

The United States was concerned about the new Soviet attitude toward Iran and decided to encourage Iran to join the Baghdad Pact. To this end, Ambassador Chapin met with the Shah and the Iranian government to discuss the benefits of joining the Baghdad Pact. Celâl Bayar, the Turkish president, would also visit Iran to promote this endeavor. On July 19, 1955, Ambassador Chapin told the Shah that the United States was willing to increase its military aid to Iran if it would join the Baghdad Pact. The Shah agreed that Iran would join the pact but he expected U.S. assistance as part of the plan.[56]

In August 1955, the Iranian government was informed by the Turkish government that Celâl Bayar would visit Iran from September 19 to 26, 1955. The Turkish president discussed with the Shah the advantages of Iran's joining the Baghdad Pact and tried to ease the Shah's concern about a Soviet backlash.[57] Pakistan's government joined the Baghdad Pact on September 23, 1955. The United States was pleased with Pakistan's membership in the pact. The State Department issued a press release stating that the United States supported those countries that sought better security through a regional defense alliance.[58]

On September 27, 1955, Nasrollah Entezam, the Iranian foreign minister, met with Ambassador Chapin. Entezam told Chapin that in the aftermath of the Turkish-Iranian discussions, the Iranian government had decided to join the Baghdad Pact.[59] The Iranian government had agreed to join for several reasons. First, the pact was a chance for Iran to protect itself from an outside attack through a regional defense alliance. Second, the Shah and the Iranian government thought that Iran would obtain more U.S. aid if it joined the pact. Third, Pakistan had also joined.

On October 8, 1955, the Shah delivered a speech to the Iranian Senate declaring his intention for Iran to join the Baghdad Pact.[60] The U.S. State Department congratulated Iran on its decision to join the pact.[61] The Soviet government delivered a letter to the Iranian government indicating its displeasure over Iran's decision to join the pact. The Soviets argued that Iran's membership in the pact would violate the terms of the Russo-Persian Treaty of 1921, since the pact was a military alliance against the Soviet Union.[62] The Iranian government replied that the Soviet Union had nothing to worry about and that Iran's membership was to promote security in the region.[63]

The five members of the Baghdad Pact met in Baghdad November 21–22, 1955 to set up an official organization. This organization would have a Council of Ministers and committees for communications, counter-subversion, economic cooperation, and military planning.[64] Its permanent headquarters was set up in Baghdad with a secretary general and staff to oversee its functions. Later in 1958, when Iraq withdrew its membership from the pact, the headquarters of this organization was moved to Ankara, and the name of the Baghdad Pact changed to the Central Treaty Organization (CENTO).

Ambassador Waldemar Gellman and Admiral John Cassady had attended the meeting in Baghdad as U.S. observers.[65] Even though the United States was behind the founding of the Baghdad Pact, it had decided not to become a full member to avoid upsetting countries such as Egypt and the Soviet Union, who were hostile to the pact. The United States, nonetheless, would join the economic and counter-subversion committees of the Baghdad Pact and maintain a permanent connection with its military planning committee. In addition, the United States provided its members with military aid.[66]

During this time, Eisenhower was considering the question of providing more financial aid to Iran, as it struggled with a large budget deficit that had persisted from the Musaddiq period. On February 20, 1956, in a meeting with members of the National Security Council, Eisenhower said that the United States would provide $20 million to the Iranian government to help with its budgetary problems.[67]

The Shah departed for a state visit to India to discuss Iran's membership in the Baghdad Pact. He met with Prime Minister Jawaharlal Nehru, who was opposed to the Baghdad Pact due to Pakistan's membership. The Shah met Secretary Dulles on March 9, 1956, in Karachi, on his return to Iran. At this meeting, the Shah asked for additional U.S. financial aid in the amount of $75 million for the next three years. Secretary Dulles replied that the amount asked by the Shah was excessive and the United States could provide no grants, only loans.[68]

During the first three weeks of April 1956, delegates from Great Britain, Turkey, Iraq, Pakistan, and an observer team from the United States, met in Tehran for the Second Baghdad Pact Conference. It was at that meeting that the United States officially joined the economic and counter-subversion committees of the Baghdad Pact and agreed to maintain a permanent connection with its military planning committee.[69] The members of the Baghdad Pact discussed certain objectives and the continuing threat from the Soviet Union. They also discussed their security concerns. Pakistan, for example, was concerned about India's plots to take full control over Kashmir. Iraq was wary of Egypt and Israel's threat to the Arab world. Britain was upset about Saudi Arabia's recent anti-British rhetoric. Turkey was worried about a possible communist coup in Syria that could threaten its borders. Iran wanted to pursue its historic claims on Bahrein.[70] The members also discussed ways in which they could better coordinate their efforts in economic cooperation and defense planning.

Meanwhile, the Shah had decided to accept the Soviet invitation for a state visit. The Shah was disappointed over the lack of U.S. financial aid, which could ameliorate Iran's financial difficulties. The Iranian government decided to ask the U.S. government for financial aid prior to the Shah's departure. On June 19, 1956, Ali Amini, the Iranian ambassador to the United States, wrote to the State Department arguing that Iran's membership in the Baghdad Pact had heightened Soviet hostility. Amini observed that the level of U.S. aid to Iran had not changed since Iran joined the pact. Amini said that prior to the Shah's departure to the Soviet Union, the United States could show its support by providing Iran financial aid. Amini also indicated that the Soviet Union was likely to offer financial aid to Iran.[71]

The State Department analyzed the contents of Amini's letter. It believed that while the Shah and his government preferred maintaining Iran's pro-Western stance, they were testing the United States to determine whether it would grant any aid to Iran. The State Department responded by reminding Amini of all the assistance the United States had provided to Iran since the end of Musaddiq's government.[72]

The Shah visited the Soviet Union from June 25 to July 13, 1956. Following his trip, the Shah met with Ambassador Chapin and recounted how the Soviet government had criticized Iran's membership in the Baghdad Pact. The Shah had tried to assure the Soviets that Iran had no intention of ever attacking the Soviet Union. He had even pledged that Iranian territory would not be used as a base to attack the Soviet Union. Even though the Soviet government had not offered any financial aid to the Shah during his visit, it indicated its willingness if Iran were to ask for it. Finally, the Soviet government had proposed an increase in its trade with Iran.[73]

Ambassador Chapin reported to the State Department about the Shah's state visit to the Soviet Union. The State Department was pleased that the Shah had defended Iran's foreign policy and his membership in the Baghdad Pact. The State Department asked President Eisenhower to send a letter congratulating the Shah on his trip, as it would help strengthen Iran's new pro-Western stance.[74] On July 25, 1956, Eisenhower congratulated the Shah for his successful trip and for pursuing policies that were beneficial to Iran.[75]

Having completed his trip to the Soviet Union, the Shah turned his attention to the state of the economy and Iran's Second Seven-Year Development Plan, which had begun in 1955 and was to continue until 1962. The oil nationalization crisis of 1951–53 had left Iran bankrupt, and the First Seven-Year Plan (1949–1955), which had been dependent on oil revenues to finance its development projects, in shambles. In 1955, the Plan Organization was to prepare and carry out the Second Seven-Year Plan. It was estimated that the Plan Organization would receive 60 to 80 percent of the funds derived from the sale of oil between 1956 and 1962.[76]

The expenditures associated with the Second Seven Year Plan were estimated to be 70 billion *rials* equivalent to $933 million. Twenty-five percent of this amount was to be utilized to complete projects that had originated during the First Seven-Year Plan. The remaining amount was to be used for projects listed under the Second Seven-Year Plan.[77] The estimated expenditures, however, turned out to be higher than the expected return from the sale of oil, which was to be given to the Plan Organization. To overcome this deficit, the Iranian government tried to obtain a loan in the amount of $75 million from the World Bank.[78]

In the latter part of 1956, the Iranian government tried to obtain a $75 million loan from the World Bank. To guarantee a return on its loan, the bank wanted the Plan Organization to pledge its oil revenues as security. At the same time, the Iranian government had to deal with a serious problem. The Iranian government had previously signed an agreement with the EXIM Bank, which had provided a credit line of $53 million to Iran for the purpose of carrying out development projects. An article in this agreement, however, said that the Iranian government could not use its revenues as security toward any future loans.[79] This article created a problem with the World Bank and the $75 million loan that the Iranian government had requested. Ambassador Amini sought a waiver from the EXIM Bank's specifications, but the bank refused. Negotiations among the three parties continued nonetheless.[80]

If the World Bank were to authorize its loan to Iran, the Iranian government would then have to submit the contract to the Majlis for approval. Therefore the Shah began to pave the way ahead of time by pressuring Majlis deputies to support the Plan Organization and Abul Hasan Ibtihaj, its director. Encouraged by the Shah, Ibtihaj also asked the Majlis to approve a draft of an agreement whereby the World Bank would provide a loan in the amount of $75 million to the Plan Organization, which the Plan Organization would repay using the money obtained from its share of oil revenues. The Majlis refused and continued to debate this issue.[81]

On December 26, 1956, Ambassador Amini presented a proposal to the EXIM Bank that addressed its controversial article. The proposal involved pledging Iran's oil revenues representing the share of the Plan Organization to the World Bank to secure the $75 million loan and pledging the remaining oil revenues to secure the EXIM Bank loans.[82] The Iranian government's proposal was accepted. On January 18, 1957, the World Bank approved a $75 million loan for Iran. The EXIM Bank, in turn, waived its special article and agreed to service its loans from Iran's oil revenues.[83]

THE CREATION OF SAVAK

In December 1956, the Shah and his government decided that it was time for Iran to have a national intelligence agency. SAVAK, *Sazman-i Ittila'at va Amniyat-i Kishvar* (Information and Security Agency of the Nation), was established in early 1957 and given special powers by the Majlis. The CIA and MOSSAD had provided guidance in creating SAVAK and the training of its agents. To maintain domestic security, SAVAK monitored the activities of opposition groups such as the National Front and the Tudeh Party. At the same time, it monitored developments related to foreign intelligence.[84]

In his memoirs, the Shah argued that SAVAK's main goal was to combat the spread of communism, which was considered a major threat to Iran. He recalled that Iranian opposition groups and the international press had attributed the worst of crimes to SAVAK. Further, it was rumored that millions of Iranians were employed by it, which the Shah found outrageous. The Shah noted that by 1978, SAVAK had 3,200 people in its service and that the figure had not gone above 4,000.[85] He added in defense of SAVAK that other countries had created similar agencies to maintain domestic security and deal with external threats, and cited the KGB and the CIA as examples. The Shah appointed General Teymour Bakhtiar, the military governor of Tehran, to lead SAVAK and chose General Hasan Alavi-Kia and General Hasan Pakravan as General Bakhtiar's deputies.[86]

When SAVAK was founded, it had eight departments, to which one more was added. The first department was actually its headquarters, which included the offices of the director, his staff and deputies. The second department was concerned with foreign intelligence. The third department was in charge of maintaining the country's domestic security. The fourth department provided security for the SAVAK personnel. The fifth department was in charge of technical matters such as surveillance. The sixth department dealt with the logistics of SAVAK's operations. The seventh department was in charge of foreign intelligence analysis. The eighth department dealt with counterintelligence. Finally, the ninth department monitored the offices issuing passports and individuals applying for visas to go overseas.[87] The SAVAK's third department was the most dreaded among the public. It was responsible for investigating and carrying out operations against political opposition groups, minority groups, the clergy, and Iranians studying abroad.[88] Having created this organization to maintain internal safety and order, the Iranian government turned its attention to its main external threat, the Soviet Union.

THE EISENHOWER DOCTRINE AND ITS IMPLICATIONS FOR IRAN

The Eisenhower administration had been concerned about the spread of Soviet influence in the Middle East. It therefore decided to warn the Soviet Union against any future actions that could generate a strong U.S. response. This warning was embodied in the Eisenhower Doctrine, which Eisenhower presented to the Congress on January 5, 1957. The Eisenhower Doctrine stated that the United States would cooperate with any Middle Eastern country, and provide economic and military assistance as necessary to help prevent the spread of communism.[89] The Iranian government was pleased by the Eisenhower doctrine, and Iranian newspapers provided full coverage of it.[90] The Iranian government also received further encouraging news from the United States. On January 18, 1957, the World Bank approved a loan in the amount of $75 million to Iran. This loan would help finance a number of projects associated with Iran's Second Seven-Year Development Plan including the improvement of agriculture, the transportation system, and social services.[91]

On January 23, 1957, the State Department produced a report regarding Iran's future prospects. The report observed that the Shah's regime depended on the Iranian Army to remain in power and that its ability to rule effectively hinged on economic development as well as social and political reforms. If there were no progress, the middle and lower classes would rebel against the monarchy. As long as the Shah remained in power, Iran would continue its pro-Western stance and resist communism. The Shah's stay in power depended on the continuance of U.S. support for Iran.[92]

At the same time, the U.S. House Committee on Government Operations issued a report regarding U.S. aid operations in Iran. The committee was critical of U.S. aid operations in Iran, especially the U.S. technical aid programs, which between 1951 and 1956 totaled a quarter of a billion dollars, and had been administered in a haphazard manner. The U.S. technical assistance program had actually been used to keep the Iranian economy alive during the oil dispute. The United States had no control over its budgetary aid to the Iranian government since 1953, and the Iranian budget deficit had worsened.[93] Although the report was critical of the U.S. aid program, the committee's main concern was for the sources of these problems to be eliminated in future operations.[94]

On February 8, 1957, the National Security Council produced a report regarding U.S. policy toward Iran. The report discussed the importance of Iran to U.S. national security. It emphasized the significance of Iran's strategic location, its oil, and maintaining Iran's sovereignty in the face of continuous Soviet threat.[95] Despite the consolidation of the Shah's rule since 1953, there were certain issues that could threaten U.S. interests in Iran. The Iranian people wanted changes in their standard of living and were angered by their weak political institutions. If the Shah's regime were to survive, he had to make changes within the political system and take steps to improve the economy.[96] What the United States did not know was that Iran's internal weaknesses would not only hamper U.S. objectives in Iran but would bring down the monarchy two decades later. The report then recounted U.S. objectives in Iran, among which were: maintaining Iran's sovereignty free from communism; supporting a government that would improve the economy and raise the people's standard of living; and strengthening the Iranian Army so that it could better provide domestic security, as well as defense.[97]

The report also projected that by the end of 1957, Iranian oil revenues were expected to increase to nearly $180 million, which would help Iran with its economic development.[98] The United States would continue its technical aid to Iran but would no longer provide budgetary aid. It would provide loans to Iran, unless unexpected circumstances justified the use of grants. The report recommended that U.S. aid be administered in a way that would induce the Iranian government to carry out much needed economic and political reforms.[99] The United States had come to the realization that its budgetary aid to Iran since 1953 had not produced any concrete results. The purpose of the budgetary aid was to keep the Iranian economy alive following the military coup that overthrew Musaddiq, but the Iranian budget deficit had continued to grow. The United States hoped that its technical aid would encourage the Iranian government to carry out much-needed reforms to improve the lives of its people.

On March 9, 1957, President Eisenhower signed House Joint Resolution 117 as an addendum to the Eisenhower Doctrine. It stated that the U.S. government would help Middle Eastern countries maintain their sovereignty against the threat of communism. Eisenhower asked Ambassador James P. Richards, his special assistant, to visit the Middle East and explain the implications of this resolution. Ambassador Richards was to discuss the issue of U.S. economic and military aid with a number of Middle Eastern countries to promote the objectives of the resolution. Ambassador Richards left on March 12, 1957, to visit fifteen countries in the region.[100]

Ambassador Richards visited Iran from March 23 to March 27, 1957. He met with Prime Minister Hussein Ala and other government officials. Ala confirmed his government's support of the Eisenhower Doctrine and the House Joint Resolution 117. Ala noted that since the security of many countries was guaranteed according to this resolution, the Iranian government could now fully pursue economic and social development with an ease of mind. Richards responded that according to the Eisenhower Doctrine, the United States would help any country resist communism.[101]

Richards noted that U.S. financial aid would be limited, given that there were fifteen countries to consider. Small amounts of aid, however, were available to fund projects that were of interest to members of the Baghdad Pact, such as the construction of roads, railways, and communications centers. Ala said that the Iranian government was interested in obtaining aid for certain projects, such as the construction of a railway linking Iran with Turkey and Pakistan, and the construction of an airport at Qum.[102]

Richards also met with the Shah, who discussed his visit to the Soviet Union during the previous year, and the difficult position he was in for abandoning Musaddiq's neutral policy. In addition to coping with hostile

Soviet propaganda, Iran had to safeguard against any communist infiltration. To overcome these problems, the Shah knew that he had to undertake economic reforms, and encourage foreign investment in Iran. The Shah wanted to develop Qum's oil fields and construct a pipeline that would carry its oil to Turkey. Yet this project required foreign aid. The Shah was worried about his army's weakness and said that additional U.S. military aid was needed to strengthen his forces. Richards emphasized the security assurances mentioned under the Eisenhower Doctrine.[103] Ala and Ambassador Richards issued a joint statement at the conclusion of the talks, with Ala reiterating his country's appreciation for the Eisenhower Doctrine.[104]

EXPERIMENTATION WITH A TWO-PARTY SYSTEM

Following the Richards mission to Iran, Prime Minister Ala resigned. Ala wanted to assume his former post of minister of court. Although Ala was a well respected politician, his government had become associated with corruption and led to intense public speculation. Manuchehr Eqbal became the new prime minister.[105] Eqbal announced the introduction of a two-party system. One would be the government party, conservative in its political orientation; the other would be the opposition party, more liberal in its orientation. The government party was to be led by Prime Minister Eqbal. The opposition party, in turn, was to be led by Assadollah Alam, the former minister of the interior. The opposition party's main emphasis was on promoting land reform, and called for absentee landlords to sell their lands to the government, who would then sell it to the peasants at a much lower price. The public ridiculed Alam's leadership of the opposition party since he was an absentee landowner. The Shah assured the public that Alam would serve as a good example in distributing land to the peasants.[106]

In his memoirs, the Shah noted that Western democracies had a two-party system, and he wanted the same for Iran. The party gaining the largest number of votes would lead the government, while the next in line would become the opposition party. The Shah also wanted smaller parties to function and not be discouraged by the two-party system.[107] The Tudeh Party and Musaddiq's National Front remained outlawed due to their threat to the Shah's regime, although the National Front returned briefly to Iranian politics between 1960 and 1962.

Meanwhile, a Soviet negotiating team had arrived in Iran in connection with the 1954 agreement between the two countries, which focused on the settlement of border disputes. The two sides also had to discuss issues such as the movement of people across the borders, and the use and navigation of the rivers along the two borders. On May 14, 1957, the two sides signed a new treaty, which entailed among other things: the regulation of border crossings; the use of rivers along the borders; and the regulation of hunting activities in the border areas.[108] This treaty, known as the Regime of the Soviet-Iranian Frontier and the Procedure for the Settlement of Frontier Disputes and Incidents, was registered with the United Nations.[109]

Following the departure of the Soviet negotiating team, Alam officially introduced the opposition party, Hizb-i Mardom (People's Party), which advocated land reform, the elimination of illiteracy, and women's suffrage. While this party was named the opposition party, its remained loyal to the Shah. The government party, which came to be known as Hizb-i Milliyun (Nationalist Party), pursued a conservative agenda. It also favored land reform, but one that would maintain the present landlord system. Nearly two-thirds of the Majlis deputies, who were mainly landowners, became members of the Milliyun Party.[110]

The Milliyun, or the government party, would not make its official debut until 1958. Although I have not come across any reasons as to why there was an interval between the time the two parties chose to come on the political scene, I offer two explanations. First, due to the complexities involved, it was not clear who would lead the government party. (This task would eventually fall to Eqbal himself.) Second, the Shah and the Iranian government thought it wise for the opposition party to make its debut first so as to give the outside world the impression that democracy was in practice.

Eqbal had taken major steps to implement political reform, yet he was aware of certain problems that could hamper his efforts. On June 14, 1957, Eqbal discussed these problems with members of the International Cooperation Administration (ICA) team, who were visiting Iran. The ICA was responsible for the evaluation and allocation of U.S. technical aid to Iran. Eqbal's concerns included: the Shah's tight grip on power, which could block Eqbal's efforts at promoting a free society; the need for the decentralization of provincial administration as part of Iran's political and economic development; and the persistent budget deficit.[111]

Meanwhile, the Tudeh Party had resumed its activities in exile. Following the 1953 coup, the Shah had declared the Tudeh Party illegal, and many of its members were forced into exile. The Tudeh Party blamed Musaddiq and his failure to accept Tudeh's offer of cooperation not only for his downfall but also the Tudeh's predicament. On July 17, 1957, the fourth meeting of the Tudeh Party's Central Committee took place in East Germany to discuss ways in which the party could be rehabilitated.[112] The Tudeh Party reached the conclusion that it had to portray itself as a progressive party that admitted to making its share of mistakes in the past but was ready to move forward with new endeavors.[113]

In the summer of 1957, Ibtihaj, the director of the Plan Organization, was in the process of creating an Economic Bureau within the Plan Organization. Ibtihaj wanted to recruit Iranian students studying abroad to serve in this bureau. In June 1957, Ibtihaj met with a doctoral student, Khodad Farmanfarmayan, who would not only become the director of the Economic Bureau but also the Plan Organization. Ibtihaj informed Farmanfarmayan that he would ask the University of Pittsburgh for a group of advisors to help with economic planning. Farmanfarmayan, recommended Harvard University, as it had already sent an advisory group to Pakistan. Ibtihaj agreed to approach Harvard University.[114]

Ibtihaj contacted the Ford Foundation and the World Bank regarding his plan to hire a group of advisors from Harvard University. Ibtihaj asked for a grant to finance the cost of hiring advisers to train the Iranian employees. Ibtihaj and Farmanfarmayan scheduled a meeting with Edward Mason, the dean of the Harvard Graduate School of Public Administration, who had supervised a similar project for Pakistan. Mason agreed to send a group of advisers to Iran to help the Economic Bureau. The Ford Foundation provided a grant that would finance the expenditures associated with the services of the American advisors, who would arrive in 1958.[115]

In the remaining months of 1957, the Shah and the Iranian government tried to obtain more military aid from the United States. On October 2, 1957, the State Department issued a report noting that the Shah wanted an increase in U.S. military aid beyond what the United States could provide. The Shah had sent General Alavi-Kia, the Deputy Director of SAVAK, to request weapons that would cost nearly $500 million. The Shah wanted more aircraft and a strong naval force. However, the United States had set aside only $40 million in military aid to Iran.[116]

The United States, nonetheless, agreed to help with the construction of an airfield in Qum. Having an airfield in Qum was important as it was located southwest of Tehran, and could be used for its defense if need be. Furthermore, oil was found in Qum, which made its future economic prospects hopeful. The State Department determined that the construction project would cost nearly $6.5 million. The Defense Department, however, argued that since the project did not fit into its military construction program, funding had to be provided by the ICA.[117]

Secretary of State Dulles replied that it was in U.S. interest to support the construction of the airfield in Qum, despite the Defense Department's refusal to accept the project. The State Department asked the ICA to finance the Qum airfield. The State Department used the aforementioned argument to convince the ICA to finance the airfield.[118] The ICA agreed to finance the project and entered into negotiations with the Defense Department. The construction of the airfield would be carried out under the supervision of the U.S. Army

Corps of Engineers. The ICA would give $6.5 million to the Defense Department from the Special Assistance Funds to finance this project.[119] While the Shah was pleased about these developments, he was to receive some disappointing news regarding future U.S. budgetary aid to Iran.

On December 15, 1957, Ambassador Chapin presented the Shah with a memorandum indicating that the United States would decrease its budgetary aid to Iran. The Shah was disappointed but focused instead on strengthening the Iranian Army and hoped that the United States would provide military aid to Iran. This aid would provide military equipment and training to the Iranian Army similar to what the United States had provided to Turkey. The Shah said that he was willing to send Iranians to the United States to be trained to use sophisticated military equipment.[120]

The Shah continued by saying that he would take into consideration the Baghdad Pact's military recommendations for Iran, which included having sixteen divisions, five skeleton divisions, and a special division to guard the Shah.[121] The Shah wanted his forces to have the best training and weaponry, given the continuous threat from the Soviet Union. Otherwise he would have to reconsider Iran's membership in the Baghdad Pact. The Shah's statement clearly indicated that he was disappointed at the low level of U.S. military and economic aid to Iran. The decrease in U.S. budgetary aid should not have come as a surprise to the Shah. The U.S. government had realized that the Shah and his government had not brought the Iranian budget deficit under control. The Congress knew that U.S. aid had been administered to Iran in a haphazard fashion. That is why the United States decided to significantly cut down its budgetary aid to Iran.

Meanwhile, the North Atlantic Council (NAC), which was the executive organ of NATO, held its annual meeting from December 16 to December 19, 1957, in Paris. Eisenhower and other Western leaders wanted to discuss the Soviet testing of an Intercontinental Ballistic Missile (ICBM), as well as the launching of Sputnik in 1957.[122] To counter these threats, Eisenhower and Dulles said that the United States would provide Intermediate Range Ballistic Missiles (IRBM) to other NATO members.[123] The U.S. decision to install IRBMs in Turkey would lead to a major Cold War crisis in the early 1960s known as the Cuban Missile Crisis.

Secretary of State Dulles visited Iran from January 24 to January 26, 1958, prior to attending a scheduled meeting of the Baghdad Pact in Ankara. In a meeting with Dulles, Eqbal said that the Iranian budget deficit was estimated to reach $100 million and asked for U.S. financial assistance. Dulles replied that the United States would consider providing up to $40 million in loans to Iran from either the Export-Import Bank or the Development Loan Fund (DLF).[124]

Dulles also met with the Shah, who discussed the future needs of the Iranian Army. The Shah wanted to increase the size of the Iranian Army in order to fulfill Iran's commitment to the Baghdad Pact. He indicated his desire to obtain missiles to defend Iran not only from the Soviet Union but also countries like Afghanistan, where Soviet influence had spread. Dulles said that the United States could not provide missiles to Iran, as they were in short supply. Dulles said that he would discuss the question of the size of the Iranian Army with the Defense Department and ask for the delivery of certain weapons, which would help strengthen it.[125]

Following the Dulles visit to Iran, the Iranian government decided to ask the U.S. government for economic aid. On January 29, 1958, in a meeting with State Department officials, Parviz Mahdavi, the Iranian consul in Washington, asked about the possibility of obtaining a $250 million credit agreement over a five-year period.[126] Murat Williams, the director of the Greece-Turkey-Iran office (GTI), was dismayed by this request. Since the State Department had not yet received an account of Secretary Dulles's discussions in Tehran, it was not aware of any agreements for the United States to provide any specific credit to Iran. In addition, credits could only be granted after applications were filed for specific projects and were approved by the Export-Import Bank or the Development Loan Fund. Williams advised Mahdavi to have the Iranian government submit applications for development projects, as there were limited funds available from the Development Loan Fund and the Export-Import Bank.[127]

Ali Amini, the Iranian ambassador to the United States, also met with State Department officials in support of Mahdavi's request. The Iranian government had asked Amini to inquire how much financial aid the United States could provide. Lampton Berry, the acting assistant secretary of NEA, reiterated the statement made by Secretary Dulles in Iran that up to $40 million in loans could be considered if the Iranian government would submit applications for worthy development projects. Berry then told Amini to have his government apply for a loan from the Development Loan Fund.[128]

Meanwhile, on February 17, 1958, Prime Minister Eqbal announced the creation of Hizb-i Mardom (People's Party), which was the government party.[129] Eqbal would lead the party. The opposition, or Nationalist Party, had appeared earlier on the political scene in the spring of 1957 with Alam as its leader. The Iranian government claimed that democracy was now in practice in Iran. Shortly thereafter, the Tudeh Party held its fifth meeting in exile. It issued a resolution that advocated overthrowing the Shah's regime and replacing it with democracy.[130]

The Tudeh Party's resolution alarmed the Iranian government. Yet the threat of a revolution did not emanate from the Tudeh Party at the time, rather from a group of prominent politicians. On February 28, 1958, SAVAK discovered that General Vali Qarani, the vice chief of staff of the Iranian Army, was planning to carry out a military coup against the Shah.[131] Also implicated were individuals such as Hasan Arsanjani, who would later carry out the land reform project in 1962, and Ali Amini, the Iranian ambassador to the United States, who would later become prime minister. Since Qarani had close relations with the American embassy, the Shah suspected that the American embassy might have been involved. The American embassy denied any involvement. The Shah's suspicion of U.S. involvement, along with the fact that those implicated were well-known officials, made him give light sentences to all involved. Qarani was imprisoned for three years, Arsanjani briefly detained, and Amini removed from his position.

Following this brief upheaval, the Iranian Plan Organization received some positive news from the DLF. On March 11, 1958, the DLF authorized a $5 million loan to Iran's Plan Organization to be utilized for its municipal development program.[132] Ibtihaj, the director of the Plan Organization, contacted Ambassador Chapin about this loan and the $40 million that had been previously requested from the DLF. Ibtihaj said that when the Plan Organization applied for the $5 million loan, it had not foreseen the need for the $40 million loan. The government's cut in the level of oil revenues given to the Plan Organization, however, necessitated the need for a $40 million loan from the DLF.[133] Ibtihaj's persistence paid off, and the Plan Organization would receive the full $40 million from the DLF.

The Iranian government also had to deal with its balance-of-trade payments. Since 1955, the level of Iran's imported goods had increased rapidly. Between 1955 and 1958, Iran's level of imported goods went from $143 million to $610 million,[134] but its level of exported goods declined considerably. In 1955, Iran had a surplus in the sale of its oil and non-oil products. In subsequent years, however, it had developed a growing trade deficit even though its oil revenues continued to rise.[135] The Iranian government had no choice but to accept stabilization measures prescribed by the IMF.

Meanwhile, the Shah was planning a state visit to the United States. Prior to his visit, the Shah met with Ambassador Chapin and said that he intended to discuss the issue of U.S. military and financial aid to Iran with U.S. officials.[136] The Shah argued that Iran was in need of financial aid, and he hoped that the United States would promote U.S. investments in Iran. In addition, he wanted the United States to provide more military weapons to Iran and to allow Iranians to be trained at U.S. naval and military schools.

The Shah had also changed his mind about the construction of the airfield in Qum. He wanted the airfield to be constructed in the Qazvin-Hamadan-Zanjan area for strategic reasons. The United States agreed but it emphasized that it would not provide more than $6.5 million in aid for this project. On May 10, 1958, the two governments signed an agreement whereby the United States would help construct an airfield in the Qazvin-Hamadan-Zanjan area and provide $6.5 million in aid for the project.[137] On May 13, 1958, Ambassador Chapin met with the Shah for the very last time as he was being replaced by Edward Wailes.[138]

Meanwhile, the State Department produced a report regarding U.S. military aid to Iran. It stated that the programs associated with military assistance to Iran had been useful in promoting U.S. objectives in the country. U.S. policy toward Iran centered on the maintenance of the Shah's regime, which was aligned with the West. Over the years, the United States had helped strengthen the Iranian Army, which had become capable of maintaining domestic security as well as resisting an outside attack. The most reliable political figure to promote U.S. interests in Iran was the Shah, who depended on the Iranian Army to remain in power. Overall, the Military Assistance Program had played an important role in promoting U.S. objectives in Iran.[139]

The report noted that a destabilizing factor in Iran was its economy, which had weakened considerably due to the budget deficit, as well as the Shah's obsession with military spending. Therefore the United States had to deal with a weak Iranian economy, the Shah's desire for more military equipment, and the availability of funds to promote its interests in Iran.[140] The report also observed, however, that the size of the Iranian Army, estimated at 140,000, had created problems for the economy.[141] For these reasons, the United States would recommend decreasing the number of Iranian troops, which the Mutual Assistance Program could support in Iran.

During this time, Secretary Dulles and the Joint Chiefs of Staff had prepared a memorandum for Eisenhower prior to the Shah's visit to the United States from June 30 to July 2, 1958. It observed that the Shah would ask for an increase in the number of his forces based on two arguments: Iran's strategic location and its close proximity to the Soviet Union; and strengthening Iran's defense capabilities as a member of the Baghdad Pact. While the Shah was primarily concerned with military matters, he was likely to ask for U.S. financial aid.[142]

Dulles was of the opinion that U.S. officials should try to convince the Shah that military buildup was harmful to the economic well being of Iran. There was no need for Iran to worry about its security since the United States supported the Baghdad Pact and its members. Further, the United Stated served as an obstacle to any Soviet plans to attack Iran. Dulles recommended that Eisenhower should listen to the Shah's request for military aid and ask what equipment and training he envisioned for his forces. Finally, the Shah had to be informed that the Development Loan Fund could provide a loan in the amount of $40 million if the Iranian government submitted detailed applications for its development projects.[143]

On June 30, 1958, Eisenhower met with the Shah. This was the Shah's first meeting with Eisenhower, who asked the Shah about the Iranian Army. The Shah replied that the Iranian Army had more than ten brigades and began to discuss the significance of Iran's strategic location. Eisenhower told the Shah not to worry about a Soviet attack on Iran. He tried to make the Shah understand that the maintenance of a large army would hurt the economy. The Shah replied that he expected considerable economic progress over the next decade. Furthermore, he emphasized the importance of his policy called Positive Nationalism, which centered on cooperation with the West for Iran's benefit.[144]

On July 1, 1958, Eisenhower, Secretary Dulles, and William Rountree from the NEA, met with the Shah and Ambassador Ali Ardalan to discuss critical political developments that had taken place in the Middle East. Both Eisenhower and the Shah were concerned about the riots that had taken place in Lebanon. The Shah thought that the United States could take action if it were to save Lebanon from communism. Eisenhower replied that the United States had to find out whether the riots had resulted from communist intrigues or were simply a rebellion among dissatisfied peasants, who wanted the Lebanese government to address their needs. If this was a rebellion against Camille Chamoun, then sending U.S. forces to Lebanon was unwise.[145]

The conversation then turned to Gamal Abdel Nasser's rule in Egypt. Ever since Nasser had overthrown the Egyptian monarchy in 1952, he had become critical of other monarchies in the region, including the Shah's. The Shah said that he had formulated the policy of Positive Nationalism to counter communism and radical political figures such as Nasser.[146] The Shah was trying to defend Iran's foreign policy and its close relations with the West. He disregarded any claims that Iran was being exploited by the United States. Instead, he argued that the U.S. technical and military aid had helped strengthen Iran.[147] The Shah also spoke about Iran's neutral stand in the past as advocated by Musaddiq and criticized him for his policy of Negative Equilibrium. Following the Shah's departure from the United States, the Development Loan Fund announced that it had authorized a loan in the amount of $40 million to Iran's Plan Organization to help finance development projects such as the construction of highways and airports.[148]

Shortly thereafter, the State Department produced a report regarding U.S. military aid to Iran. It stated that the United States had decided to send additional military equipment to Iran in response to the Shah's request. In addition, the United States would increase Iran's share in its MAP program from nine to eleven divisions by 1965.[149] One might question why, despite its reservations, the United States would provide additional military aid to Iran. At least two reasons come to mind. First, the Shah was a valuable ally and the only reliable figure, who could promote U.S. interests in Iran. Since strengthening the Iranian forces was a favorite theme of the Shah, this request was granted within the limits of MAP. Second, the United States was aware of the social unrest in Iraq that could lead to the fall of the monarchy. British influence in Iraq had declined between 1946 and 1958. The United States, however, had not taken any measures to replace British influence in Iraq nor any measures to intervene in the social unrest that eventually led to a military coup that overthrew the Iraqi monarchy in 1958.[150] Whether the United States could have done anything to change the course of events in Iraq is still a matter for debate.

THE IRAQI REVOLUTION AND ITS EFFECT ON IRAN

On July 14, 1958, General Abd al-Karim Qasim and his officers overthrew the Iraqi monarchy. Members of the Iraqi royal family and Prime Minister Nuri al-Said were executed. The Shah watched these developments with disbelief and thought that the Soviet Union was the mastermind behind revolutionary movements in the Middle East that strove to overthrow monarchies. The Shah knew that the overthrow of the Iraqi monarchy could not be taken lightly as what happened in Iraq could happen again.[151]

The Shah's fears subsided when the State Department notified him of additional U.S. military aid, which was designed to strengthen the Iranian Army. The United States had agreed to send Iran tanks, aircraft, and minesweepers.[152] In addition, the State Department emphasized two important points regarding the size and training of the Iranian Army. First, it appeared that 37,000 men had to be added to the original size of the army in order to achieve optimum strength. Second, the United States would provide special military training programs for the army to achieve the necessary strength.[153]

On July 28, 1958, the Ministerial Council of the Baghdad Pact held a meeting in London. The Iraqi representative had not attended the meeting. In fact, by early 1959, Qasim officially withdrew Iraq's membership from the pact, after which the pact was renamed CENTO (Central Treaty Organization) and its headquarters moved to Turkey. At the meeting, the members discussed the Iraqi coup and reaffirmed their commitment to preserve collective security. U.S. representatives, who had also attended this meeting, said that the United States would negotiate bilateral defense agreements with Iran, Pakistan, and Turkey.[154]

On August 10, 1958, the Shah met with Major General John Seitz, chief of the U.S. Military Assistance Group in Iran. The Shah argued that given the events that had taken place in Iraq, his army needed to be strengthened. He noted that previously, Iraq had pledged to assist Iran in case of a Soviet attack. Given the downfall of the Iraqi monarchy and Qasim's hostility toward the Shah, the size of the Iranian Army had to be increased even more than what was projected before. Seitz replied that the United States would not support an increase, because Iran did not have the means to maintain a large army.[155] The Shah then asked for sophisticated military equipment to counteract the threat from Qasim's regime. Seitz said that the United States would consider providing tanks and special rifles to strengthen Iran's defense.[156]

On August 26, 1958, the CIA and the intelligence organizations of the U.S. State Department, army, navy, and air force, prepared a report analyzing Iran's future prospects.[157] The report stated that the fall of the Iraqi monarchy had frightened the Shah, who was also facing opposition within Iran. If the Shah were to reform Iran's political and economic systems, he could remain in power. Otherwise, his regime would be overthrown. The report noted the possibility of certain opposition groups forcing the Shah into becoming a constitutional monarch. Although these groups would push for political and economic reforms, it remained to be seen whether they would have more success than the Shah. The reported ended by saying that the prospects of a military coup in Iran was unlikely, given the army's loyalty to the Shah.[158]

Shortly thereafter, the Shah carried out an anticorruption campaign. He held several press conferences stating that he would end corruption and carry out reforms. He asked Prime Minister Eqbal to introduce a bill in the Majlis that would prohibit government employees from participating in business transactions with the government. This measure was especially directed at Majlis deputies, who had been involved in such dealings and made large sums of money. The Shah said that members of the royal family would also be subject to this bill. Another bill that was introduced required government employees to declare their earned income and wealth and to explain any unusual increases.[159]

Meanwhile, the Soviet Union had begun its negative propaganda against a possible U.S-Iranian bilateral agreement, which the United States had announced at the Baghdad Pact Ministerial Council meeting in London. The Soviets thought that this agreement would lead to the establishment of U.S. military bases in Iran. On October 31, 1958, the Soviet government sent a letter to the Iranian government, accusing it of wanting to negotiate a military agreement with the United States, which was in violation of the Russo-Persian Treaty of 1921. The letter concluded that the Soviet Union would not remain silent on this issue, which posed a threat to its security.[160]

The Iranian government did not to reply to the Soviet government and instead concentrated on obtaining more U.S. financial and military aid. On December 3, 1958, Ibtihaj, the director of the Plan Organization, sent a message to the State Department asking the U.S. government to reconsider its level of financial and military aid to Iran given the growing negative Soviet propaganda against Iran. Ibtihaj said that U.S. financial aid in the amount of $75 to $100 million was justified if it were to keep Iran on the side of the West.[161] The State Department observed that the Iranian government's request for more U.S. aid that year had resulted from a number of factors, including the negative Soviet propaganda regarding the proposed U.S.-Iranian bilateral agreement and concern over the spread of Soviet influence in the Middle East.[162]

Following Ibtihaj's message, Douglas Dillon, the under secretary for economic affairs, met with Eugene Black, president of the World Bank, to discuss Iran's financial problems. Dillon disagreed with Ibtihaj's argument that Iran's financial problems had resulted from U.S. pressure on the Shah to maintain an expensive army. Dillon then referred to a message previously sent by Ibtihaj to the State Department, which requested more U.S. military and economic aid due to Soviet hostility. Dillon, at the same time, understood the pressure Iran was facing from the Soviets, which was also a major source of concern to the United States.[163]

Eugene Black reviewed Iran's economic problems. The World Bank had initially agreed to provide a loan in the amount of $72 million for the construction of a highway, yet two factors hindered this process. First, the Iranian government had been unable to balance its budget. Second, the Shah intended to divert the bulk of the Plan Organization's share of oil revenues to the government budget. Dillon shared Black's concern over Iran's budget deficit. At the end of the meeting, Black was unsure about what the bank had to do. Dillon recommended finding a solution to allow for the construction of the highway project to take place.[164]

IRAN ON THE VERGE OF A SECOND COLD WAR CRISIS

Iran found itself on the verge of another Cold War crisis during 1958–59. This crisis was in part precipitated by the Shah's disappointment over the lack of U.S. military and financial aid and his willingness to consider a non-aggression pact with the Soviet Union that would allay his fear of a future Soviet attack. On December 24, 1958, Ambassador Nikolai Pegov notified Foreign Minister Ali Asghar Hekmat that the Soviet Union wanted to negotiate a non-aggression pact with Iran. Pegov added that the Soviet Union would give military and financial aid to Iran if the Iranian government stopped its negotiations for a bilateral defense agreement with the United States.[165]

The Iranian government took its time to respond to the Soviet offer. On December 28, 1958, the Soviet government sent a letter to the Iranian government stating that Iran could become a U.S. military base from which the Soviet Union could be attacked. The letter once again made reference to the pending U.S.-Iranian bilateral defense agreement, adding that it would put the Soviet Union in danger. The letter ended with the Soviet Union's emphasis on negotiating with the Iranian government and encouraging it to take a neutral stance.[166] The Iranian government decided to negotiate a non-aggression pact with the Soviet government, which became a major source of concern for the United States.

On January 7, 1959, the Development Loan Fund announced that it would provide a loan in the amount of $47 million to Iran's Plan Organization to help finance development projects.[167] The timing of this loan might have been connected to the fact that the United States did not want Iran to sign a non-aggression pact with the Soviet Union. Throughout 1958, Ibtihaj and the Iranian government had been continuously pushing for a DLF loan but to no avail. The United States was indeed worried about the next move the Shah and his government would make.

Secretary of State Dulles sent a telegram to Ambassador Wailes reiterating U.S. concern over the Shah's decision to negotiate a non-aggression pact with the Soviet Union. The two men understood the Shah's fears, given the downfall of the Iraqi monarchy and the constant threat emanating from the Soviet Union. Yet by negotiating an agreement with the Soviet Union, the Shah could place his country in a position that he would later come to regret. Dulles asked Wailes to meet with the Shah and reassure him of continuous U.S. support for Iran.[168]

Shortly thereafter, Iran was discussed at a National Security Council meeting. Allen Dulles, director of the CIA, discussed Iran's decision to negotiate a non-aggression pact with the Soviet Union. His brother, Secretary of State Dulles, said that the non-aggression pact was similar to the bilateral defense agreement that the United States wanted to negotiate with Iran. The Iranian government, however, wanted commitments far beyond what the United States could provide. Secretary of States Dulles concluded that the United States should not worry about keeping the Shah content at all times.[169]

On January 29, 1959, a Soviet negotiating team led by Vladimir Semeonov, deputy minister of foreign affairs arrived in Tehran for negotiations. The Iranian government said that it would sign a non-aggression pact with the Soviet Union if Iran could keep its membership in the Baghdad Pact, and that the Soviets would cancel Article VI of the Russo-Persian Treaty of 1921, which authorized the Soviets to send their troops to Iran if their borders were ever threatened.[170]

The United States was very upset about these developments. On January 30, 1959, Eisenhower sent a letter to the Shah regarding his decision to negotiate a non-aggression pact with the Soviet Union. Eisenhower warned that the Soviet Union had negotiated such pacts with other countries before to deceive them, and used China and Finland as examples. Eisenhower added that the Soviet Union had used its economic influence over both countries to interfere in their domestic affairs.[171]

Eisenhower said that the Soviet objective was to separate Iran from its Western allies and destroy the defense pact to which Iran belonged. He added that the U.S. government understood the pressures Iran was facing from the Soviet Union and that despite some differences between Iran and the United States regarding the proposed bilateral agreement, the United States would provide continuous support to Iran. Eisenhower encouraged the Shah not to take actions that would harm not only Iran but its relations with the West.[172]

On February 7, 1959, the Shah met with Ambassador Wailes and said that he had decided to sign a bilateral agreement with the United States. At the same time, he would consider signing a non-aggression treaty with the Soviet Union if it would accept the terms put forth by the Iranian government. The Shah said that if he did not consider the treaty with the Soviets, Iran could be thrown into political turmoil, as the treaty had also offered the benefits of economic and military aid. Furthermore, the Soviets were willing to dissolve Article VI of the Russo-Persian Treaty of 1921 and agree to Iran's membership in the Baghdad Pact.[173]

The Soviets were upset with the fact that while they were in the process of negotiating with the Shah, he was also considering signing a bilateral treaty with the United States. On February 10, 1959, the Soviet embassy announced that the Iranian government had no intention of signing a treaty with the Soviet Union and criticized the Shah for pursuing plans that he could not follow through.[174] The Soviet negotiating team left Iran following this announcement.

The departure of the Soviet negotiating team from Iran was followed by an intense, hostile propaganda campaign against the Shah and the United States. I have identified this period as the second flare-up of Cold War tensions in Iran following the first incidence in 1946. The important question here is whether the Shah had planned this scenario in order to obtain more U.S. military and economic. Secretary Dulles was of the opinion that the Shah was blackmailing the United States, but President Eisenhower believed that the Shah had to be encouraged not to give in to the Soviets. My own analysis suggests that while the Shah was trying to get rid of Article VI of the Russo-Persian Treaty of 1921, he was also using this opportunity to obtain more aid from the United States. After all, the Shah had made it clear to the Soviets that Iran would not withdraw from the Baghdad Pact. It also became evident to the Soviets during their negotiations that the Shah was also considering signing a bilateral agreement with the United States.

On February 11, 1959, the Shah responded to President Eisenhower's letter. The Shah said that the purpose of his negotiations with the Soviet Union was to improve relations between the two countries and mitigate the Soviet threat to Iran. The Shah had made it clear to the Soviets that Iran would remain in the Baghdad Pact and maintain its relations with the United States. The Soviets had offered to dissolve Article VI of the Russo-Persian Treaty of 1921 if Iran would not sign a bilateral treaty with the United States. At the end of his letter, the Shah reassured Eisenhower of Iran's close relations with the United States.[175]

On February 12, 1959, Tass, the Soviet news agency, accused the Shah of being dishonest with the Soviet Union, which would have serious repercussions.[176] Nikita Khrushchev also attacked the Shah's regime in a speech and said that the Shah had contradicted his own proposals to the Soviet Union due to U.S. pressure. Khrushchev added that the U.S.-Iranian bilateral agreement would lead to the creation of a permanent U.S. military base in Iran. He concluded that the Shah's fears regarding the overthrow of the Iraqi monarchy had led him to negotiate a treaty with the United States.[177] Khrushchev repeated these remarks on February 24, 1959, in a speech regarding the Soviet Union's relations with Iran and Iraq. Khrushchev ridiculed the Shah and U.S. efforts to keep his regime in power.[178]

On February 28, 1959, the Iranian government announced that Ibtihaj had resigned as director of the Plan Organization. He had resigned due to differences between the Plan Organization and the Iranian government, which had cut down the Plan Organization's share of oil revenues that were to be used for development projects. The Plan Organization was to receive 80 percent of the oil revenues, yet the Iranian government refused to pay and even told the Plan Organization to borrow money from abroad.[179]

Ibtihaj became angry with the Iranian government and decided to strike back during the U.S. chief of staff's visit to Iran. Admiral Arthur W. Radford wanted to discuss Iran's military establishment and its needs in relation to the bilateral agreement that was to be signed between Iran and the United States. Ibtihaj told Radford that Iran needed economic development and not a military buildup. The best defense for Iran was to improve the people's standard of living.[180] Ibtihaj's angry words had their own consequences. The Iranian government had a bill passed that would put the prime minister in charge of the Plan Organization. Ibtihaj resigned and Khosrow Hedayat became the new director of the Plan Organization.[181]

The Iranian government was now preparing to sign a bilateral agreement with the United States. Emboldened by this fact, the Iranian government declared on March 2, 1959, that it would no longer observe Article VI of the Russo-Persian Treaty of 1921. At the same time, the Iranian government emphasized that it would abide by the remaining articles of the treaty. The Soviet government, in turn, responded that the terms of the treaty could not be changed.[182] The United States signed bilateral agreements with the governments of Turkey, Iran, and Pakistan in Ankara on March 5, 1959. The United States emphasized that it would send its forces to aid these countries if they were attacked by another country, and would continue to provide military and financial assistance to the three. The agreements made between the United States and the three countries had been authorized by Congress under the auspices of the Mutual Security Act of 1954 and the joint resolution of March 1957 to promote security and peace in the Middle East.[183]

The Soviet Union continued its hostile propaganda against the Iranian government and the United States. On April 22, 1959, Ali Qoli Ardalan, the Iranian ambassador to the United States, met with William Rountree, assistant secretary of state for Near Eastern Affairs, to discuss the hostile Soviet propaganda. Ardalan said that the Iranian government was considering filing a complaint against the Soviet Union at the United Nations. The Iranian government had two specific complaints against the Soviet Union: one was its continuous negative propaganda against Iran and the other was the flight of Soviet aircraft over Azerbaijan.[184]

Rountree said that he would discuss Iran's idea of a filing complaint at the United Nations with the State Department and the U.S. ambassador to the United Nations. Rountree then brought up the issue of Soviet flights over Azerbaijan and asked when they had taken place. Ardalan said that he was not sure except that they had occurred recently. Rountree said that the radar system that was in the process of being established in northern Iran would help trace the origin and destination of these flights. Ardalan asked whether the United States would support Iran if it were to file a complaint against the Soviet Union. Rountree replied that the United States would indeed support Iran.[185]

Hostile Soviet propaganda against the Shah's regime continued both in the Soviet press and radio broadcasts. On May 5, 1959, Foreign Minister Hekmat announced that the Iranian government would not continue diplomatic relations with the Soviet Union unless that country ended its negative propaganda attacks. Hekmat also complained about the flight of Soviet aircraft over Iranian air space. On the same day, Radio Moscow stated that Iranian complaints regarding the flight of Soviet aircraft over Iranian territory was false and the Iranians had simply no proof.[186]

Meanwhile, the World Bank announced that it would provide a loan in the amount of $72 million to the Iranian Plan Organization to finance the construction of roads and highways.[187] Shortly after this announcement, on May 24, 1959, the U.S. government announced that Secretary of State Dulles had died. President Eisenhower appointed Christian Herter to succeed him.

The Soviets continued their negative propaganda against Iran by attacking the Shah more fiercely. On June 1, 1959, Radio Moscow stated that the Shah had sold Iran to the United States and had stolen Iran's oil revenues by maintaining $500 million in personal bank accounts worldwide.[188] It added that the Shah was stifling the people's freedom by having SAVAK torture many political prisoners. Radio Moscow continued these attacks on the Shah throughout the remainder of June.

On July 21, 1959, the State Department prepared a report regarding the hostile Soviet propaganda against Iran and the possibility of Iran's filing a complaint in the United Nations. The report observed that Iran's breaking of negotiations with the Soviet Union had resulted in relentless Soviet propaganda attacks against Iran. These attacks included newspaper publications and radio broadcasts saying that Iran was in danger of falling apart due to foreign influence and the corruption of its leaders. The Soviets encouraged the Iranian people to rebel against the Shah and rid their country of any foreign influence.[189] The report also noted that the hostile Soviet propaganda could be prevented by the United Nations, which condemned any propaganda that was aimed at undermining a country's sovereignty.[190]

Meanwhile, the U.S. and the Soviet governments were trying to set up a meeting to improve their relations. Khrushchev announced that he would visit the United States from September 15 to 27, 1959. Following this announcement, the Shah addressed a letter to President Eisenhower in which he reviewed the events of the past year and thanked the United States for its continuous support and assistance through the years. The Shah then asked Eisenhower to announce right before his meeting with Khrushchev that the United States would provide financial and military aid to Iran.[191,191]

Secretary of State Herter prepared a memorandum for Eisenhower explaining that the Shah had asked for more U.S. military and economic aid because he was worried about Iran's security. The Shah was concerned about Khrushchev's trip to the United States and referred to the continuous hostile propaganda against him that had resulted from the U.S.-Iranian bilateral treaty. Herter advised Eisenhower to reiterate his support for the Shah and also mention that he would pay a state visit to Iran in the near future.[192] Eisenhower replied to the Shah's letter, assuring him of continuous U.S. support.

Eisenhower said that he would remind Khrushchev of his country's negative propaganda campaign against Iran, and that Iran was protected under the terms of the Eisenhower Doctrine.[193]

Khrushchev met with Massud Ansari, the Iranian ambassador to the Soviet Union, prior to his departure to the United States. Ansari criticized the negative Soviet propaganda to which Iran was subjected. Khrushchev replied that Soviet hostility would cease if the Iranian government adopted a neutral stance and reduced its cooperation with the United States. If Iran were to adopt a neutral foreign policy, it could receive the same benefits as Afghanistan, who was receiving Soviet aid. Khrushchev denied that any improper language had been used in Soviet broadcasts against the Shah and said he had nothing against the Shah's regime. To this end, he was willing to send Ambassador Pegov back to Iran. Pegov had left his six months earlier due to the deterioration of diplomatic relations between Iran and the Soviet Union.[194] Khrushchev then went for his first state visit to the United States. He met with Eisenhower at Camp David, and the two men decided to attend a multilateral summit in Paris scheduled for May 1960. Eisenhower agreed to visit the Soviet Union in June 1960. The Soviet shooting of an American U-2 aircraft engaged in espionage in May 1960, however, would lead to the cancellation of both visits.[195]

On September 19, 1959, the United States signed an agreement with the Turkish government to install IRBMs in Turkey.[196] The United States had agreed to provide IRBMs available to NATO countries in the aftermath of the Soviet testing of an ICBM and the launching of Sputnik in 1957. The placement of IRBMs in Turkey would later provoke the Cuban Missile Crisis and produce further ramifications in Iran. During this time, the Iranian government was preparing for the seventh meeting of the Ministerial Council of CENTO, which was to be held in Washington, D.C., from October 7–9, 1959. During these talks, Vice President Nixon and Secretary of State Herter emphasized the importance of CENTO as a shield against communism, and reiterated U.S. support for its members. The United States and the participants also discussed the negative Soviet propaganda against Iran and admired the Shah and his government for their strength. They hoped that those involved in the negative propaganda attacks against Iran would observe the U.N. resolution adopted on August 21, 1958, which warned members states not to interfere in each other's internal affairs.[197]

Following this announcement, the U.S. and the Iranian governments signed an agreement on October 7, 1959, whereby the Development Loan Fund (DLF) would provide a loan in the amount of $25 million to Iran to finance the construction of highways. On October 9, President Eisenhower also met with Prime Minister Eqbal, who was representing his country at the meeting. Eisenhower supported Iran's stand against the hostile Soviet propaganda and reaffirmed his country's support for Iran's sovereignty.[198] Upon Eqbal's return to Iran, the Shah asked him to draft a land reform bill to be presented to the Majlis. This draft underwent several changes before its final approval by the Majlis.

Meanwhile, Eisenhower had decided to visit a number of countries, including Turkey, Greece, and Iran, from December 3 to December 22, 1959. The president arrived in Tehran early morning on December 14 and left for Athens later that afternoon. During his brief visit to Iran, Eisenhower discussed with the Shah and Eqbal Iran's military establishment, the issue of land reform, and the developments in Iraq. The Shah said he had reviewed Iran's military problems and concluded that Iran needed additional aircraft as well as missiles.[199] The Shah added that the Iraqis had constructed six airfields that could be used to carry out strikes against Iran. That is why he wanted to build three airfields, one located in close proximity to Iraq and the other two in northeast Iran. Eisenhower told the Shah that he would have his administration look into this matter. Finally, with regard to land reform, the Shah said he would take measures to improve agrarian conditions in Iran.[200]

Before his departure, President Eisenhower went before the Majlis and issued a joint statement with the Iranian government. The statement emphasized that the visit had strengthened the friendship between the two countries. While the two sides pledged their support of CENTO, they agreed that in the interest of peace, adequate disarmament had to take place. The Shah then discussed Iran's economic and social transformation and thanked the United States for all its help. Eisenhower congratulated the Shah for his attempts at maintaining stability and promoting economic development in the country.[201] As might have been expected, hostile Soviet propaganda now centered on Eisenhower's visit to Iran and his meeting with the Shah. Radio Moscow announced that Eisenhower's visit to Iran had added another year to the Shah's regime and accused the Eisenhower administration of orchestrating a coup that overthrew Musaddiq's government in 1953.[202]

NOTES

1. Department of State *Bulletin* 29, no. 749 (14 September 1953): 349.
2. Department of State *Bulletin* 29, no. 749 (14 September 1953): 349–50.
3. Department of State *Bulletin* 29, no. 749 (14 September 1953): 350.
4. U.S. Department of State, *United States Treaties and Other International Agreements*, 4 (22 September 1953): 2809.
5. U.S. Embassy in Tehran, "Iranian Political Developments from the Advent of the Zahedi Government to the Arrival of the British Diplomatic Mission, August

19–December 21, 1953," 21 January 1954, RG 84, Box 7, Classified General Records 1953–1955, National Archives, College Park, Md.

6. U.S. Embassy in Tehran, "Iranian Political Developments from the Advent of the Zahedi Government to the Arrival of the British Diplomatic Mission, August 19–December 21, 1953."

7. U.S. Embassy in Tehran, "Iranian Political Developments from the Advent of the Zahedi Government to the Arrival of the British Diplomatic Mission, August 19–December 21, 1953."

8. Department of State *Bulletin* 29, no. 748 (26 October 1953): 553.

9. *Foreign Relations of the United States, 1952–1954*, 10: 814–15.

10. Department of State *Bulletin* 29, no. 749 (28 December 1953): 894–96.

11. U.S. Department of State, RG 59, Decimal File 788.00/12-1953, 19 December 1953, National Archives, College Park, Md.

12. U. S. Department of State, RG 59, Decimal File 788.00/12-1953, 19 December 1953, National Archives, College Park, Md.

13. Benjamin Shwadran, *The Middle East, Oil, and the Great Powers* (New York: Praeger, 1955), 181.

14. *Foreign Relations of the United States, 1952–1954*, 10: 850–52.

15. U.S. Department of State, RG 59, Decimal File788.00/12-2153, 21 December 1953, National Archives, College Park, Md.

16. U.S. Department of State, RG 59, Decimal File 788.00/12-2253, 22 December 1953, National Archives, College Park, Md. For a discussion of Musaddiq's trial see Jalil Buzurg-Mehr, *Dr. Muhammad Musaddiq va Residigi-yi Farjami dar Divan-i Kishvar* (Dr. Muhammad Musaddiq and the Investigation in the Supreme Court) (Tehran: Shirkat-i Sahami-yi Intishar, 1367/1988); and Gholam Husein Nejati, ed., *Dar Kenar-i Pedaram: Khatirat-i Dr. Ghulam Husein Musaddiq* (By My Father's Side: The Memoirs of Dr. Ghulam Husein Musaddiq), 126–42.

17. *Foreign Relations of the United States, 1952–1954*, 10: 865–89.

18. *Foreign Relations of the United States, 1952–1954*, 10: 865–89.

19. *Foreign Relations of the United States, 1952–1954*, 10: 898.

20. "Oil Concerns Reassured, Anti-Trust Immunity Granted 5 in Iran Negoiations," *New York Times*, 31 January 1954, 27.

21. *Foreign Relations of the United States, 1952–1954*, 10: 928.

22. *Foreign Relations of the United States, 1952–1954*, 10: 929.

23. U.S. Department of State, RG 59, Decimal File 788.00/3-1854, 18 March 1954, National Archives, College Park, Md.

24. *Foreign Relations of the United States, 1952–1954*, 10: 972–74.

25. *Foreign Relations of the United States, 1952–1954*, 10: 987–1000.

26. Department of State *Bulletin* 31, no. 790 (16 August 1954): 230–31.

27. Department of State *Bulletin* 31, no. 790 (16 August 1954): 232–33.

28. *Foreign Relations of the United States, 1952–1954*, 10: 1044–46.

29. U.S. Embassy in Tehran,"Extension of Martial Law," 9 August 1954, RG 84, Box 7, Classified General Records, 1953–1955, Lot File 60F86, National Archives, College Park, Md.

30. Timur Bakhtiar, *Kitab-i Siyah Darbareyeh Sazman-i Afsaran-i Tudeh* (A Black List on Tudeh Party Officers) (Tehran: Kayhan Press, 1334/1955), 1–3.

31. Timur Bakhtiar, *Kitab-i Siyah Darbareyeh Sazman-i Afsaran-i Tudeh* (A Black List on Tudeh Party Officers), 32–72.

32. Kianuri, *Khatirat-i Nur al-Din Kianuri* (The Memoirs of Nur al-Din Kianuri), Tehran: Ittila'at Press, 1371/1992, 286–88.

33. U.S. Department of State, RG 59, Decimal File 788.00/9-2954, 29 September 1954, National Archives, College Park, Md.

34. *Foreign Relations of the United States, 195–1954*, 10: 1062.

35. Department of State *Bulletin* 31, no. 804 (22 November 1954): 776.

36. Department of State *Bulletin* 31, no. 804 (22 November 1954): 776.

37. J. C. Hurewitz, *Diplomacy in the Near and Middle East: A Documentary Record, 1914–1956*, vol. 2 (New Jersey: D. Van Nostrand, 1956), 385–90; U.S. Embassy in Tehran, "Iranian-Soviet Treaty on Frontier and Financial Matters," 30 November 1954, RG 84, Box 5, Lot 60F86, Classified General Records, 1953–1955, National Archives, College Park, Md.

38. *Foreign Relations of the United States, 1952–1954*, 10: 1066–67.

39. *Foreign Relations of the United States, 195–1954*, 10: 1072.

40. John C. Campbell, *Defense of the Middle East: Problems of American Diplomacy* (New York: Harper & Brothers, 1958), 39–49. The term Northern Tier refers to Middle Eastern countries that either share a border or are located near the former Soviet Union.

41. Department of State *Bulletin* 28, no. 729 (15 June 1953): 831–35.

42. Campbell, *Defense of the Middle East*, 50.

43. Campbell, *Defense of the Middle East*, 50–52.

44. Campbell, *Defense of the Middle East*, 51.

45. *Foreign Relations of the United States, 1955–1957*, vol. 12, *The Near East Region, Iran, and Iraq* (Washington, D.C.: Government Printing Office, 1991), 683.

46. *Foreign Relations of the United States, 1955–1957*, 12: 683.

47. *Foreign Relations of the United States, 1955–1957*, 12: 683.

48. Campbell, *Defense of the Middle East*, 52–53.

49. *Foreign Relations of the United States, 1955–1957*, 12: 97; Hurewitz, *Diplomacy in the Near and Middle East*, vol. 2, 390–91.

50. Campbell, *Defense of the Middle East*, 57–58.

51. *Foreign Relations of the United States, 1955–1957*, 12: 726–29.

52. Department of State *Bulletin* 32, no. 826, 25 April 1955, 696.

53. *Foreign Relations of the United States, 1955–1957*, 12: 733.

54. *Foreign Relations of the United States, 1955–1957*, 12: 748.

55. *Foreign Relations of the United States, 1955–1957*, 12: 748–50.

56. *Foreign Relations of the United States, 1955–1957*, 12: 820.

57. U.S. Department of State, RG 59, Decimal File 788.00/9-1955, 19 September 1955, National Archives, College Park, Md.

58. *Foreign Relations of the United States, 1955–1957*, 12: 158.

59. *Foreign Relations of the United States, 1955–1957*, 12: 775–76.

60. *Foreign Relations of the United States, 1955–1957*, 12: 789.

61. Department of State *Bulletin* 33, no. 853 (24 October 1955): 653; *Foreign Relations of the United States, 1955–1957*, 12: 168–69.

62. Mahdavi, *Tarikh-i Ravabit-i Khariji-yi Iran* (A History of Iran's Foreign Relations), 133; U.S. Embassy in Tehran, "Political Summary for the Month of October, 1955," 8 November 1955, RG 84, Box. 5, Classified General Records, Lot 60F86, National Archives, College Park, Md.

63. U.S. Embassy in Tehran, "Political Summary for the Month of October, 1955," 8 November 1955, RG 84, Box. 5, Classified General Records, Lot 60F86, National Archives, College Park, Md.

64. Campbell, *Defense of the Middle East*, 60.

65. Department of State *Bulletin* 33, no. 858 (5 December 1955): 926.

66. Campbell, *Defense of the Middle East*, 60–61; Department of State *Bulletin* 33, no. 858 (5 December 1955): 926; *Foreign Relations of the United States, 1955–1957*, 12: 240–41; Mark J. Gasiorowski, *U.S. Foreign Policy and the Shah: Building a Client State in Iran* (Ithaca, N.Y.: Cornell University Press, 1991), 122.

67. *Foreign Relations of the United States, 1955–1957*, 12: 805.

68. U.S. Department of State, RG 59, Decimal File 788.00/4-756, 7 April 1956, "Political Summary for the Month of March 1956," 3, National Archives, College Park, Md.

69. U.S. Department of State, RG 59, Decimal File 788.00/5-1156, 11 May 1956, "Political Summary for the Month of April 1956," 6–7, National Archives, College Park, Md.

70. U.S. Department of State, RG 59, Decimal File 788.00/5-1156, 11 May 1956, "Political Summary for the Month of April 1956," 7–8, National Archives, College Park, Md.

71. U.S. Department of State, RG 59, Decimal File 788.5-MSP/6-2256, 22 June 1956, National Archives, College Park, Md; *Foreign Relations of the United States, 1955–1957*, 12: 820.

72. *Foreign Relations of the United States, 1955–1957*, 12: 820–25.

73. *Foreign Relations of the United States, 1955–1957*, 12: 838.

74. *Foreign Relations of the United States, 1955–1957*, 12: 839.

75. *Foreign Relations of the United States, 1955–1957*, 12: 840.

76. H. Motamen, "Development Planning in Iran,' in *Middle East Economic Papers*, Beirut, 1956, 109, as cited in Julian Bharier, *Economic Development in Iran, 1900–1970*, 9; Plan Organization, *The Second Seven-Year Development Plan of Iran* (Tehran: Public Relations Bureau, 1956), 1–5.

77. Jahangir Amuzegar and M. Ali Fekrat, *Iran: Economic Development Under Dualistic Conditions* (Chicago: University of Chicago Press, 1971), 42; Bharier, *Economic Development in Iran*, 90; Homayoun Katouzian, *The Political Economy of Modern Iran: Despotism and Pseudo-Modernism, 1926–1979* (New York: New York University Press, 1981), 203.

78. Bharier, *The Economic Development in Iran*, 90–91; Plan Organization, *The Second Seven Year Development Plan of Iran*, 7–10.

79. *Foreign Relations of the United States, 1955–1957*, 12: 845.

80. *Foreign Relations of the United States, 1955–1957*, 12: 846.

81. U.S. Department of State, RG 59, Decimal File 788.00/12-456, 4 December 1956, "Political Summary for the Month of November 1956," National Archives, College Park, Md.

82. *Foreign Relations of the United States, 1955–1957*, 12: 865.

83. *Foreign Relations of the United States, 1955–1957*, 12: 875.

84. See General Hasan Alavi-Kia, in an interview recorded by Habib Ladjevardi, March 1, 1983, Paris, France, bMS Persian 39 (9), tape no. 1, Iranian Oral History Collection, Houghton Library, Harvard University. This citation is by permission of the Houghton Library. Thomas Plate, *Secret Police: The Inside Story of a Network of Terror* (New York: Doubleday, 1981), 59.

85. Muhammad Reza Pahlavi, *Answer to History* (New York: Stein & Day, 1980), 156.

86. See General Hassan Alavi-Kia, in an interview by Habib Ladjevardi, March 1, 1983, bMS Persian 39 (9), tape no. 1, Iranian Oral History Collection, Houghton Library, Harvard University (this citation is by pemission of the Houghton Library); Pahlavi, *Answer to History*, 156–57.

87. Gasiorowski, *U.S. Foreign Policy and the Shah*, 153–54; Earnest Orney, "The Eyes and Ears of the Shah," *The Intelligence Quarterly* 1, 4 (February 1986): 1–2; Plate, *Secret Police: The Inside Story of a Network of Terror*, 319–20.

88. Gasiorowski, *U.S. Foreign Policy and the Shah*, 153; Orney, "The Eyes and Ears of the Shah," 1.

89. Campbell, *Defense of the Middle East*, 120–23; Benson Lee Grayson, *United States–Iranian Relations* (Lanham, Md.: University Press of America, 1981), 136.

90. *Ittila'at* and *Kayhan*, 6 January 1957.

91. Department of State *Bulletin* 36, no. 920 (11 February 1957): 217; *Foreign Relations of the United States, 1955–1957*, 12: 874.

92. U.S. Department of State, NIE-34-57, "The Outlook for Iran," 23 January 1957, as cited in *Foreign Relations of the United States, 1955–1957*, 12: 874–80.

93. United States Congress, House of Representatives, Committee on Government Operations, *Hearings*, 85th Congress, 1st Session, House Report no. 10, "United States Aid Operations in Iran," 28 January 1957, 3–5.

94. United States Congress, House of Representatives, Committee on Government Operations, *Hearings*, 85th Congress, 1st Session, House Report no. 10, "United States Aid Operations in Iran," 28 January 1957, 5–6.

95. *Foreign Relations of the United States, 1955–1957*, 12: 901.

96. *Foreign Relations of the United States, 1955–1957*, 12: 902–903.

97. *Foreign Relations of the United States, 1955–1957*, 12: 904–905.

98. *Foreign Relations of the United States, 1955–1957*, 12: 903.

99. *Foreign Relations of the United States, 1955–1957*, 12: 906–907.

100. Department of State *Bulletin* 37, no. 948 (26 August): 339.

101. *Foreign Relations of the United States, 1955–1957*, 12: 922–23.

102. *Foreign Relations of the United States, 1955–1957*, 12: 923.

103. *Foreign Relations of the United States, 1955–1957*, 12: 926–28.

104. Department of State *Bulletin* 36, no. 932 (6 May 1957): 727–28.

105. U.S. Department of State, RG 59, Decimal File 788.00/6-357, 27 April 1957, "An Analysis of the Eqbal Government," 7, National Archives, College Park, Md.

106. U.S. Department of State, RG 59, Decimal File 788.00/6-357, 27 April 1957, "An Analysis of the Eqbal Government," 9, National Archives, College Park, Md.

107. Pahlavi, *Mission For My Country*, 172.

108. Rouhollah K. Ramazani, *Iran's Foreign Policy, 1941–1973* (Charlottesville: University of Virginia Press, 1975), 305–306; United Nations, *Treaty Series* 457, no. 6586 (1963): 161–262.

109. United Nations, *Treaty Series* 457, no. 6586 (1963): 161–262.

110. Hafiz Farmanfarmayan, "Politics During the Sixties," in Ehsan Yarshater, ed., *Iran Faces the Seventies* (New York: Praeger, 1971), 92.

111. U.S. Department of State, RG 59, Decimal File 788.00/6-1457, 14 June 1957, "Memorandum of Conversation Between ICA Evaluation Team and Prime Minister," National Archives, College Park, Md.

112. Sepehr Zabih, *The Communist Movement in Iran* (Berkeley: University of California Press, 1966), 220–21.

113. Zabih, *The Communist Movement in Iran*, 221.

114. See Khodadad Farmanfarmaiyan, in an interview recorded by Habib Ladjevardi, November 10, 1982, Cambridge, Mass., bMS Persian 39 (37), tape no. 1, Iranian Oral History Collection, Houghton Library, Harvard University. This citation is by permission of the Houghton Library.

115. See Khodadad Farmanfarmaiyan, in an interview recorded by Habib Ladjevardi, November 10, 1982, Cambridge, Mass., bMS Persian 39 (37), tape no. 2, Iranian Oral History Collection, Houghton Library, Harvard University. This citation is by permission of the Houghton Library.

116. U.S. Department of State, RG 59, Decimal File 788.5-MSP/10-257, 2 October 1957, "U.S. Aid for Iran: Qum Airfield," National Archives, College Park, Md.

117. U.S. Department of State, RG 59, Decimal File 788.5-MSP/10-257, 2 October 1957, "U.S. Aid for Iran: Qum Airfield," National Archives, College Park, Md.

118. U.S. Department of State, GTI Files: Lot 60 D 533, Iran 1951–1958, "The Qum Airfield," 15 November 1957, as cited in *Foreign Relations of the United States, 1955–1957*, 12: 953.

119. *Foreign Relations of the United States, 1955–1957*, 12: 953–54.

120. *Foreign Relations of the United States, 1955–1957*, 12: 959.

121. *Foreign Relations of the United States, 1955–1957*, 12: 960.

122. Philip Nash, *The Other Missiles of October* (Chapel Hill: University of North Carolina Press, 1997), 6.

123. Philip Nash, *The Other Missiles of October*, 7.

124. U.S. Department of State, RG 59, Decimal File, 788.5-MSP/1-3058, 30 January 1958, "Iran's Desire for Financial Assistance," National Archives, College Park, Md.

125. U.S. Department of State, 25 January 1958, "Audience with the Shah-Iranian Defense Assistance," RG 59, Box 10, GTI *Files*: Lot 60 D 533, Iran 1951–1958, National Archives, College Park, Md.

126. U.S. Department of State, RG 59, Decimal File 788.5-MSP/1-2958, 29 January 1958, "Iran's Desire for Financial Assistance," National Archives, College Park, Md.

127. U.S. Department of State, RG 59, Decimal File 788.5-MSP/1-2958, 29 January 1958, "Iran's Desire for Financial Assistance," National Archives, College Park, Md.

128. U.S. Department of State, RG 59, Decimal File 788.5-MSP/2-458, 4 February 1958, "Iran's Desire for Financial Assistance," National Archives, College Park, Md.

129. *Ittila'at* and *Kayhan*, 17 February, 1958.

130. Central Committee of the Tudeh Party,"Resolution of the Fifth Plenum, March 1958," *Masael-i Hizbi* [Party Problems], no. 5 (April 1958): 44, as cited in Zabih, *The Communist Movement in Iran*, 221.

131. Cottam, *Iran and the United States: A Cold War Case study* (Pittsburgh: University of Pittsburgh Press, 1988), 128; *Foreign Relations of the United States, 1958–1960*, vol. 12, *The Near East Region, Iraq, Iran, and the Arabian Peninsula* (Washington, D.C.: Government Printing Office, 1993), 42–43; Gasiorowski, *U.S. Foreign Policy and the Shah*, 174.

132. U.S. Department of State, RG 59, Decimal File 788.00/3-1158, 11 March 1958, National Archives, College Park, Md.

133. U.S. Department of State, RG 59, Decimal File 788.00/3-1158, 11 March 1958, National Archives, College Park, Md.

134. Vizarat-i Iqtisad, *Amar-i Bazargani-yi Khariji-yi Iran* (Official Foreign Trade Statistics by the Ministry of the Economy) 1966, as cited in Katouzian, *The Political Economy of Modern Iran*, 206.

135. Massoud Karshenas, *Oil, State, and Industrialization in Iran* (Cambridge: Cambridge University Press, 1990), 214–20; Katouzian, *The Political Economy of Modern Iran*, 206–207.

136. U.S. Department of State, RG 59, Decimal File 788.11/5-658, 6 May 1958, National Archives, College Park, MD.

137. U.S. Department of State, RG 59, Decimal File 788.5-MSP/5-1558, 13 May 1958, National Archives, College Park, Md.

138. U.S. Department of State, RG 59, Decimal File 788.5-MSP/5-1558, 13 May 1958, National Archives, College Park, Md.

139. U.S. Department of State, RG 59, Decimal File 788.5-MSP/6-958, 9 June 1958, 1–2, National Archives, College Park, Md.

140. U.S. Department of State, RG 59, Decimal File 788.5-MSP/6-958, 9 June 1958, 2, National Archives, College Park, Md.

141. U.S. Department of State, RG 59, Decimal File 788.5-MSP/6-958, 9 June 1958, 2, National Archives, College Park, Md.

142. *Foreign Relations of the United States, 1958–1960*, 12: 562.

143. *Foreign Relations of the United States*, 12: 564–65.

144. *Foreign Relations of the United States*, 12: 566–67.

145. *Foreign Relations of the United States*, 12: 570–71.

146. *Foreign Relations of the United States*, 12: 573–75.
147. Pahlavi, *Mission for My Country*, 130.
148. Department of State *Bulletin* 39, no. 996 (28 July 1958): 154.
149. U.S. Department of State, "U.S. Military Assistance to Iran," 11 July 1958, RG 59, Box 10, GTI: Lot 60 D 533, Iran 1951–1958, National Archives, College Park, Md.
150. Frederick W. Axelgard, "U.S. Support for the British Position in Pre-Revolutionary Iraq," in Robert A. Fernea and William R. Louis, eds., *The Iraqi Revolution of 1958: The Old Social Classes Revisited* (London: Tauris, 1991), 78.
151. Chubin, *The Foreign Relations of Iran*, 171; Cottam, *Iran and the United States*, 119; Ramazani, *Iran's Foreign Policy, 1941–1973*; 281.
152. U.S. Department of State, "Special Military Assistance for Turkey, Iran, and Pakistan in Light of Iraq Situation,' 21 July 1958, RG 59, Box 11, GTI Files: Lot 60 D 533, Iran 1951–1958, National Archives, College Park, Md.
153. U.S. Department of State, "Special Military Assistance for Turkey, Iran, and Pakistan in Light of Iraq Situation,' 21 July 1958, RG 59, Box 11, GTI Files: Lot 60 D 533, Iran 1951–1958, National Archives, College Park, Md.
154. Department of State, *Bulletin* 39, no. 999 (18 August 1958): 273.
155. U.S. Department of State, RG 59, Decimal File 788.5 MSP/8-1158, 11 August 1958, National Archives, College Park, Md.
156. U.S. Department of State, RG 59, Decimal File 788.5 MSP/8-1158, 11 August 1958, National Archives, College Park, Md.
157. Department of State, INR-NIE Files, SNIE 34–58,"Stability of the Present Regime in Iran," 26 August 1958, as cited in *Foreign Relations of United States, 1958–1960*, 12: 586.
158. Department of State, INR-NIE Files, SNIE 34–58,"Stability of the Present Regime in Iran," 26 August 1958, as cited in *Foreign Relations of United States, 1958–1960*, 12: 586.
159. *Foreign Relations of the United States, 1958–1960*, 12: 598.
160. U.S. Department of State, "U.S.S.R.-Iranian Relations," 30 June 1959, 2, RG 59, Box 1, GTI Files: 60 D 533, Iran 1951–1958, National Archives, College Park, Md.
161. *Foreign Relations of the United States, 1958–1960*, 12: 615.
162. *Foreign Relations of the United States, 1958–1960*, 12: 616.
163. *Foreign Relations of the United States, 1958–1960*, 12: 619–20.
164. *Foreign Relations of the United States, 1958–1960*, 12: 620–21.
165. U.S. Department of State, "U.S.S.R.-Iranian Relations," 30 June 1959, 3, RG 59, Box 1, GTI Files: 60 D 533, Iran 1951–1958, National Archives, College Park, Md.
166. *Current Digest of the Soviet Press* 11, 3 (25 February 1959): 25; U.S. Department of State, "U.S.S.R.-Iranian Relations," 30 June 1959, 3, RG 59, Box 1, GTI Files: 66 D 173, Iran 1958–1963, National Archives, College Park, Md.
167. Department of State, *Bulletin* 40, no. 1022 (26 January 1959): 136.
168. *Foreign Relations of the United States, 1958–1960*, 12: 622.
169. *Foreign Relations of the United States, 1958–1960*, 12: 625–26.

170. U.S. Department of State, "U.S.S.R.-Iranian Relations,' 30 June 1959, 4, RG 59, Box 1, GTI Files: 66 D 173, Iran 1958–1963, National Archives, College Park, Md.

171. *Foreign Relations of the United States, 1958–1960*, 12: 627–28.

172. *Foreign Relations of the United States, 1958–1960*, 12: 628–29.

173. *Foreign Relations of the United States, 1958–1960*, 12: 636.

174. Royal Institute of International Affairs, *Documents on International Affairs, 1959* (London: Oxford University Press, 1963), 352–56.

175. U.S. Department of State, RG 59, Decimal File, 788.5 MSP/2-1159, 11 February 1959, National Archives, College Park, Md.

176. "Soviet Cuts Off Iran Talks," *New York Times*, 13 February 1959, 1.

177. *Mizan Newsletter* 1, 3 (March 1959): 1–2, as cited in Ramazani, *Iran's Foreign Policy, 1941–1973*, 299.

178. *Mizan Newsletter* 1, 3 (March 1959): 2–4, as cited in Ramazani, *Iran's Foreign Policy, 1941–1973*, 299.

179. Abu al-Hasan Ibtihaj, *Khatirat-i Abu al-Hasan Ibtihaj* (Memoirs of Abu al-Hasan Ibtihaj), vol. 1, (Tehran: Ilmi, 1371/1992), 444. Also see Khodadad Farmanfarmayan, in an interview recorded by Habib Ladjevardi, November 10, 1982, Cambridge, Mass., bMS Persian 39 (37), tape no. 3, Iranian Oral History Collection, Houghton Library, Harvard University. This citation is by permission of the Houghton Library.

180. See Khodadad Farmanfarmaiyan, in an interview recorded by Habib Ladjevardi, November 10, 1982, Cambridge, Mass., bMS Persian 39 (37), tape no. 4, Iranian Oral History Collection, Houghton Library, Harvard University. This citation is by permission of the Houghton Library. Also see Abul Hasan Ibtihaj, in an interview recorded by Habib Ladjevardi, November 30, 1981, Cannes, France, bMS Persian 39 (32), tape no. 8, Iranian Oral History Collection, Harvard University. This citation is by permission of the Houghton Library.

181. Ibtehaj, *Khatirat-i Abu al-Hasan Ibtihaj* (The Memoirs of Abu al- Hasan Ibtihaj), vol. 1, 444–47.

182. *Ittila'at Havai*, 4 March 1959.

183. Department of State *Bulletin* 40, no. 1030 (23 March 1959): 416–17; Department of State, *Treaties and Other International Acts Series*, no. 4189 (5 March 1959): 1–3.

184. U.S. Department of State, RG 59, Decimal File 788.00/4-2359, 23 April 1959, "Soviet Pressures and Propaganda Against Iran," 1–2, National Archives, College Park, Md.

185. U.S. Department of State, RG 59, Decimal File 788.00/4-2359, 23 April 1959, "Soviet Pressures and Propaganda Against Iran," 2, National Archives, College Park, Md.

186. U.S. Department of State, RG 59, Decimal File 788.00/5-859, 8 May 1959, National Archives, College Park, Md.

187. See Khodadad Farmanfarmaiyan, in an interview recorded by Habib Ladjevardi, November 10, 1982, Cambridge, Mass., bMS Persian 39 (37), tape no. 2, Iranian Oral History Collection, Houghton Library, Harvard University. This citation is by permission of the Houghton Library.

188. U.S. Department of State, RG 59, Decimal File 788.00/6-659, 6 June 1959, National Archives, College Park, Md.

189. Department of State, GTI Files: Lot 66 D 173, Iran 1958–1963, "Soviet Propaganda Attacks on Iran," 21 July 1959, 1, RG 59, Box 1, National Archives, College Park, Md.

190. Department of State, GTI Files: Lot 66 D 173, Iran 1958–1963, "Soviet Propaganda Attacks on Iran," 21 July 1959, 2, RG 59, Box 1, National Archives, College Park, Md.

191. U.S. Department of State, RG 59, Decimal File 788.5-MSP/8-1759, 17 August 1959, RG 59, National Archives, College Park, Md.

192. *Foreign Relations of the United States, 1958–1960*, 12: 649–51.

193. *Foreign Relations of the United States, 1958–1960*, 12: 651.

194. Department of State, "Analysis of Khrushchev's Remarks to the Iranian Ambassador in Moscow on September 2, 1959," 14 September 1959, RG 59, Box 1, GTI Files: Lot 66 D 173, Iran 1958–1963, National Archives, College Park, Md.

195. Raymond L. Garthoff, *Assessing the Adversary: Estimates by the Eisenhower Administration of Soviet Intentions and Capabilities* (Washington, D.C.: Brookings Institution, 1991), 40–41.

196. Nash, *The Other Missiles of October*, 66.

197. Department of State *Bulletin* 41, no. 1061 (26 October 1959): 581–86.

198. Department of State *Bulletin* 41, no. 1061 (26 October 1959): 587.

199. *Foreign Relations of the United States, 1958–1960*, 12: 658.

200. *Foreign Relations of the United States, 1958–1960*, 12: 659.

201. Department of State *Bulletin* 42, no. 1072 (11 January 1960): 53–54.

202. U.S. Department of State, RG 59, Decimal File 788.00/12-1959, 19 December 1959, National Archives, College Park, Md.

Chapter Five

The End of Cold War Tensions in Iran

In the aftermath of the oil nationalization crisis, economic and political problems continued to persist in Iran despite the Shah's and the Iranian government's attempts to stabilize the country. Even though the Eisenhower administration had provided substantial budgetary aid to Iran to help rehabilitate its economy, it had proved unsuccessful. To alleviate economic difficulties, the Iranian government took measures such as submitting a land reform bill to the Majlis to improve agrarian conditions, and adopted an economic stabilization program as prescribed by the International Monetary Fund (IMF). In an effort to solve political problems, the Iranian government held elections for the Twentieth Majlis in 1960, but these elections proved controversial, as they had been rigged. As a result, new elections were held in 1961.

Also in 1961, John F. Kennedy, a Democrat, took office as the new president of the United States. The Shah and the Iranian government were uncertain about the new Kennedy administration and what its policy would be toward Iran. The Kennedy administration made it clear to the Shah and the Iranian government that no U.S. aid would be forthcoming unless the Iranian government carried out much needed reforms. It emphasized economic reform over military buildup in Iran. This carrot-and-stick approach over the issue of aid, plus the constant fear that Iran could still fall to communism, induced the Shah to carry out a comprehensive reform program that came to be known as the White Revolution.

In September 1962, the Iranian government took an unexpected step that led to a thaw in Soviet-Iranian relations. The precipitating event was the Iranian government's pledge to the Soviet Union not to allow any foreign missile bases on its soil. This pledge can only be understood in terms of the Cold War crisis heating up a hemisphere away in Cuba, as well as the Shah's disappointment with the Kennedy administration over the lack of U.S. aid to Iran. In the fall of 1962, the United States and the Soviet Union remained locked in animosity. The Soviets were concerned about the Jupiter missiles the United States had installed in Turkey, and had reacted by installing missile bases in Cuba. Iran's pledge to the Soviets of no missile bases allayed their fear that the United States might install missiles in Iran. The United States voiced no opposition to the Shah's pledge because of the way he had phrased it. The significance of this pledge is that it not only helped bring an end to the Cold War tensions in Iran but also helped improve Soviet-Iranian relations.

IRAN'S ATTEMPTS AT ECONOMIC STABILIZATION

Before the end of 1959, the Shah had asked Prime Minister Eqbal to prepare a draft of a land reform bill. The purpose of this bill was to reduce the amount of land owned by absentee landlords, and at the same time help many poor peasants. On January 1,1960, the Shah presented the bill to the Majlis.[1] The Shah's experimentation with land reform could be traced back to 1951, when he had issued a decree for royal estates to be divided and sold to peasants. In 1952, Musaddiq had also tried to reduce the income of wealthy landowners obtained from their estates and set up village councils to represent the interests of the peasants. Yet these measures did not improve the peasants' standard of living nor provide adequate representation for them on the councils.[2]

When Musaddiq's government was overthrown, the Shah decided to continue with the sale of royal estates to peasants. Many landowners were opposed to this move, since the peasants expected landowners to follow the Shah's example. The Shah then asked Eqbal to draft a land reform bill to be presented to the Majlis. This bill specified that an individual could not own more than 988 acres of irrigated land, or 1, 976 acres of land that was not irrigated.[3] Any land cultivated by mechanized means was excluded from this bill.

After presenting the bill to the Majlis, the Shah sent a letter to Eisenhower asking for more military aid in the face of the communist threat, which he perceived was coming from Iraq and Afghanistan. This aid was to be utilized for the construction of airbases and radar stations at Dezful and Zahedan. The Shah also wanted to strengthen the Iranian Army so that it could withstand any external attacks. Eisenhower asked the Department of Defense to prepare a report that would provide an estimate of the costs associated with the Shah's request.[4] While the Shah was waiting for Eisenhower's reply, he received news that the World Bank had agreed to provide a loan in the amount of $42 million to Iran's Plan Organization to complete a project regarding the Dez Dam.[5]

Meanwhile, opposition to the Shah's proposed land reform bill was growing among different groups of landowners, including the clergy. On February 13, 1960, Ayatollah Hussein Borujerdi, the Shiite *Mujtahid* (religious leader), sent a letter to the Majlis complaining that the land reform bill was contrary to Islamic law and the Iranian Constitution. In order to keep Ayatollah Borujerdi and the clergy quiet, the government and the majlis decided to modify the contents of the land reform bill. As a result, lands held by the clergy in the form of pious endowments were exempted from the bill.[6]

Meanwhile, the Department of Defense had reviewed the Shah's letter and summarized its content in a report that was given to Eisenhower. The report noted that the military equipment requested by the Shah would cost nearly $600 million and that the Shah had exaggerated the communist threat from Iraq and Afghanistan. The Iranian Army was capable of defending Iran against an attack from those countries. Finally, the U.S.-Iranian bilateral defense agreement guaranteed Iran's security against any outside aggression.[7] Eisenhower therefore rejected the Shah's request for more military aid, noting the high cost associated with the purchase and maintenance of the military equipment, which also required special training.[8] The Shah, disappointed at the president's reply, turned his attention to the land reform bill and pressured the Majlis for its approval. On March 15, 1960, the Majlis passed the bill.

The Shah's paranoia with the spread of communism in the region once again led him to request military assistance from the United States. In a letter to Eisenhower on March 30, 1960, the Shah recounted his concern about the spread of Soviet influence in Afghanistan and Iraq and mentioned his disappointment over the fact that the United States had refused to provide weapons that could help strengthen his army. Secretary of State Herter informed Eisenhower that there was no need to reply to the Shah just yet as this was an ongoing debate.[9]

The National Security Council held a meeting on April 7, 1960, to discuss international developments that could affect U.S. interests abroad. General Charles Cabell, a CIA representative, said that there had been no changes in Soviet-Iranian relations. At the same time, there were procommunist groups in Iran and abroad, who had increased their activities against the Shah's regime. Cabell then recounted SAVAK's recent report that it had discovered a ring of procommunist officers in the Iranian Army. In addition, Berlin radio continued to support the Tudeh Party and encouraged it to strengthen itself. Despite these developments, the Shah was under the impression that his land reform bill had led to more public support for the monarchy. Cabell did not agree with the Shah's views and thought that land reform bill had led to the alienation of wealthy landowners and the clergy, who opposed the Shah.[10]

If the U.S. government and the CIA thought that they had a firm grasp of world events affecting U.S. security, they were soon disappointed. On May 5, 1960, Khrushchev announced that an American U-2 aircraft had been shot down on May 1, while flying over the Soviet Union. Khrushchev had kept this information quiet for days to see how the United States would react. Khrushchev warned the members of the CENTO that if it became known that they had provided a base for the U-2 flight, there would be serious repercussions.[11]

The United States announced on May 5 that the plane was a U-2 aircraft that had been involved in climate studies over Turkey and was forced to land when the pilot reported mechanical difficulties.[12] On May 7, 1960, Khrushchev announced that the Soviet government had proof that the U-2 had been involved in espionage against the Soviet Union. The U-2's flight plan began in Pakistan and was to end in Norway, covering the Soviet Union in between, but was shot down by a Soviet missile inside the Soviet Union. Francis Gary Powers, the pilot was captured, brought to trial, and imprisoned. The plane's wreckage was taken to Moscow, where it was kept.[13]

Khruschev's announcement about the U-2 incident humiliated the United States. The question of the U.S.-Soviet détente and the forthcoming summit between the two sides that was to take place in Paris remained uncertain. On May 7, 1960, the United States publicly admitted that the purpose of the U-2 flight had been to obtain information about the Soviet Union and that these flights had been taking place since 1955 as part of its Open Skies program.[14]

Iranian newspapers began their coverage of the U-2 incident on May 7, 1960, following Khrushchev's public announcement, focusing in particular on his warning to the members of CENTO.[15] Masoud Entesar, the Iranian ambassador to the Soviet Union, met with the Shah to discuss the U-2 incident. Entesar said that while Khrushchev had named Iran among the list of countries that may have provided a base for the U-2 flight, he knew that Iran was not involved in the incident. Entesar advised the Shah to enter into a dialogue with the Soviet Union to improve relations between the two sides.[16]

On May 12, 1960, Foreign Minister Andrei Gromyko announced that Iran had not been involved in the U-2 incident and warned other members of CENTO not to participate in any future activities that would aggravate the Soviet Union.[17] Despite this announcement, the Soviet government was upset about the fact that Iran had allowed the United States and the members of CENTO to use the Iranian air space for a display of fighter jet maneuvers, called Shahbaz II, that were to be held May 14–18, 1960. The Soviet government warned the Iranian government that these activities would be considered a violation of the Russo-Persian Treaty of 1921.[18] The Iranian government paid no attention and allowed the maneuvers to take place.

Despite the U-2 incident, Eisenhower and Khrushchev attended a summit on May 17, 1960, in Paris. The two sides wanted to discuss the question of East Germany and the U.S.-Soviet détente. The summit failed, however, because Khrushchev was angry over the fact that the United States had continuously provided weapons to West Germany. In response to the U-2 incident, Khrushchev rescinded his invitation for Eisenhower to visit the Soviet Union.[19]

On May 25, 1960, the Soviet government reiterated its statement that Iran had not been involved in the U-2 incident.[20] Why the Soviet government would repeat this statement, given its displeasure at the Iranian decision to proceed with the CENTO operations over the Iranian air space, is an interesting question. The Soviet government was desperately seeking to sign an agreement with Iran in which the latter would agree not to allow any foreign missile bases on its soil. This urgency can be traced to a deepening Cold War rivalry between the Soviet Union and the United States.

The Shah took his time to consider the resumption of normal relations with the Soviet Union. He was to receive some shocking news from neighboring Turkey, which would add to his fears of external threats to his regime. On May 31, 1960, a military coup overthrew the government of Prime Minister Adnan Menderes. The United States did not seemed surprised by this event, since the Turkish government had been experiencing economic and political problems. In 1950, Turkey had transformed itself into a multiparty democracy, yet the government had engaged in reckless spending and incurred a large debt. Menderes had dealt harshly with any political opposition. As a result, his government was overthrown by a military coup in 1960 in an effort to restore democracy.

The U.S. National Security Council held a meeting on May 31, 1960. Robert Amory of the CIA discussed the political situation in Iran. Amory observed that the Turkish military coup had its own effect on Iran, in that several opposition groups had stepped up their activities against the Shah. Amory added that the Iranian Army did not have the same prestige as the Turkish Army and was unlikely to overthrow the Shah. The Shah had remained on shaky ground ever since the fall of Musaddiq's government.[21]

In the aftermath of the Turkish military coup, the United States took steps to guide Iran into pursuing economic stabilization. The United States was well aware that the deteriorating economy had played a major role in bringing about the Turkish military coup. The United States knew that the Shah was the only political figure who would promote U.S. interests in Iran. At the same time, the U.S. government could not force the Shah to carry out political reforms at the risk of losing him. With these facts in mind, the United States asked the Iranian government to send a negotiating team to Washington to discuss an economic stabilization program for Iran.

The Iranian negotiating team visited the United States from June 23 through July 1, 1960, and met with State Department and IMF officials. During these talks, the United States indicated that U.S. financial aid could be provided if the Iranian government would undertake an economic stabilization program as prescribed by the IMF. The Iranian government agreed to these plans and pledged to pursue initiatives that would lead to economic growth.[22]

On July 6, 1960, the National Security Council produced a report on U.S. policy toward Iran. The report emphasized that the best way for the United States to promote its interests in Iran was to continue its support of the Shah. The important question was how best to influence the Shah to carry out much-needed reforms. The Shah had to satisfy the needs of the people without losing the support of conservative groups, such as the wealthy landowners and the clergy, which could endanger the monarchy. The Shah had been critical of U.S. efforts to encourage him to carry out reforms. The report observed that if the Shah were pushed too hard, he could pursue a neutral stance and gravitate toward the Soviet Union. The report concluded that the United States had no choice but to maintain a balance between persuading and pressuring the Shah to carry out reforms.[23]

Meanwhile, the Shah struck back at Nasser and his supporters for their constant criticism of the Pahlavi regime. On July 24, 1960, which coincided with the eighth anniversary of the Egyptian military coup that had overthrown the monarchy, the Shah announced Iran's support for Israel and emphasized that such support had existed since 1949.[24] The Shah's announcement angered Nasser and the Arab world. Nasser ended his country's diplomatic relations with Iran, and Egyptian media portrayed the Shah as an outcast in the region.[25]

The National Security Council met on July 25, 1960, to discuss international developments that could affect U.S. interests and security. Allen Dulles noted that the Soviet government had asked the Shah and the Iranian government about the possibility of the two sides giving a pledge that no foreign country would be allowed to station its forces on either side. This was due to the U-2 incident, and the Soviets did not want Iran to be used as a base to carry out activities against the Soviet Union. The Shah had not replied immediately and had taken his time to reflect on the issue.[26]

The Shah set aside his concerns over the Soviet Union and Egypt to focus on Iran's economic stabilization program, which had become necessary due to the balance-of-payments problem. In order to remedy this situation, the Shah and the Iranian government knew that they had to increase the tariffs on imported goods. In addition, the Iranian government asked the United States to terminate the reciprocal trade agreement of 1943.[27] The United States agreed, knowing that these measures were part of Iran's economic stabilization program.

In early August 1960, the Iranian government held elections for the Twentieth Majlis, during which the Mardom (People's Party) and Milliyun (Nationalist Party) competed. In order to give the appearance of a democratic election, the Shah had also allowed candidates from the National Front to compete. The National Front had been banned since the fall of Musaddiq's government, yet by early 1960, it had become popular especially among university students. On August 3, 1960, the Shah met with Ambassador Wailes to discuss the elections. The Shah was upset with Iranian newspapers for printing stories about election fraud. The Shah said that government investigations indicated that elections were conducted unfairly in Tabriz and other cities, but he had ordered new elections to be held. Wailes responded that the Shah's views about holding free elections had produced a positive image of the Shah both inside and outside Iran. The Shah said that many of these problems had resulted from inadequate election laws, which were in need of reform. The Shah ended by saying that he would work with the Majlis to have a new law enacted that would specify the need for proper voter registration and identification prior to voting.[28]

The Shah's assurances to Wailes may not have been enough, as violence broke out throughout the country. Iranian newspapers published several stories about election fraud when it was announced that the Milliyun (Nationalist Party), the party of the government, had won. The Shah, who felt threatened by these developments, held a press conference on August 27, 1960. He voiced his dismay with the elections and blamed the problems on the electoral laws. The next day, Prime Minister Eqbal, who had led the Milliyun (Nationalist Party), resigned. While the public considered Eqbal as one of the individuals behind the election fraud, Eqbal felt that he had become a scapegoat for following the Shah's orders. The Shah refrained from blaming Eqbal and appointed Ja'far Sharif-Emami as the next prime minister.[29] On September 1, 1960, the Shah issued an order calling on the recently elected deputies to the Majlis to resign and for the Majlis to establish a committee to either revise the election law or produce a new one.[30]

While the Iranian government was busy dealing with election fraud and the appointment of a new prime minister, the Tudeh Party held its seventh annual meeting in Berlin from August 19–29, 1960. The Tudeh Party discussed its political program and future plans. It stated that Iran was plagued by feudalism and imperialism. The only remedy was for a revolution to take place that would take power away from the wealthy upper class and create a democratic government. Such a government, in turn, would represent different classes and would eradicate any remnants of feudalism and imperialism.[31]

Meanwhile, Ja'far Sharif-Emami asked the United States to send a negotiating team to Iran to continue discussions regarding the implementation of an economic stabilization plan that would revive the Iranian economy. During the Iranian team's visit to Washington earlier in the year, they were told that the United States would send its team to Iran to discuss the issue of U.S. financial aid if the Iranian government would carry out an economic stabilization plan as prescribed by the IMF. The State Department informed Sharif-Emami that on October 8, 1960, it would send a negotiating group composed of members from the State department, the Development Loan fund (DLF), and the Exim Bank to Iran.[32]

Before the end of the year, Khosrow Hedayat, the director of the Plan Organization, visited the United States to finalize discussions that had taken place in October. The talks focused on the economic stabilization plan for Iran that was designed to prevent inflation and bankruptcy. The talks ended with a number of incentives for Iran. The DLF provided a loan to Iran in the amount of $26.2 million for the construction of roads and highways linking southern Iran to the Caspian Sea region. The Exim Bank provided a loan in the amount of $15 million to help with the purchase of U.S. machinery needed to carry out Iran's developmental projects. The ICA authorized a defense grant in the amount of $22 million and the IMF provided $50 to help Iran with its economic stabilization program.[33]

During this time, the U.S. government had been caught up in presidential elections, which would herald a new era with victory for the Democratic Party. In November 1960, John F. Kennedy defeated Richard Nixon after eight years of a Republican administration. Kennedy was elected president with Lyndon Johnson as vice president. Kennedy named Dean Rusk secretary of state. During his presidential campaign, Kennedy had criticized the Eisenhower administration for the missile gap that had developed between the United States and the Soviet Union and for the rapid spread of communism in Third World countries, including Cuba. It was Neil McElroy, Eisenhower's secretary of defense, who had previously discussed the issue of a missile gap and predicted that by the early 1960s, the Soviets would be ahead of the United States in terms of possessing ICBMs.[34] As a result, Kennedy focused on expanding the size of the U.S. military and made changes to the U.S. missile programs. Kennedy's concerns as it turned out were exaggerated and his emphasis on a U.S. military buildup further fueled Cold War tensions.

For the sake of national security, Kennedy had advocated the expansion of U.S. conventional forces and missile programs in dealing with the Soviet Union. He had a different view, however, regarding the containment of communism abroad. Kennedy thought that the advancement of economic development and social justice were the best defense against the spread of communism. To help Third World countries with the above objectives, the Kennedy administration put forth a series of programs including the Peace

Corps and Food for Peace. Kennedy's election as president would signal new beginnings for Iran in the realm of reform, but reform would also have its repercussions in Iran.

IRAN ON THE VERGE OF A POLITICAL CRISIS

On January 10, 1961, new elections were held for the Twentieth Majlis with candidates from the Milliyun (Nationalist) and Mardom (People's) parties, and the National Front competing against each other. These elections did not fare well. The Milliyun (Nationalist) Party won once again, and only one National Front deputy was elected. In response, the Mardom Party, the National Front, and other opposition parties accused the government of election fraud. Shortly thereafter, thousands of university students demonstrated against the fraudulent elections. The government responded by shutting down the headquarters of the National Front.

The Tudeh Party took this opportunity to establish contact with the National Front. In 1953, the Tudeh Party had tried a conciliatory approach with the National Front and even warned Musaddiq of an impending military coup but to no avail. After the fall of Mussaddiq's government, there had been no contact between the National Front and the Tudeh Party, whose activities had been banned by the Shah. On February 9, 1961, the Tudeh Party sent a letter to the National Front asking for an alliance between the two parties and reminding the National Front of their past defeat, which had resulted from the lack of cooperation with one another. The letter mentioned certain tasks that needed to be carried out by both sides to overthrow the monarchy, including the recruitment of more members and organizing campaigns against the Shah's regime.[35] The National Front, suspicious of the Tudeh Party, refused to cooperate.

Meanwhile, the Shah had instructed General Bakhtiar, the director of SAVAK, to deliver a letter to President Kennedy. Bakhtiar was to meet with a number of U.S. officials to discuss the Kennedy administration's policy toward Iran under.[36] On February 21, 1961, Bakhtiar met with Secretary of State Rusk and other State Department officials. Bakhtiar said that the purpose of his visit was to give the Kennedy administration an update on the political situation in Iran. Bakhtiar noted that Iran continued to endure a Soviet threat due to its strategic location as well as its commitment to CENTO. Bakhtiar said that Iran needed a strong economy that could provide a decent standard of living for its people as well as a strong military to protect the country. Iran could not achieve these goals without the help of the United States.[37] Bakhtiar also noted that Iraq and Afghanistan were receiving financial and military aid from the Soviet Union. He argued that Iran needed assistance from the United States to withstand any threats from these countries.[38]

Rusk replied that the United States did not believe that Iran faced any military threat from Iraq or Afghanistan. The only possible threat was the Soviet Union. In this regard, Iran need not worry, as the United States was monitoring the situation. Rusk added that the best defense against communism entailed the promotion of economic and social reforms and did not rely on a military buildup. Rusk ended by saying that since the Kennedy administration had been in office for just one month and was in the process of putting its foreign aid program together, he could not make any statements regarding the question of U.S. aid to Iran.[39]

On March 1, 1961, Bakhtiar met with President Kennedy and presented a letter written by the Shah. After reading the letter, Kennedy said that his administration would review the issue of U.S. aid to Iran. Bakhtiar discussed Iran's economic problems, including the financing of development projects and maintaining a strong army. Kennedy replied that his administration knew about Iran's problems and asked Bakhtiar to convince the Shah of the continuous U.S. support. At the end of the meeting, Kennedy said that he would send Ambassador Harriman to Iran as a follow up to their conversation.[40] Ambassador Harriman visited Iran on March 14, 1961. Harriman's trip was not productive and further upset the Shah, as he was expecting news regarding the question of U.S. aid to Iran. Harriman told the Shah that the Kennedy administration was supportive of the Shah but that he was not sure about the question of U.S. financial and military aid to Iran.[41]

On March 17, 1961, Rusk prepared a memorandum for Kennedy that discussed a possible reply to the Shah's letter. A letter was to be delivered to Ambassador Wailes in Iran, who would then give it to the Shah. The letter would emphasize the importance of promoting economic and social reforms that were crucial in maintaining Iran's stability. At the time, however, the United States could not give the Shah any information about its level of aid to Iran, as its foreign aid programs were still under review. The letter advised the Iranian government to modify its budget and expenditures so that it could meet the level of U.S. aid. The letter ended by reassuring the Shah and his government of the continuous U.S. support for Iran.[42]

On March 22, 1961, Kennedy presented his administration's foreign aid program to Congress. Kennedy advocated long-term planning for the economic development of countries receiving U.S. aid, which would allow the United States to get involved in all aspects of how its aid was being used. The Foreign Assistance Act of 1961 enabled the United States to participate in the economic and social reconstruction of the country receiving aid on the grounds that U.S. aid had to be utilized effectively.[43]

It may be recalled that in the aftermath of the 1953 coup, the Eisenhower administration had provided Iran with emergency aid, as it was estimated that it would take at least three years from the settlement of the oil dispute for Iran's oil revenues to reach a level where it could finance its own development projects. But by 1958, Iran's oil revenues were still not enough to finance development projects. Furthermore, the government had begun to divert a large part of the Plan Organization's share of oil revenues to cover its administrative expenses. These difficulties persisted throughout 1960, when Eisenhower's term in office came to an end, and continued to persist while Kennedy was in office. The Kennedy administration was aware that U.S. aid to Iran during the Eisenhower years had produced few concrete results. Kennedy therefore ordered a review of all U.S. financial and military aid to Iran and set up an Iran Task Force to examine political developments in Iran and produce special reports. These reports would determine the level of U.S. financial and military aid provided to Iran.[44]

Meanwhile, Ambassador Harriman met with State Department officials on his return from Iran. Harriman was happy with the progress made in Iran in the course of a decade. It may be recalled that during the oil nationalization crisis, Harriman had met with Musaddiq to mediate the oil dispute. Harriman said that the Shah had aligned Iran with the West and would not take a neutral stance because it would leave the country vulnerable to the spread of communism. The economic problems had resulted from excessive government expenditures. The rapid growth of the private sector had led to a foreign exchange deficit. An estimated $40 million was needed to keep the Iranian economy functioning until the start of Third Economic Plan in 1962.[45] Harriman did not foresee an immediate crisis in Iran but emphasized that the Shah had to undertake much needed reforms. Harriman emphasized that the Kennedy administration had to specify its level of financial and military aid to Iran and inform the Shah accordingly. Finally, the Kennedy administration had to convince the Shah to focus more on economic and social reforms as opposed to military buildup.[46]

The Shah was displeased with the Kennedy administration's insistence on Iran's need for reforms, given the lack of U.S. financial support. He was also upset over what he thought was the administration's failure to understand the importance of Iran's strategic location and the ongoing threat from the Soviet Union. In an interview with an American news magazine in March 1961, the Shah discussed the continuous communist threat to his regime and what seemed to be the Kennedy administration's lack of comprehension of this issue.[47]

The subject of Iran came up a few weeks later when, on April 10, 1961, Walter Lippmann, a well-known American reporter, interviewed Nikita

Khrushchev. Khrushchev said that Iran would experience a future revolution due to the corruption in the Shah's regime, which had led to the suffering of the Iranian people. Khrushchev believed that the United States could not prevent this revolution from taking place with all its insistence on the Shah carrying out democratic reforms. When Kennedy found out about this interview, he became determined to prove Khrushchev otherwise by pushing the Shah to carry out much needed reforms in Iran.[48]

Kennedy's attention was temporarily diverted from Iran to Cuba. On April 17, 1961, a group of Cuban exiles attempted to invade Cuba with the help of the CIA. The invasion of Cuba at the Bay of Pigs failed because it was poorly planned and carried out. Castro's forces had responded efficiently and captured 1,113 Cuban rebels.[49] Despite this humiliating incident, the Kennedy administration began to prepare for an upcoming Vienna Summit, where Khrushchev and Kennedy were to discuss U.S.-Soviet détente and the question of East Germany.

Meanwhile, the ninth CENTO council meeting took place in Turkey, from April 27 to 28, 1961. Hussein Qods-Nakhai, the Iranian foreign minister, met with Secretary Rusk, Ambassador Wailes, and Philip Talbot, the director of the Iran Task Force. During this meeting, Qods-Nakhai discussed the continuous danger of communism and negative Soviet propaganda against Iran. Qods-Nakhai said that the Iranian government had become aware that many Iranian students studying abroad were falling under the influence of communist ideology. He added that the Egyptians were involved in spreading communism among Iranian students in the West. The Egyptian government was in the process of publishing a book that condemned the Shah's regime. Qods-Nakhai said that Iran was not ready to embrace democracy, as the people had no confidence in the elections or in the Majlis. The discussion ended with Qods-Nakhai asking for more U.S. aid.[50]

IRAN'S ATTEMPTS AT POLITICAL STABILIZATION

Political turmoil was on the rise in Iran as dissatisfied teachers, students, and workers had begun to demonstrate against the government and the deteriorating economy. On May 2, 1961, primary and secondary school teachers went on strike asking for higher pay. The strikes spread throughout the country but were especially intense in Tehran, where the schools were closed. On May 4, nearly 50,000 students joined the teachers in their strike. Clashes with the police led to one death and many injuries. A number of arrests were also made when the police were hurt. Government employees also threatened to join the strike.[51]

The Shah had to find a way to end this crisis as soon as possible. He knew that the fraudulent elections of 1960 and 1961 and the deteriorating economy had fueled this crisis. On May 4, 1961, the Shah met with Generals Bakhtiar and Alavi-Kia, the director and deputy director of SAVAK, who told the Shah to dismiss Prime Minister Sharif-Emami and appoint Ali Amini.[52] Amini was an experienced politician who had played an important part in the settlement of the oil nationalization dispute and served as ambassador to the United States. In addition, he was pro-reform and had maintained good relations with several opposition groups, including the National Front and the clergy. The Shah, who wanted to bring an end to the chaos, agreed to appoint Amini the next prime minister.

On May 5, 1961, Prime Minister Sharif-Emami and his cabinet resigned. On the same day, the U.S. National Security Council met to discuss Iran's deteriorating situation. The National Security Council asked the Iran Task Force to prepare a report on Iran for the council's forthcoming meeting scheduled for May 19.[53] On May 6, the Shah appointed Amini his new prime minister. Amini, in turn, asked the Shah to accept certain conditions prior to the start of his post. Among these were Amini's right to choose the government ministers, except for the minister of war; ending the current Majlis, as the majority of deputies were powerful landowners opposed to land reform; and the establishment of a special court that would prosecute cases of corruption.[54] The Shah agreed to those terms.

Amini began to recruit reform-minded individuals to his cabinet. Among them were Hasan Arsanjani, who became minister of agriculture, and Muhammad Derakhshesh, who became minister of education. Arsanjani had sufficient knowledge about rural Iran and was committed to economic and political reform. Derakhshesh was a teacher who had helped organized the Iran Teachers Association. Amini had appointed Derakshesh as minister of education to negotiate with the teachers in reaching a settlement.[55] The Shah dissolved the Twentieth Majlis in order to give Amini more freedom to carry out much-needed reforms. Amini banned demonstrations while he and Derakhshesh met with teachers to negotiate. As a result, the teachers' strike ended and schools reopened.[56]

In the meantime, the Iran Task Force had prepared its first report on the political situation in Iran, which was to be presented to the National Security Council on May 19. The report noted that even though Iran had taken a pro-Western stance, it continued to struggle under the Shah's dictatorship. Economic and social reforms were not being pursued effectively. The Soviet Union was encouraging Iranians to revolt against the Shah's regime.[57] According to the report, the primary objective of the United States was to maintain Iran's sovereignty. To this end, the United States had to accomplish certain goals, among which were to keep the monarchy intact and encourage the Shah and his government to continue with economic development to prevent the spread of communism in Iran.[58]

Before this report was presented to the National Security Council, the Iran Task Force asked the American embassy in Tehran for advice about the extent to which the United States should support Amini's government. Ambassador Wailes replied that the United States should not make any public statements in support of Amini's government because the Shah was still the monarch, and Amini his prime minister. It was not wise for the United States to publicly support a prime minister whose future was unknown.[59]

Even though the United States was privately supportive of Amini's government, it was hesitant to publicly identify with him. On the Iranian side, there are few objective views of Amini's rise to power and any U.S. involvement. This is understandable, given the strict censorship and fear of SAVAK during that period. In his memoirs, Amini stated that it was the Shah who had circulated rumors that he was handpicked by the United States. In fact, decades later, in 1978, when Iran was on the verge of a revolution and the United States was being blamed for all its problems, the Shah had the Iranian newspapers print that the United States had forced him to appoint Amini in 1961. Amini was very upset and told Prime Minister Hoveyda that the Shah had put Iran to shame with this statement.[60]

The Shah has not mentioned Amini in any of his books or memoirs. This is not surprising, given the fact that the Shah did not like Amini and had been compelled to appoint him in order to avert further political chaos in 1961. In the aftermath of the Islamic Revolution of 1979, General Hussein Fardust, the previous deputy director of SAVAK and a close friend of the Shah, also made a similar statement in his memoirs about Amini's nomination, but with a special twist. Fardust stated that the Kennedy administration had pushed the Shah to accept Amini's nomination. In return, the United States agreed to give a loan in the amount of $35 million to Iran's Plan Organization. Fardust had quoted Armin Meyer, the former assistant secretary of the Office of Near Eastern and African Affairs (NEA) and ambassador to Iran (1965 to 1969), for making this statement at a conference in Washington, D.C. in October 1977.[61]

The National Security Council met on May 15, 1961, and approved the recommendations that had been presented by the Iran Task Force. Shortly thereafter, the CIA and other U.S. intelligence agencies prepared a report about Amini's government. The report observed that Amini's challenge was to deal with both economic problems and political opposition. The Soviets were also attacking Amini with negative propaganda, charging that he was being guided by the United States to save the Shah's regime. The Soviet

Union hoped that Amini's failure would lead to a revolution in Iran that would bring an end to the Shah's regime. The report concluded by saying that Amini's appointment had been an important step toward the spread of democracy in Iran.[62]

On May 24, 1961, President Kennedy approved certain recommendations put forth by the State Department regarding U.S. policy toward Iran. Among these were that the United States would encourage Amini's government to carry out much-needed reforms in Iran, and that the United States would emphasize economic development over military buildup in Iran.[63] On May 25, 1961, Ambassador Wailes met with Amini and Khodadad Farmanfarmayan, Amini's economic adviser, to discuss Iran's economic problems. Amini and Farmanfarmayan requested a U.S. loan in the amount of $40 million to deal with two critical problems: the depletion of foreign exchange reserves; and ending a number of the Plan Organization's development projects due to the lack of money. Wailes said that he would notify the United States regarding this request. In a telegram to Secretary Rusk, Wailes observed that Amini's government would not survive without financial aid.[64]

The State Department asked Ambassador Wailes to meet with the Shah for the last time prior to his departure. Wailes was being replaced by Julius Holmes. On June 6, 1961, Wailes met with the Shah and said that the United States was content with Amini's appointment and that the Shah should support Amini's efforts at solving national problems and carrying out much-needed reforms. Wailes reminded the Shah about the National Front and its grievances against the government, which had to be addressed. Finally, Wailes emphasized that the United States did not agree with the idea of expanding the size of the Iranian Army, as it would further weaken the economy.[65]

Meanwhile, the Vienna Conference had taken place on June 3 and 4, 1961. President Kennedy and Premier Khrushchev discussed the issue of détente and the possibility of negotiating a nuclear test ban treaty.[66] The subject of Iran was also discussed during those talks. Khrushchev stated that the Shah's regime would crumble due to the deteriorating economic and political conditions in Iran. These comments must have affected Kennedy, for he asked the State Department to prepare a report regarding the stability of the Shah's regime. He also became determined to change the Shah's focus from military matters to carrying out economic, political, and social reforms.[67]

Khrushchev's observations on the deteriorating economic and political conditions in Iran were accurate. The National Front had organized demonstrations against Amini's government and its failure to act on its promises. On June 21, the Iranian police attacked a group of demonstrators, and several members of the National Front were arrested.[68] Yet the National Front continued its activities against Amini's government. The National Front called for a public gathering on July 21, 1961, to commemorate Musaddiq's victory over Qavam on that day in 1952. Amini ordered the police to prevent any disorder and blamed the Soviet Union and the Tudeh Party for encouraging the National Front to revolt. On July 23, 1961, the Iranian foreign minister met with the Soviet ambassador and gave him a letter protesting Soviet interference in Iranian affairs. The Soviet press responded with a harsh criticism of Amini.[69]

In a radio announcement, Amini accused the National Front of collaborating with the Tudeh Party and defended his reliance on the police to maintain order. The National Front denied Amini's charges and accused him of following the Shah's orders to crack down on the opposition.[70] In his memoirs, Shahpur Bakhtiar, a prominent member of the National Front and the prime minister of Iran in 1978, criticized Amini's crackdown on the National Front. Bakhtiar believed that Amini had acted against the National Front and arrested several of its members in order to satisfy the Shah. Bakhtiar, who was among those arrested, saw Amini's actions as a betrayal of the National Front.[71]

On August 2, 1961, the Iran Task Force prepared its second report regarding political and economic developments in Iran. It observed that Amini's government was plagued by political and economic problems, and if the economic problems continued to the point where the Shah's regime was threatened, U.S. aid would be required. The report also noted that an Iranian negotiating team was in the process of presenting an overview of its Third Economic Development Plan to the World Bank, and that it would be best if the United States supported this plan. The report recommended that the United States consider providing the Iranian government a grant in the amount of $5 million to help improve its budget deficit.[72]

Meanwhile, Cold War tensions in Berlin had led to a major crisis. Khrushchev was upset by the fact that thousands of people were fleeing East Germany to seek refuge in West Germany. In order to prevent this, the Soviets began to build a wall in East Berlin on August 13, 1961 to separate the two sides. During the first week, the wall consisted of barbed wire, which failed to stop people from crossing into West Germany. Cement blocks were soon used to build a wall that separated East and West Germany.[73] The Kennedy administration did not challenge the Soviet Union, as inhumane as its actions were. The international community, including Iran, was stunned at the news of the Berlin Wall. At the time, however, the Iranian government had to deal with two important developments. The first was the upcoming ninth annual meeting of the Tudeh Party, which would result in its declaration to overthrow the Shah's regime. The second was the delivery of a paper at a conference in the United States by Ibtehaj, the former director of the Plan Organization, which would deeply embarrass the Iranian government.

The Tudeh Party held its ninth annual meeting in East Berlin September 10–16, 1961. This meeting focused on promoting revolutionary movements in Iran for the purpose of establishing a democracy. The Tudeh Party observed that while the overthrow of the Shah's regime was its main concern, revolutionary movements in Iran were not yet sophisticated enough to accomplish this task. Nonetheless, the Tudeh Party pledged that upon assuming power, it would promote free elections in Iran and would continue its struggle against imperialism.[74] It is important to note that this was the Tudeh Party's last meeting before its dissolution, which became effective in 1965. Two factors would lead to the demise of the Tudeh Party. The first was a significant improvement in Soviet-Iranian relations in 1962 and the second was the rift among Tudeh Party leaders.[75]

On September 21, 1961, Ibtihaj, the former director of the Plan Organization, attended a conference at the Stanford Research Institute in California, where he presented a paper. Ibtihaj had become critical of the Shah after being removed from his post as director of the Plan Organization in 1957. Ibtihaj was worried about inflation and the lack of coordination in economic planning, and he criticized the Shah for spending Iran's oil revenues on purchasing military weapons instead of promoting economic development projects.

At the conference, Ibtihaj stated that U.S. attempts to negotiate bilateral defense agreements with Third World countries were harmful, as those countries became obsessed with expanding their military establishment and paid little attention to economic development. Opposition groups in countries receiving U.S. aid charged that their governments were selling out to the imperialist powers. With regard to Iran, Ibtihaj said, "Not long ago, the United States was loved and respected in Iran without having given a penny of aid. Now after more than a $1 billion of loans and grants, the United States is neither loved nor respected; she is distrusted and hated by many."[76] Upon his return to Iran, Ibtihaj was imprisoned for several months. The Iranian government made no mention of his controversial paper but said that the arrest had resulted from Ibtihaj's inappropriate behavior before the Iranian Civil Service Tribunal.[77]

On October 9, 1961, the Iran Task Force prepared its third report on Iran. The report said that the key U.S. objective in Iran was to prevent it from falling to communism. To this end, it was in the best interests of the United States to support a pro-Western government that would carry out reforms and promote modernization in Iran. The report noted that progress had been made in Iran due to continuous U.S. support and pressure. Iran was no longer experiencing political disorder. The Shah had accepted the reduction in U.S. military aid, as well as stabilization measures to improve the economy.[78]

On October 17, 1961, Ambassador Holmes sent a telegram to the State Department notifying the latter about some serious political developments in Iran that could end Amini's premiership. It appeared that the Shah was thinking about holding elections in the near future as a way to get rid of Amini. Holmes then asked if he could advise the Shah not to hold elections and instead let Amini's government continue with its tasks.[79] Armin Meyer, the assistant secretary of state, discussed the telegram with Secretary Rusk. Meyer noted that Rusk's recommendations were in tune with U.S. policy objectives as discussed in the Task Force Report. Secretary Rusk agreed with Holmes's recommendations.[80]

On October 30, 1961, Holmes met with the Shah and told him about the advantages of having a capable prime minister. The Shah said that he would not oppose Amini if he cooperated with the Shah in implementing reforms. The Shah explained what he intended to do with regard to land reform as well as plans for the reform of the education system, civil service, and the judicial system.[81] The Shah then discussed the issue of elections, saying that free elections were not possible, as the majority of the people did not know much about political parties and party politics. The Majlis still had deputies who wanted Iran to take a neutral stance in international affairs. The Shah said he had two choices to consider. Either have the people vote during elections to elect a traditional government or for the Shah to rule by decree without the Majlis for two years while his reforms continued. The latter choice had to do with the fact that the majority of the Majlis deputies were wealthy landowners and businessmen, who were opposed to the Shah's reforms, as it threatened their interests. The Shah then asked Holmes about his views regarding the two choices. Holmes replied that a government without a Majlis for two years would be better than having another fraudulent election, provided that economic and social reforms would continue.[82]

It is apparent from this statement that the U.S. government was pushing for economic and social reforms in Iran, regardless of the fact that the Majlis would not be in session. The United States was concerned that a Majlis in session could lead to the defeat of the Shah's reforms, given the fact that the deputies were primarily landowners or conservative members of society, who opposed any reforms that would threaten their interests. To avoid any social disorder, the Shah decided to allow the Majlis to remain in session, while he continued with his reforms.

On November 11, 1961, the Shah ordered Amini's government to study and prepare the way for a comprehensive reform program known as the White Revolution.[83] The Shah had chosen the term white to signify the fact that this was a progressive movement where no blood would be shed in carrying out these reforms. The White Revolution initially consisted of six points to which others were added within a decade. On November 14, 1961, Amini announced that the Shah had granted him executive power to carry out the White Revolution. The National Front did not agree with Amini's new powers and began to speak out against him in the public. Amini responded by having the leaders of the National Front and other opposition groups detained. The Shah told the public that he had granted Amini executive powers to carry out much needed reforms.[84]

Before the end of the year, the United States signed an agreement for economic cooperation with the Iranian government. Although this agreement did not specify any specific amount of money in terms of loans or grants, it stated that the United States would continue to provide technical aid to Iran. In return, the U.S. personnel in Iran under the terms of this agreement would be exempt from paying taxes to the Iranian government. Furthermore, these personnel would have diplomatic immunity.[85]

In early January 1962, Amini asked Hasan Arsanjani, the minister of agriculture, to revise the 1960 land reform law, which he thought was ineffectual. It fell upon Arsanjani to reduce the power of wealthy landowners by limiting their land ownership to one village. Landowners with more than one village had to sell their land to the government, which in turn, would sell them to the peasants at a much lower price. Arsanjani wanted to empower peasants into making their own decisions about issues pertaining to the well being of their village. The Iranian government would provide low-interest loans to rural cooperatives, which would provide the peasants with the needed credits. The hope was to eradicate the feudal system and replace it with an independent farming system.[86]

The first phase of land reform began with an amended land reform bill, signed into law on January 9, 1962. Arsanjani announced that land reform would first begin in the Azerbaijan province followed by the remaining provinces throughout the country.[87] Arsanjani, who was aware that the new land reform bill was detested by many landowners and the clergy, emphasized that it was not contrary to Islamic law or the Constitution.[88]

On January 18, 1962, the Iran Task Force prepared its fourth report on political developments in Iran. The report discussed Amini's achievements as prime minister. Amini had managed to bring the teachers' strike under control and had the Shah's support in carrying out reforms. In addition, Amini had taken measures to combat corruption, inflation, and foreign exchange problems.[89] The report observed that the United States would eventually have to choose between two strategies: either support the Shah and his prime minister or support representatives from opposition groups such as the National Front. The report, however, cautioned that if the National Front were to come to power, it could end the U.S. military mission in Iran, withdraw Iran's membership from CENTO, and collaborate with pro-communist groups.[90] For these reasons, it was in the best interests of the United States to support the Shah, and at the same time, to encourage him to carry out much-needed reforms.

The National Front was disappointed with Amini for not holding new elections as he had previously promised. On January 22, 1962, several National Front leaders were arrested. This action led to demonstrations by Tehran University students, where the National Front was popular. Iranian police clashed with the students, which led to many being injured and others taken into custody. As a result, Tehran University was shut down for several months.[91] Amini accused the Tudeh Party of encouraging the National Front to carry out these demonstrations and for the disorder that had resulted.[92]

The Iranian clergy were also concerned about these demonstrations. Ayatollah Muhammad Behbahani wrote to the Shah asking for an investigation, as one of his relatives had been arrested during the demonstrations. Behbahani also asked the Shah to order Amini to hold elections for a new Majlis. The call for elections had been of the National Front's grievances against Amini's government. The Shah was upset with Behbahani's demands and did not answer him.[93] The United States had been monitoring these developments with concern. The State Department sent a memorandum to the president's assistant for National Security Affairs, recommending that the Shah be invited to the United States for a visit. The State Department then suggested that Chester Bowles, the president's special representative to Iran, who was about to visit Iran, to invite the Shah for a state visit by early October 1962.[94]

Coincident with this memorandum, a World Bank negotiating team had arrived in Iran to review Iran's Third Development Plan, which was to be implemented in September 1962. The members of this team were in Iran for six weeks to review the plan.[95] The purpose of Iran's Third Plan was to increase the country's GNP above the level that had prevailed between 1955 and 1962. It entailed a five and a half year period beginning in September 1962, and its expenditures were estimated to be $5 billion.[96] While the Third Plan's main objective was to increase Iran's GNP, its secondary objectives included the creation of more job opportunities and improving the people's standard of living.[97] If the World Bank were to approve Iran's Third Plan, it would seek donors such as the United States and Great Britain to discuss the question of financing.[98]

Meanwhile, Kennedy had asked Chester Bowles, one of his advisers, to visit to Iran from February 10 to 14, 1962, and to prepare a report regarding Iran's political, economic, and social development. Bowles was to invite the Shah for a state visit to the United States. In a meeting with Bowles, Amini discussed his concerns over Iran's military spending. Bowles suggested that it would be worthwhile if surplus conscripts were organized into special units that would serve as the Corps of Engineers, who could help out with development construction projects. Bowles described how the United States for example relied on its Army Corps of Engineers, who were involved in many domestic projects.[99]

Bowles also met with Minister of Agriculture Arsanjani to discuss the issue of land reform. In response to Arsanjani's complaint over the lack of machinery and equipment, Bowles said that it was feasible to look into the construction of tube wells. The construction of these wells was an acceptable project to obtain loans, as it signified that land reform was in progress. Bowles then met with officials from the Plan Organization and congratulated them on their efforts to improve agriculture and rural conditions as part of Iran's Third Economic Plan.[100]

Bowles also met with the Shah and invited him for a state visit to the United States, which the Shah accepted. The Shah requested financial and military aid from the United States to alleviate the budget deficit and at the same time modernize the Iranian Army. He was still upset about Turkey's receiving more military aid than Iran and asked for the United States to examine Iran's military establishment and its needs. Bowles refrained from discussing military issues and instead emphasized that Iran's well being depended on its success at economic and social reform.[101] As far as Soviet-Iranian relations were concerned, Bowles believed that in the ensuing months, the Soviets would either step up their negative propaganda attacks against the Shah, as they had done in the past, or take a different approach and try to forge new relations with Iran.

Meanwhile, the Shah's dissatisfaction with the Kennedy administration over the lack of U.S. military aid reached a boiling point. On March 5, 1962, Ambassador Holmes reported to the State Department that the Shah had sent him a disturbing message. The Shah said that the Kennedy administration did not seem to understand that the reason why Iran needed a strong military force was because of its vulnerability and the threats it was facing from within and outside the country. If nothing was done to strengthen his forces, the Shah could not remain as the commander in chief.[102] On March 7, 1962, Holmes met with the Shah and told him he could not understand how the Shah could give up his position of commander in chief. The Shah replied that either the United States did not understand the consequences of losing Iran to the Soviets or did not care.[103]

Holmes had replied to the Shah that his statement would not be accepted in the United States, and he reiterated the Kennedy administration's emphasis on economic reform over military buildup to achieve stability in Iran. Holmes added that the United States received several requests for aid each year, yet it had to distribute its aid in ways that would prove beneficial to the country receiving it.[104]

The Shah then began to compare the U.S. treatment of Turkey with that of Iran. Holmes replied that the Shah was wrong to assume that the United States had categorized its allies and distributed its economic and military aid accordingly. Holmes continued that sometimes a country's resources were not enough to carry out the intended reforms and this is where U.S. aid was used to supplement a country's resources. Turkey required more aid than Iran, because Iran was receiving nearly $ 300 million a year from its oil revenues. Turkish forces had to be upgraded due to Turkey's obligations to NATO.[105]

Finally, Holmes told the Shah that the United States was reviewing the level of its financial and military aid to Iran and that the Shah would be informed accordingly. The Shah said that Iran's stability depended on him and the army. He did not want to push the United States to have his demands met. In the aftermath of this meeting, Holmes told the State Department that the United States had no choice but to support the Shah, as there was no other reliable figure, who would promote U.S. interests in Iran.[106] The State Department, in turn, began to think about obtaining an aid package that Holmes could present to the Shah. In addition, it recommended to President Kennedy to move up the date of the Shah's state visit to the United States.[107]

On March 8, 1962, Fowler Hamilton, the administrator of the Agency of International Development (AID), presented a report to the National Security Council emphasizing that the United States had to convince the Shah to reduce the size of his military forces due to the deteriorating political and economic situation in Iran.[108] Hamilton said that in order for the United States to shift the Shah's attention from military issues to economic and social reform, certain objectives had to be met. Among these were: the United States would provide nearly $300 million in military aid to Iran between 1962 and 1967 if the Shah agreed to reduce his forces to 150,000; and the United States would help Iran's Third Economic Plan by seeking donors for its financing.[109]

On March 8, 1962, the State Department forwarded a memorandum to Kennedy requesting that the date of the Shah's visit to the United States be changed. The memorandum noted that the Shah was upset over the decrease in U.S. military aid and the Kennedy administration's lack of appreciation for Iran. The Shah had indicated that he wished to visit the United States in spring instead of autumn.[110] A week later, the Shah was invited to visit the United States in April instead of September 1962. The State Department was determined to persuade the Shah to reduce the size of his military force.

Meanwhile, the United States was seeking diplomatic immunity for its military personnel in Iran. The United States suggested to the Iranian government that all the U.S. military personnel in Iran be considered administrative and technical personnel, as mentioned in the Vienna Convention on Diplomatic Intercourse and Immunities. If the Iranian government were to accept this proposal, criminal jurisdiction would be given to American authorities.[111] The idea of diplomatic immunity can be traced back to August 1959. During that time, the Defense Department had submitted a report to a subcommittee of the Senate Armed Services Committee chaired by Sam J. Ervin Jr. (later of Watergate fame) stating that the Iranian government had not granted immunity to four American servicemen who had been involved in traffic accidents in Iran that had resulted in the deaths of pedestrians.[112]

In 1960, the Defense Department had reported incidents about U.S. military personnel in Iran to the Ervin subcommittee. One case involved an American sergeant who had killed an Iranian pedestrian while driving. The sergeant was found guilty by an Iranian court, which sentenced him to two months in prison and the payment of a fine. Another case involved an American major who had also killed a pedestrian in a traffic accident. The major was sentenced to six months in prison. Iran had refused to grant diplomatic immunity in both cases.[113] During a hearing before Congress in July 1961, the Defense Department reported sixteen cases in which Iran had refused to grant diplomatic immunity. The Defense Department's testimony before Congress also affected the State Department, which knew that the Defense Department was intent upon achieving diplomatic immunity for U.S. military personnel in Iran.[114]

On March 14, 1962, Kennedy asked his military adviser, General Maxwell Taylor, to prepare a report on whether there was any truth to Iran's accusation that it was being discriminated against when it came to the U.S. Military Assistance Program, in comparison to countries such as Turkey and Pakistan. Taylor reported that it was difficult to compare these countries, as their needs varied. Turkey received more military aid because of its membership in NATO and CENTO. Furthermore, the Turkish Army was larger than the Iranian Army, and Turkey had allowed the United States to set up air and military bases on its soil.[115] Taylor observed that U.S. military aid given to Pakistan was similar to that given to Iran. The only difference was that since the Pakistani Army was trained by the British, it was in a better position to learn to utilize the military equipment than the Iranian Army. For these reasons, U.S. military aid to Pakistan was expected to decrease. Taylor therefore saw no basis for Iran's claim of discrimination.[116]

On March 16, 1962, the State Department notified Ambassador Holmes that the president had moved up the date of the Shah's visit to mid-April. Holmes was told to assure the Shah of U.S. support, and to return to Washington a week before the Shah's visit.[117] Holmes presented the Shah with the new invitation to visit the United States on April 10, 1962.[118] On March 19, 1962, the United States asked the Iranian government to grant diplomatic immunity to its military personnel in Iran.[119] Whether this came as a surprise to the Iranian government was never mentioned, and the Iranian government would in fact take a whole year to reach a decision. What is important is that the State Department had cleverly discerned the right time to approach the Shah, given the fact that the Shah was eager to step up the date of visit and see what the United States would offer in terms of military and economic aid.

The Shah visited the United States from April 10 to 18, 1962 and met with President Kennedy, Secretary of State Rusk, Defense Secretary McNamara, William Gaud, the Assistant AID Administrator, and other State Department officials.[120] The Shah discussed Iran's need of U.S. military aid. The president replied that a military buildup in Iran would not protect it from a Soviet attack. Therefore, there was no need for Iran to have a large army. The Shah then complained about the amount of military aid given by the United States to Turkey. The president replied that Iran's main problem was its economy and that there was no need to worry about military issues, as they would be discussed in the near future. He complimented the Shah for supporting Amini and his efforts to reform Iran. In the days that followed, the president and his team continued to discuss military and economic issues with the Shah.[121]

Military matters were discussed on different levels. The Shah was concerned about the issue of Soviet military aid to Afghanistan and the country's future prospects. He also discussed political developments in Iraq and criticized Qasim for establishing a military dictatorship, and for his crackdown on the Kurds. The Shah was worried that the Kurds in Iran would be influenced by what was happening to the Kurds in Iraq. For these reasons, the Shah argued that he needed to strengthen his army, and he asked for more aircraft. He noted that if the Soviets were to interfere with the Kurdish issue, it would complicate the situation. The Shah noted that the Soviets had already provided military aid to Qasim and that Qasim had rejected a treaty of friendship with Iran. Relations between Iraq and Iran remained strained over the issue of the Shatt al-Arab waterway. The 1937 treaty had given Iraq the right to administer it.[122]

The Shah then discussed Arab countries such as Egypt and Syria and how they were benefiting from Soviet military aid. The Shah observed that Nasser's Pan-Arabism had failed in Egypt, and that is why Nasser was now pursuing socialism. The Shah warned that Nasser's policies could lead to a communist takeover in Egypt, which could have repercussions for Iran.[123] Kennedy asked the Shah to discuss the issue of Soviet aid to these countries with the Senate Foreign Relations Committee. Kennedy added that his administration was aware that many Arab states had become politically unstable, but if they were to attack any country, it would be Israel.[124]

President Kennedy asked Defense Secretary McNamara to report on Iran's military establishment. McNamara reported that the Iranian Army was large and not adequately equipped. Therefore it would be wise to reduce its size. To this end, the United States was willing to supervise a special program for Iran and provide military aid if the Shah agreed to reduce the size of his army. The Shah asked how this reduction would fit within CENTO's requirements, which wanted its members to have large forces. McNamara said that this issue would be discussed at a later time with the Defense Department. Secretary of State Rusk, however, told the Shah that CENTO should not be used as a point of reference. The president said that if Iran were to be attacked by the Soviets, it was unlikely to get much help from Turkey or Pakistan, as those countries had to deal with their own problems. So far, the United States had managed to convince the Soviets that it would continue to protect Iran.[125]

During the meetings with the Shah, Kennedy also asked Secretary of State Rusk to discuss the issue of U.S. financial aid to Iran. Rusk talked about the importance of economic development over military buildup and observed that progress was being made in Iran. The Shah described Iran's Third Development Plan, noting the problem of unemployment, which had resulted from the stabilization program prescribed by the IMF. The Shah said that Iran needed budgetary aid from the United States. The President replied that Iran could not expect any aid in the future because of congressional cuts in foreign aid.[126] William S. Gaud, the assistant administrator of AID, discussed steps the Iranian government could take to alleviate its budgetary problems. Gaud said that the Iranian government should consider combining its economic and military budgets, and take measures to increase its revenues.[127]

The Shah also discussed reducing the size of Iran's military forces with Secretary McNamara and members of the Joint Chiefs of Staff (JCS). The Shah once again mentioned CENTO and whether its requirements had to be used as criteria for restructuring the Iranian military forces. McNamara said that the strength of the Iranian forces had to be gauged more in terms of withstanding threats coming from neighboring countries other than the Soviet Union.[128] The discussion then turned to the question of maintaining a 150,000 troop level in Iran. The Shah said that it would actually be wise to increase the number to avoid giving the wrong impression that Iran's borders no longer required defense. McNamara proposed sending a team from the JCS to Iran to further discuss the issue of the size of Iran's military forces.[129] Finally, McNamara discussed the proposed U.S. military aid to Iran, which was to be distributed within a five-year period from mid-1962 to 1967. McNamara informed the Shah that he would be given a list prior to his departure of the U.S. military equipment that the United States would send to Iran as part of its aid package.[130]

On April 13, 1962, the Shah met with Averell Harriman. The Shah said that while he was pleased to meet President Kennedy, he was disappointed about his discussions with the Defense Department. The Shah argued that due to Iran's strategic location, it needed more military equipment and aircraft. The Shah then talked about land reform and hoped that there would be positive results in the near future. While he was concerned about Iran's high unemployment rate that had resulted from the economic stabilization program, the Shah hoped that Iran's economic situation would continue to improve.[131]

Harriman congratulated the Shah for pursuing economic development plans and at the same time encouraged him to maintain good relations with opposition groups including intellectuals and university students to preserve order in the country. Harriman added that Iran's security was in a large part due to continuous U.S. support and not the Iranian Army. Iran's greatest danger was the spread of communism, not a military attack from the Soviet Union. The Shah agreed and said he hoped for changes in Iran's economic development.[132]

Prior to his departure, the Shah met again with President Kennedy and members of the Defense and State departments. The president and the Shah examined the draft of a joint statement, which was to be issued prior to the Shah's departure. Secretary of Defense McNamara handed the Shah the list of military equipment to be provided to Iran, pointing out the aircraft and weapons that had been added to the original list. The President said that nothing contributed more to Iran's standing in the international community than its economic development program, and he congratulated the Shah for appointing Amini to carry out this task.[133] The Shah replied that while Iran's economic development was his key goal, Iran needed security to implement its economic development plans. Iran was capable of resisting communism if it possessed a strong army, and it could serve as a good example for other countries in the Middle East.[134]

The Shah had not given the Kennedy administration an immediate response as to whether he had agreed to Iran's force reduction and the proposed U.S. military plan for the country. Ambassador Holmes informed the State and Defense Departments that he was sure that the Shah would agree with the plan, but the Shah first wanted the JCS team to visit Iran. The Shah wanted to persuade U.S. military officials that Iran needed higher levels of U.S. military aid.[135] The State and Defense Departments indicated that they would not object to the Shah's request for additional weapons, as it could prove valid in the future. The JCS team, was working closely with the ARMISH/MAAG in Tehran, the U.S. Permanent Military Deputy to CENTO, and the Commander in Chief/Europe (CINCEUR), and had to report its findings by July 1, 1962. The tasks of the JCS team was to: reorganize the Iranian Army to reach the reduced level; develop an early warning plan for Iran; and resolve the discrepancy between CENTO's requirements for Iran and those requirements negotiated as part of the U.S.-Iranian bilateral defense agreement.[136]

As might have been expected, the Shah's trip to the United States did not sit well with the Soviet Union, which struck back with hostile propaganda. On April 20, 1962, a Russian newspaper claimed that the Shah wanted to purchase missiles from the United States. The article warned that it was not in the Shah's interest to use those missiles to intimidate other countries in the region.[137] The article emphasized that the Shah's visit to the United States would not help Iran's deteriorating economy as Iran's budget was utilized for military purposes due to Iran's membership in CENTO and its close relations with the United States. The article accused Amini of being an American puppet and said that the Shah had been forced to appoint him to appease the United States. The article concluded that Iran should take a neutral stance in international affairs.[138] Months later, despite its bitter criticism of the Shah's trip to the United States, the Soviet Union changed its stance dramatically and approached the Iranian government to conclude a significant agreement that would lead to better relations between the two countries.

Meanwhile, the State Department was becoming concerned over the problems Amini was facing in Iran. It asked the American embassy in Tehran to prepare a report regarding Amini's economic policies.[139] Ambassador Holmes was in the United States at the time, therefore Stuart W. Rockwell had to prepare the report. On June 12, 1962, Rockwell sent a report to the State Department observing that Amini's government had weakened because of the deteriorating economy. Amini had carried out an anticorruption campaign and launched land reform. But he had not dealt effectively with the budget deficit. He had inherited a deteriorating economic situation from previous governments and had been unable to increase revenues. Amini was aware that these financial problems could lead to the collapse of his government.[140]

Iran's budget deficit was estimated at $250 million, of which $160 million had to do with government spending and about $90 million in connection with the pursuance of economic development projects.[141] Government spending was high due to economic recession and the government's failure to implement new tax measures. The completion of the Second Economic Plan and other development projects required additional funding. The Iranian military expected an increase in its spending, which would worsen the country's budget deficit. The report also stated that while the Shah had agreed to reduce Iran's military budget that was unlikely to happen.

The National Security Council presented a memorandum about Iran to McGeorge Bundy, the president's special assistant for National Security Affairs. The memorandum discussed the observations of Edward S. Mason, the president's special economic consultant, after completing a trip to Iran. Mason had sent a team from Harvard University to visit Iran in 1957 to provide guidance to the Plan Organization regarding economic planning and the implementation of development plans. Mason said that Iran's economy had deteriorated and Amini was unable to do anything about it. For these reasons, Mason had decided to withdraw his advisory team from Iran when its contract expired in September 1962.[142] The memorandum ended by suggesting that the president send a message to the Shah urging him to take immediate action. Otherwise, it would be impossible for the Third Economic Plan to begin.[143]

Meanwhile, Secretary of State Rusk had read Stuart Rockwell's report regarding the political and economic situation in Iran. Rusk replied that it was the Iranian government's responsibility to deal with its budget deficit. The Iranian government could not expect the United States to help it with its financial problems. Rusk observed that Amini was not to blame since budgetary problems had existed long before he became prime minister. The Shah hesitated to help Amini, worrying that he would be blamed for interference. At the same time, the deteriorating economy posed a major threat to the Shah's rule. Rusk suggested that when Ambassador Holmes returned to Iran, he should encourage the Shah to support Amini in reducing the budget deficit.[144]

Rusk also discussed Iran's Third Economic Plan, which was to begin in September 1962. He thought if the Iranian government failed to take any actions, there was no point in sending an international consultative group to Iran in September 1962. This group was to review and discuss Iran's Third Economic Plan. The United States wanted proof that the Iranian government was involved in economic management, and if it failed to do so, there was no point in providing foreign aid.[145] Following Ambassador Holmes's return to Iran, the State Department notified him about the Kennedy administration's concern over the deteriorating economic situation in Iran and advised that these concerns be relayed to the Shah.[146] Prior to his meeting with the Shah, Holmes met with Amini to get an update regarding the political and economic situation in Iran. Amini said that he intended to reduce the budget deficit by cutting the budget of the government ministries.[147]

Amini was unable to quote Holmes an approximate number as to where Iran's budget deficit stood and said that the Iranian Finance Ministry would come up with an estimate by June 30, 1962. Amini said that he wanted to reduce the military budget and hoped that the Shah would agree.[148] Amini then asked for U.S. financial aid for the purpose of maintaining political stability. Holmes said that Iran could not rely on any budgetary aid from the United States. At the end of the meeting, Amini said he would try to take measures to improve the taxation system. Holmes informed the State Department that he would not be able to give any recommendations to the Kennedy administration as to how to deal with Iran until the final estimate for the Iranian budget deficit became available.[149] On July 9, 1962, the Shah wrote a letter to President Kennedy about the difficulty of controlling Iran's budget deficit and asked for U.S. financial aid. At the same time, the Shah asked for more U.S. military equipment in addition to what had been previously offered to Iran.[150] As may have been expected, President Kennedy did not respond immediately, as he had already advised the Shah on what needed to be done in Iran.

Meanwhile, on July 16, 1962, the National Security Council staff prepared a memorandum for President Kennedy regarding Iran. The memorandum discussed Amini's failure to reduce the budget deficit, which had resulted from a number of factors such as: inflation; the increase in salaries for teachers; the costs associated with land reform; and the Shah's refusal to reduce military spending. The Iranian government was disappointed by the U.S. refusal to provide any budgetary aid. The memorandum recommended that despite Amini's problems, the United States had to continue to support him and pressure the Shah to reduce Iran's military spending.[151] These recommendations, however, were too late, for on July 18, 1962, Amini resigned.

Years later, in his memoirs, Amini offered an explanation for his resignation: the Shah's inability to comprehend the severe nature of the budget crisis; and his refusal to cooperate with Amini to rectify this problem. In particular, Amini criticized the Shah on three key issues. First, the Shah had been pressing Amini to bring Assadollah Alam, one of his trusted friends, into his cabinet. Amini had refused, wanting no interference from the Shah. The Shah, however, appointed Alam prime minister in the aftermath of Amini's resignation. Second, Amini was frustrated by the Shah's paranoia on the matter of who was in charge of running the country. Amini was particularly annoyed that the Shah wanted to know the exact details of each ministry and the budget allotted to it. Third, the Shah, in his preoccupation with the military budget, seemed little concerned about the budget deficit. When Amini suggested that each ministry's budget be cut, the Shah wanted the total sum to be transferred to the military budget instead of resolving the budget deficit.[152]

With regard to the third point, Amini said that the Shah had tried to persuade him to agree, hinting that it was all right to twist the truth. Amini had replied that the Defense Ministry should not have priority over the ministries of Public Health and Agriculture. After all, which country was Iran preparing to combat? The Shah had named Iraq. Amini had countered that it was not in Iraq's interest to fight with Iran, and even if it came to a war with the Soviets, Iran could never win. Stockpiling military weaponry was useless and the oil revenues had to be spent more wisely.[153] For these reasons, Amini had resigned and the Shah appointed Assadollah Alam, his close friend and a former leader of the Mardom Party, the new prime minister. It is interesting to note that in the aftermath of Amini's resignation, the Shah asked Arsanjani to retain his post as minister of agriculture. The Shah was aware of Arsanjani's contribution to land reform and was intent on keeping him.

Following Amini's resignation, the Kennedy administration received reports that Amini blamed his government's downfall on the U.S. refusal to provide economic aid to Iran. In a memorandum that was prepared for President Kennedy on July 18, 1962, the National Security Council reflected that Amini had blamed the United States because he was unable to mention the real reason behind his downfall, which was the Shah's refusal to reduce military spending.[154] The State Department released a statement to the press in response to reports that Amini had blamed the United States for his downfall. It noted that during Amini's term in office, the United States had provided financial aid in the amount of $67.3 million consisting of grants and loans as well as an additional $20 million for a development project.[155]

In his memoirs, Amini never claimed that insufficient U.S. financial aid was behind his government's downfall. Rather, what Amini said was that in his discussions with the Shah about the budget deficit, he had reminded the Shah that the United States had made it clear that it could offer no help.[156] While privately Amini may have blamed the United States, he never admitted it in the public. In fact, at a press conference on the day following his resignation, Amini denied any reports that he blamed the United States. The State Department's press release regarding the $67.3 million in U.S. financial aid to Iran, as well as Amini's denial of blaming the United States, received full coverage in Iranian newspapers.[157]

On July 19, 1962, the National Security Council staff prepared a report about factors that had led to Amini's resignation. The report observed that Alam's government would be less effective than Amini's in reducing the budget deficit because it was under the Shah's direct control. A persistent problem was Iran's growing military budget. The report then recommended that the United States ask the Shah to take measures to reduce the budget deficit. Holmes did not agree with pushing the Shah and instead recommended keeping the Shah content, as it would be in the best interests of the United States.[158]

On August 1, 1962, Kennedy replied to the Shah's letter of July 9, writing that he was disappointed at Amini's resignation, as Amini had tried to implement the Shah's reforms. Kennedy reiterated that he was aware of Iran's budget deficit problems but that the Shah and his government had to care of the deficit without depending on foreign aid. Kennedy encouraged the Shah and his government to take steps to bring these problems under control.[159] Kennedy then expressed his appreciation for U.S.-Iranian relations and the Shah's continuous fight against the spread of communism. In order to strengthen Iran's security, it was necessary for the Shah to carry on with economic and social reforms. Kennedy also reminded the Shah of U.S. military aid program proposed to him earlier, which was the most that the United States could offer.[160] The tone of this letter made it obvious that the Kennedy administration would not help the Iranian government with its budget deficit crisis.

Kennedy asked Lyndon Johnson to pay a state visit to Cyprus, Greece, and Turkey, and Iran. During his visit to Iran from August 24–26, 1962, Johnson met with the Shah and Prime Minister Alam, and he emphasized the significance of social and economic reforms over a military buildup.[161] On August 28, 1962, Johnson reported to the president regarding his trip to Iran. Johnson noted that despite the Shah's problems, he remained the most reliable figure in Iran to promote U.S. interests. The United States should try to influence the Shah to move forward with his reforms to prevent the downfall of the monarchy. Further, the United States had to determine the requirements for Iran's military establishment on a continuous basis and allocate U.S. military aid accordingly.[162]

While the United States may have held back financial aid to the Iranian government, it did not withhold humanitarian aid in times of need. In September 1962, a powerful earthquake hit Iran that resulted in nearly 20,000 dead and thousands injured. It had taken the Iranian rescue teams several hours to reach the area of the quake, as it was in a remote part of the country. The Iranian Red Cross asked the United States for tents, blankets, and an American-manned field hospital to provide care for the injured.[163] President Kennedy offered immediate U.S. assistance to Iran.

Ambassador Holmes gave the Iranian Red Cross a check in the amount of $10,000 from the American embassy's special emergency fund. The next day he gave another $10,000 to assist in the distribution of needed supplies, such as powdered milk and flour. In addition to providing transportation for the field hospital, the U.S. Air Force flew Iranian doctors and medical students from Europe to provide service for the injured. The Shah thanked President Kennedy and his administration for their generosity during this tragic time.[164]

IRAN'S PLEDGE OF NO MISSILE BASES TO THE SOVIETS

In the early 1960s, the Shah had began to think about pursuing a new direction for Iran's foreign policy, an Independent National Policy (siyasat-i mustaqilli melli), which came to replace his former policy of Positive Nationalism.[165]

This new direction in Iran's foreign policy would lead to the Iranian government's pledge to the Soviet Union not allow the establishment of any foreign missile bases in Iran. The Shah was well aware of the controversy brewing over the Soviet missile bases in Cuba and did not want the same to happen to Iran. At the same time, the Shah had become disillusioned with the lack of U.S. financial aid to Iran by the Kennedy administration and its insistence on reform. The pledge to the Soviets was a chance for the Shah to prove to everyone that he was not a puppet of the United States and could carry out policies that were in Iran's best interests.

The Soviet Union was eager to set aside years of unhappiness at the Shah's close relations with the United States and approach the Iranian government seeking better relations. The Soviet government hoped for the issuance of a joint statement with the Iranian government pledging that no foreign missile bases would be allowed on Iranian territory. This significant move on the part of the Soviets can only be understood within the context of the Cold War and the events leading up to the Cuban Missile Crisis in 1962. Since the early 1960s, the Soviets had been aware of the installation of U.S. Jupiter missiles in Turkey targeted at the Soviet Union. The Soviets had retaliated by installing missiles in Cuba pointed at the United States, and were determined not to allow this situation to repeat itself in their own neighborhood.

The Shah's uncertainty about signing a fifty-year non-aggression treaty with the Soviets and his immediate move to sign a bilateral defense agreement with the United States in 1959 had led to the cooling of Iran's relations with the Soviet Union. The Soviets had responded by stepping up their negative propaganda campaign against the Shah and his government, which was to continue into the early 1960s. The hostile nature of this propaganda and the resulting war of nerves had made the Iranian government consider filing an appeal to the U.N., but in the end it decided not to, as it was faced with other pressing matters in the country.

On September 12, 1962, the Soviet government asked the Iranian government for a joint statement stating that Iran would allow no foreign missile bases on its soil. The U.S. government believed that the Soviets had asked for a joint statement to make the issue of foreign bases in Iran subject to Soviet consultation. The Iranian government disagreed. Instead, on September 15, 1962, the Iranian Ministry of Foreign Affairs offered a unilateral statement to the Soviet government giving assurances that no foreign missile bases would be installed on Iranian territory.[166] The Soviets tried to change this statement, but the Iranians remained adamant. The United States was also satisfied with Iran's unilateral statement, as it proved that Iran was in charge of its own affairs and was not belligerent toward the Soviet Union.[167]

The United States was not interested in placing missiles in Iran, when Turkey had already been designated as the perfect site. In 1961, the United States had installed Jupiter missiles in Turkey. In time however, the Joint Committee on Atomic Energy recommended the use of the Polaris missiles, which were launched from submarines, in place of the Jupiter missiles, because they were a stronger retaliatory force.[168] From a position in the Mediterranean, the Polaris missiles could easily attack areas stretching from the Ukraine to Central Asia.[169] Given these technological advancements, there was no need for the United States to keep its missile bases in Turkey or install any in Iran. Yet the presence of the Jupiter missiles in Turkey would precipitate the Cuban Missile Crisis.

The United States now wanted the Shah to sign the five-year military aid package that had been presented to him in April 1962, during his state visit to the United States. On September 18, 1962, Secretary of State Rusk asked Ambassador Holmes to discuss this matter with the Shah and inform him that the United States had agreed to add warships and radar equipment. Rusk, however, asked Holmes to make it clear to the Shah that this was all the United States could offer at the time. It fell to Ambassador Holmes to divert the Shah's attention from the issue of military buildup to the need for economic and social reforms.[170]

Holmes met with the Shah on September 19, 1962, to discuss the U.S. proposal regarding the Five Year Military Program for Iran and present the Shah with a list of the new military weapons. The Shah said he would sign the agreement if the United States would provide additional tanks and install radar stations between Babol, Mashhad, and Zahedan.[171] The proposed military plan would also be subject to change if Iran were to come under attack by any nation. The Shah said that the items in connection with the first two requests could be delivered in the future. He asked Ambassador Holmes to prepare a memorandum to this effect for him to sign.

The Cold War rivalry and tensions between the United States and the Soviet Union over Iran subsided in the aftermath of Iran's pledge of no missile base to the Soviets, but they were to flare up over the Cuban Missile Crisis of October 1962. The Soviet Union remained insecure regarding the issue of its military strength compared to that of the United States. Khrushchev was agitated over the Jupiter missiles in Turkey that were in close proximity to the Soviet Union. He sought to reduce the threat by placing medium and intermediate-range missiles in Cuba pointed at the United States.[172]

In early September 1962, the Soviet government had asked Anatoly Dobrynin, its ambassador to the United States, to discuss the possibility of a nuclear test ban treaty with the United States. In a meeting with Robert Kennedy, Dobrynin had said that the Soviets would negotiate an atmospheric test ban treaty with the United States. Kennedy said he would relay this message to the president. Robert Kennedy then told Dobrynin that the United States was concerned about the missiles that the Soviet Union was sending to Cuba. Dobrynin told Kennedy that there were no missiles in Cuba and that there was no need for the United States to be concerned.[173]

Dobrynin's words were refuted by photos obtained from U-2 flights over Cuba. The Kennedy administration was convinced that the Soviets had installed missiles in Cuba. On October 18, 1962, Foreign Minister Gromyko met with President Kennedy, who asked about the shipping of Soviet missiles to Cuba. Gromyko replied that the Soviet Union had only sent a small supply of arms as well as advisers to Cuba to train the Cubans.[174] Kennedy had two choices: to blockade or invade the island. On October 20, 1962, the president ordered a blockade of any ship sailing to Cuba. At the same time, he ordered the Defense Department to prepare for further military action. Secretary of State McNamara listed U.S. military preparation as follows: a ground force of 250,000 men; 90,000 marines as part of the invasion force; and air attacks to be carried out against targets in Cuba.[175]

The next seven days was a period of intense diplomatic negotiation between the Soviet Union and the United States. The U.N. Secretary General U Thant acted as mediator between the two sides. On October 26, 1962, Khrushchev wrote to Kennedy agreeing to withdraw the missiles from Cuba if the United States would not invade Cuba and remove its missiles from Turkey.[176] Kennedy replied that Khrushchev's proposals contained the basis for an understanding between the two sides. On October 28, both sides issued statements outlining their arrangements.[177] Both sides quietly dismantled their respective missile bases in Turkey and Cuba.

OPPOSITION TO THE SHAH'S WHITE REVOLUTION

In October 1962, Alam's government approved a law regarding the election of representative local councils. The Iranian clergy opposed this law for a number of reasons: the candidates running for office did not have to be Muslim; the elected candidates had to take the oath of office on their own holy book; and Iranian women were granted the right to vote.[178] It was over this law that Ayatollah Ruhollah Khomeini became well known. Ayatollah Khomeini and the clergy argued that this law would increase the number of religious minorities in the Iranian government and the army. Furthermore, granting Iranian women the right to vote would lead to their decadence.[179]

Ayatollah Khomeini and other clergy began to send telegrams to the Shah and Prime Minister Alam protesting this law. The clergy began to preach against the law at mosques and in religious schools. Neither the Shah nor Alam responded to these telegrams, which angered the clergy and they chose November 1, 1962, as a national day of protest. In order to end this crisis, Alam's government decided to temporarily suspend the new law. On November 1, Alam sent telegrams to a number of clergy informing them of the government's decision.[180]

The clergy was not the only opposition group that the Iranian government had to deal with. It also faced opposition from the National Front. Alam had released several National Front leaders sentenced by Amini's government, and even met with Allahyar Saleh, the leader of the National Front, and asked for his advice as to how the government could solve its problems. The National Front agreed to cooperate with Alam if the Shah became a constitutional monarch and elections were held immediately.[181] In contrast to the clergy, the National Front supported the Local Council Elections bill, which granted women the right to vote. The National Front continued to ask for the Shah to become a constitutional monarch and for the Iranian government to hold elections. Since Alam could not meet these demands, talks broke down between the two sides.[182]

The National Front decided to step up its activities against Alam's government. It reorganized itself and allowed other groups, such as the Iran Party and the National Freedom Movement, to join as members. It then organized a campaign against the Shah's regime. Whereas in 1961, the Shah had attempted to negotiate with the National Front by appointing Ali Amini, in 1963 he would not put up with it, and ordered SAVAK to arrest members of the party. As a result, the activities of the National Front ended abruptly.

Before the end of the year, the Iranian government expected a visit from a Soviet negotiating team to further improve relations between the two countries. On December 19, 1962, a Soviet mission headed by Sergei Lapin, the Deputy Foreign Minister, visited Iran to discuss a number of issues including economic, technical, and cultural cooperation between the two sides. The Iranian government concluded an agreement that would reopen a route from Iran to Western Europe through the Soviet Union. This was important because nearly sixty-five percent of Iran's trade was with Western Europe.[183]

While the U.S.-Soviet rivalry over Iran had subsided by the end of 1962, the repercussions of the superpower rivalry and U.S. policy toward Iran would reverberate through 1963. The Kennedy administration had pushed the Shah to implement his White Revolution not only to keep the populace content and free from communist influence, but also to keep the Shah in power. The Shah remained adamant about the full implementation of the White Revolution, despite mounting opposition. In order to defeat the opposition, the Shah decided to hold a referendum so that the people would vote for his White Revolution. On January 8, 1963, the Shah announced that a referendum would be held regarding the six points of the White Revolution. The six points were land reform; the nationalization of the forests; the sale of shares in industries owned by the government; factory workers sharing the profits at their workplace; reform of the electoral law; and the creation of a literacy corps.[184]

The clergy organized a large demonstration at the bazaar in Tehran, where they distributed anti-referendum flyers to the people. The clergy had also entered an alliance with the National Front to oppose the Shah. In response, Prime Minister Alam threatened to crush any opposition.[185] On January 23, thousands of women condemned the clergy and distributed their own flyers urging women to protest against discrimination and fight for their right to vote.[186] On the same day, the American embassy in Tehran reported that the Iranian government was organizing pro-referendum demonstrations and was prepared to use the police to maintain order.[187]

On January 26, 1963, the referendum on the Shah's six points was held in Iran. The government had been worried about the issue of women voting, and had temporarily held back the Local Council Elections bill to calm the clergy. On the morning of January 26, however, the Iranian radio announced that women were allowed to vote. The results of the referendum indicated that 5,598,711 individuals had voted in favor of the Shah's reform program while 4,115 had voted against it.[188] The public had overwhelmingly approved the Shah's reform program. As a result, the Shah issued a decree that his government would implement the six-point program. President Kennedy congratulated the Shah adding that it would help better the lives of the people.[189]

The Kennedy administration was to receive further encouraging news from Iran. On March 11, 1963, nearly a year after the U.S. request for diplomatic immunity for its military personnel in Iran, the Iranian government responded, but it made a distinction between senior U.S. military advisers and the remaining staff. It decided to grant diplomatic immunity to senior members, as they possessed a diplomatic passport, but with regard to other staff members, it said that the matter would be studied further.[190] The Iranian government said that the 1961 Vienna Convention on Diplomatic Relations was not enough to grant diplomatic immunity to all U.S. military personnel and that the approval of the Majlis was needed.[191] In 1964, however, the Iranian government granted full immunity to all the U.S. military personnel in Iran.

Finally, Leonid Brezhnev visited Iran November 16–23, 1963. Brezhnev was pleased about the Soviet Union's improved relations with Iran. He stated that the new relationship between the two countries would serve as a model for other countries. As a result of this visit, border agreements were ratified, and an important economic and technical cooperation agreement was concluded that provided for the joint use of the Aras and Atrak rivers and the construction of a dam on the Atrak River. The Soviet government also pledged to provide a $30 million credit to the Iranian government.[192] A Soviet-Iranian Cultural Relations Society was also set up in Moscow, to promote cultural exchanges between the two countries.

Brezhnev left Iran on November 23, 1963, the day after President Kennedy was assassinated. The Kennedy administration had successfully pushed the Shah in the direction of reform. At the same time, the White Revolution had unleashed unexpected reactionary forces against the Shah and his reforms. This time it was not the communists or the National Front that would challenge the Shah's rule or the United States for its support of the Shah. The Iranian opposition had found its voice in Ayatollah Khomeini and the clergy, who not only opposed the Shah's White Revolution but called for the downfall of the monarchy. Khomeini was placed under house arrest in 1963 for his relentless activities against the Shah and sent into exile a year later. From exile, Khomeini continued his activities against the Shah's regime that culminated in the Islamic Revolution that overthrew the monarchy. The Shah left Iran in January 1979 never to return. Khomeini returned to Iran in February 1979 and established an Islamic republic, which remains intact to this day.

NOTES

1. Eric Hooglund, *Reform and Revolution in Rural Iran* (Austin, Tx.: University of Texas Press, 1982), 46.
2. Ann K. Lambton, "Land Reform and the Rural Cooperative Societies," in Ehsan Yarshater, ed., *Iran Faces the Seventies* (New York: Praeger, 1971), 14.
3. Lambton, "Land Reform and the Rural Cooperative Societies," in Yarshater, ed., *Iran Faces the Seventies*, 15–16.
4. U.S. Department of State, RG 59, Decimal File 788.5-MSP/1-1260, 12 January 1960, National Archives, College Park, Md.
5. *Kayhan*, 1 February 1960.
6. Lambton, "Land Reform and the Rural Cooperative Societies," in Yarshater, ed., *Iran Faces the Seventies*, 16; *Echo of Iran*, 17 February 1962, vol. 6, no. 334, 4, as cited in Willem M. Floor, "The Revolutionary Character of the Iranian Ulema," *International Journal of Middle Eastern Studies* 12 (1980): 504–505.
7. *Foreign Relations of the United States, 1958–1960*, 12: 666–67.
8. *Foreign Relations of the United States, 1958–1960*, 12: 674.
9. *Foreign Relations of the United States, 1958–1960*, 12: 674.
10. *Foreign Relations of the United States, 1958–1960*, 12: 671.
11. Special Supplement to *Soviet Weekly*, 5 May 1960.
12. Department of State *Bulletin* 42, no. 1091 (23 May 1960): 817–18.

13. *Soviet News*, 9 May 1960 as cited in G. Barraclough, "The Long Road to the Summit," *Survey of International Affairs 1959–1960*, 1964, 62. For an interesting account from the pilot see Francis Gary Powers, *Operation Overflight* (New York: Holt, 1970).

14. Department of State *Bulletin* 42, no. 1091 (23 May 1960): 818.

15. *Ittila'at* and *Kayhan*, 7–9 May 1960.

16. *Kayhan*, 10 May 1960.

17. *Kayhan*, 12 May 1960.

18. *The Current Digest of Soviet Press*, 12, 21 (22 June 1960): 18.

19. *Kayhan*, 17 May 1960.

20. *Kayhan*, 25 May 1960.

21. *Foreign Relations of the United States, 1958–1960*, 12: 675.

22. *Foreign Relations of the United States, 1950–1960*, 12: 679; *Kayhan*, 2 July 1960.

23. Department of State, S/S-NSC Files: Lot 63 D351, NSC 6010, "U.S. Policy Toward Iran," 6 July 1960, as cited in *Foreign Relations of the United States, 1958–1960*, 12: 680–88.

24. *Foreign Relations of the United States, 1958–1960*, 12: 647; James F. Goode, *The United States and Iran: In the Shadow of Musaddiq* (London: Macmillan, 1997), 165; Avner Yaniv, *Deterrence Without the Bomb: The Politics of Israeli Strategy* (Lexington, Mass., D. C. Heath, 1987), 94.

25. *al-Ahram*, 26 July 1960; *al-Akhbar* 30 July 1960; *al-Gomhouriah*, 26 July 1960; *The Egyptian Gazette*, 30 July 1960, as cited in Goode, *The United States and Iran*, 165, n. 38.

26. *Foreign Relations of the United States, 1958–1960*, 12: 690–91.

27. Department of State *Bulletin* 43, no. 1103 (15 August 1960): 261.

28. *Foreign Relations of the United States, 1958–1960*, 12: 692–93.

29. *Ittela'at* and *Kayhan* 28 August 1960.

30. *Foreign Relations of the United States, 1958–1960*, 12: 699; *Ittila'at* and *Kayhan*, 1 September 1960.

31. "Tarh-i Barnameh va Assassnami-yi Mossaveb-i Plenom-i Haftom va Konferanc-i Vahdat" (Draft Party Program and Statute Adopted by 7th Plenum and Unity Conference), *Nashriyeh -i Hezbi*, September–October 1960, as cited in Sepehr Zabih, *The Communist Movement in Iran* (Berkeley: University of California Press, 1966), 221–22.

32. Department of State, GTI Files: Lot D66 173, Iran 1958–1963, 5 October 1960, "New United States Loans to Iran," RG 59, Box 8, National Archives, College Park, Md.

33. *Department of State Bulletin* 44, no. 1124 (9 January 1961): 49–50 ; *Foreign Relations of the United States, 1958–1960*, 12: 712.

34. James N. Giglio, *The Presidency of John F. Kennedy* (Lawrence: University Press of Kansas, 1991), 45; Diane B. Kunz, ed., *The Diplomacy of the Crucial Decade* (New York: Columbia University Press, 1994), 2; Richard J. Walton, *Cold War and Counterrevolution* (New York: Viking Press, 1972), 7.

35. "Open Letter to the National Front," 9 February 1961, as cited in Zabih, *The Communist Movement in Iran*, 230–31.
36. *Foreign Relations of the United States, 1961–1963*, vol. 17, *The Near East, 1961–1962* (Washington D.C.: Government Printing Office, 1994), 25.
37. *Foreign Relations of the United States, 1961–1963*, 17: 32.
38. *Foreign Relations of the United States, 1961–1963*, 17: 32–33.
39. *Foreign Relations of the United States, 1961–1963*, 17: 33.
40. *Foreign Relations of the United States, 1961–1963*, 17: 39–40.
41. *Ittila'at* and *Kayhan*, 15 March 1961.
42. U.S. Department of State, RG 59, Decimal File 788.00/3-1761, 17 March 1961,"Suggested Reply to the Shah," National Archives, College Park, Md.
43. C. D. Carr, "The United States–Iranian Relationship 1948–1978: A Study in Reverse Influence," in Hussein Amirsadeghi, ed., *The Security of the Persian Gulf* (New York: St. Martin's Press, 1981), 66–67.
44. Carr, "The United States-Iranian Relationship 1948–1978," 67; Arthur Schlesinger, *One Thousand Days* (London: André Deutsch, 1965), 360.
45. *Foreign Relations of the United States, 196–1963*, 17: 54.
46. *Foreign Relations of the United States, 1961–1963*, 17: 55.
47. *U.S. News and World Report*, 6 March 1961, 64–65 as cited in James Bill, *The Eagle and the Lion: The Tragedy of American-Iranian Relations* (New Haven: Yale University Press, 1988), 137.
48. Walter Lippmann, *The Coming Tests with Russia* (Boston: Little, Brown, 1961), 16.
49. Giglio, *The Presidency of John F. Kennedy*, 53–58; David L. Larson, ed., *The Cuban Crisis of 1962* (Boston: Houghton, Mifflin, 1963), 303; Walton, *Cold War and Counterrevolution*, 34–47.
50. *Foreign Relations of the United States, 1961–1963*, 17: 89–90.
51. *Foreign Relations of the United States, 1961–1963*, 17: 98.
52. Department of State, GTI Files: Lot 66 D 173, Iran 1958–1963, "CIA Draft: Internal Situation in Iran," 10 May 1961, RG 59, Box 8, National Archives, College Park, Md.
53. *Foreign Relations of the United States, 1961–1963*, 17: 98–99.
54. *Ittila'at*, 6 May 1961; *Foreign Relations of the United States, 1961–1963*, 17: 99; *Kayhan*, 6 May 1961.
55. Bill, *The Eagle and the* Lion, 143.
56. *Foreign Relations of the United States, 1961–1963*, 17: 99; *Ittila'at* and *Kayhan*, 13 May 1961.
57. Department of State, GTI Files: Lot 66 D 173, Iran 1958–1963, Box 4, "Iran Task Force," 9 May 1961, RG 59, National Archives, College Park, Md.
58. Department of State, GTI Files: Lot 66 D 173, Iran 1958–1963, Box 4, "Iran Task Force," 9 May 1961, RG 59, National Archives, College Park, Md.
59. *Foreign Relations of the United States, 1961–1963*, 17: 105–106.
60. Habib Ladjevardi, ed., *Khatirat-i Ali Amini* (The Memoirs of Ali Amini) (Cambridge, Mass.: Harvard University, Center for Middle Eastern Studies, 1995), 99–100.

61. Husein Fardust, *Zuhur va Sughut-i Saltanat-i Pahlavi* (The Rise and Fall of the Pahlavi Dynasty) (Tehran: Ittila'at, 1368/1989), 306–308; Armin Meyer, in Abbas Amirie and Hamilton Twitchell, eds., *Iran in the 1980s* (Tehran: Institute for International Political and Economic Studies, 1978), 382.

62. Department of State, SNIE 34.2-61, "Short Term Outlook For Iran," 23 May 1961, as cited in *Foreign Relations of the United States, 1961–1963*, 17: 122–25.

63. U.S. Department of State, RG 59, Decimal File 788.00/5-2961, 24 May 1961, Telegram, Rusk to Wailes, National Archives, College Park, Md.

64. U.S. Department of State, RG 59, Decimal File 788.00/5-2561, 25 May 1961, Telegram, Wailes to Rusk, National Archives, College Park, Md.

65. *Foreign Relations of the United States, 1961–1963*, 17: 152–54.

66. Giglio, *The Presidency of John F. Kennedy*, 72–78; Kunz, *The Diplomacy of the Crucial Decade*, 153.

67. Carr, "The United States-Iranian Relationship," 68.

68. Willem Floor, "The Revolutionary Character of the Iranian Ulama: Wishful Thinking or Reality?" *The International Journal of Middle Eastern Studies* 12 (Spring 1980): 506.

69. *Ittila'at Havai*, 23 and 27 July 1961, as cited in rouhollah K. Ramazani, *Iran's Foreign Policy, 1941–1973* (Charlottesville: University of Virginia Press, 1975), 303.

70. U.S. Department of State, RG 59, Decimal File 788.00/7-2561, 25 July 1961, Telegram, Wailes to Rusk, National Archives, College Park, Md.

71. Ladjevardi, ed., *Khatirat-i Shahpur Bakhtiar* (The Memoirs of Shahpur Bakhtiar), 46–47.

72. *Foreign Relations of the United States, 1961–1963*, 17: 199–206.

73. John C. Ausland, *Kennedy, Khrushchev, and the Berlin-Cuba Crisis, 1961–1964* (Oslo: Scandinavian University Press, 1996), 23–24; Giglio, *The Presidency of John F. Kennedy*, 83–84.

74. "Communiqué of the 9th Plenum of the Central Committee of the Tudeh Party," 1–2, as cited in Zabih, *The Communist Movement in Iran*, 236–37.

75. Zabih, *The Communist Movement in Iran*, 242–43.

76. Abu al-Hasan Ibtihaj, *Khatirat-i Abu al -Hasan Ibtihaj* (The Memoirs of Abu al-Hasan Ibtihaj), vol. 2 (Tehran: Ilmi, 1371/1992), 485–86; Abul Hasan Ibtihaj, "A Program of Economic Growth," paper delivered at *International Industrial Conference*, Stanford Research Institute, San Francisco, 21 September 1961, as cited in Frances Bostock and Geoffrey Jones, *Planning and Power in Iran: Ebtehaj and Economic Development under the Shah* (London: Frank Cass, 1989), 159–61.

77. Ibtihaj, *Khatirat-i Abu al -Hasan Ibtihaj* (The Memoirs of Abu al-Hasan Ibtihaj), vol. 2, 491–93; Bostock and Jones, *Planning and Power in Iran*, 162.

78. Department of State, GTI Files: Lot 66 D 173, Iran 1958–1963, "Task Force Report: Iran," 9 October 1961, 2–8, RG 59, Box 3, National Archives, College Park, Md.

79. *Foreign Relations of the United States, 1961–1963*, 17: 303–305.

80. *Foreign Relations of the United States, 1961–1963*, 17: 303–304.

81. *Foreign Relations of the United States, 1961–1963*, 17: 316–17.

82. *Foreign Relations of the United States, 1961–1963*, 17: 316–17.

83. Edward Bayne, *Persian Kingship in Transition* (New York: American Universities Field Staff, 1968), 255.

84. Floor, "The Revolutionary Character of the Iranian Ulama," *International Journal of Middle Eastern Studies* 12 (Spring 1980): 507.

85. Department of State, *TIAS*, no. 4930, "Economic, Technical, and Related Assistance: Agreement Between the United States of America and Iran," 21 December 1961.

86. Hasan Arsanjani, "The Issue of Land Reform in Iran," *Majaleh-yi Masael-i Iran* 1 (December 1962): 97–104; Hooglund, *Land Reform and Revolution in Iran*, 50–51; Lambton, Land Reform and Rural Cooperative Societies," in Yarshater, ed., *Iran Faces the Seventies*, 15–17.

87. *Ittila'at* and *Kayhan*, 9 and 14 January 1962; Lambton, "Land Reform and the Rural Cooperative Societies," in Yarshater, ed., *Iran Faces the Seventies*, 19.

88. *Echo Reports*, a weekly publication of the Echo of Iran, 6 (17 February 1962): 5, as cited in Floor, "The Revolutionary Character of the Iranian Ulema," *International Journal of Middle East Studies* 12 (1980): 507, 518.

89. *Foreign Relations of the United States, 1961–1963*, 17: 416–17.

90. *Foreign Relations of the United States, 1961–1963*, 17: 418.

91. Bill, *The Eagle and the Lion*, 146; *Ittila'at*, 22 January 1962; Floor, "The Revolutionary Character of the Iranian Ulema," *International Journal of Middle Eastern Studies* 12 (1980): 508; *Kayhan*, 22 January 1962; Marvin Zonis, *The Political Elite of Iran* (Princeton, N.J.: Princeton University, 1971), 72–73.

92. *Ittila'at* and *Kayhan*, 23 January 1962.

93. *Echo of Iran*, 6 (19 February 1962): 6–7, as cited in Floor, "The Revolutionary Character of the Iranian Ulema," *International Journal of Middle East Studies* 12 (1980): 508, 518.

94. *Foreign Relations of the United States, 1961–1963*, 17: 450.

95. *Kayhan*, 1 February 1962.

96. U.S. Department of State, RG 59, Decimal File 788.00/2-2862, 28 February 1962, Memorandum, "Iran's Economic Development Plan," National Archives, College Park, Md.

97. U.S. Department of State, RG 59, Decimal File 788.00/2-2862, 28 February 1962, Memorandum, "Iran's Economic Development Plan," National Archives, College Park, Md.

98. U.S. Department of State, RG 59, Decimal File 788.00/2-2862, 28 February 1962, Memorandum, "Iran's Economic Development Plan," National Archives, College Park, Md.

99. "Message from United States Ambassador in Tehran (Holmes) to the President and Secretary of State on Chester Bowles's visit to Iran," 19 February 1962, as reprinted in Yonah Alexander and Allan Nanes, eds., *The United States and Iran: A Documentary History* (Frederick, Md.: Aletheia Books, 1980), 345–46.

100. "Message from United States Ambassador in Tehran (Holmes) to the President and Secretary of State on Chester Bowles's visit to Iran," 19 February 1962, as reprinted in Alexander and Nanes, eds., *The United States and Iran: A Documentary History*, 346.

101. "Message from United States Ambassador in Tehran (Holmes) to the President and Secretary of State on Chester Bowles's visit to Iran," 19 February 1962, as reprinted in Alexander and Nanes, eds., *The United States and Iran: A Documentary History*, 347.

102. *Foreign Relations of the United States, 1961–1963*, 17: 508.
103. *Foreign Relations of the United States, 1961–1963*, 17: 508–509.
104. *Foreign Relations of the United States, 1961–1963*, 17: 509.
105. *Foreign Relations of the United States, 1961–1963*, 17: 509–10.
106. *Foreign Relations of the United States, 1961–1963*, 17: 510–11.

107. Department of State, S/S Files: Lot 66D 147, "Secretary's Small Staff Meeting," 8 March 1962, as reprinted in *Foreign Relations of the United States, 1961–1963*, 17: 511, n. 3.

108. NSC Action No. 2447 was taken at a meeting of the National Security Council on 18 January 1962 as reprinted in *Foreign Relations of the United States, 1961–1963*, 17: 512, n. 1.

109. *Foreign Relations of the United States, 1961–1963*, 17: 512.
110. *Foreign Relations of the United States, 1961–1963*, 17: 516–18.
111. *Foreign Relations of the United States, 1961–1963*, 17: 519.

112. U.S. Congress, Senate, Committee on Armed Services, *Operation of Article VII*, Hearing before a subcommittee of the Committee on Armed Services, 86th Congress, 1st Session, 1959, 27; Steven Pfau, "The Legal Status of American Forces in Iran," *Middle East Journal* 28 (Spring 1974): 145.

113. Pfau, "The Legal Status of American Forces in Iran." *Middle East Journal* 28 (Spring 1974): 146–47.

114. Pfau, "The Legal Status of American Forces in Iran." *Middle East Journal* 28 (Spring 1974): 147.

115. *Foreign Relations of the United States, 1961–1963*, 17: 532–33.
116. *Foreign Relations of the United States, 1961–1963*, 17: 532.
117. *Foreign Relations of the United States, 1961–1963*, 17: 532–33.
118. *Foreign Relations of the United States, 1961–1963*, 17: 533, n. 2.

119. Roy Mottahedeh, "Iran's Foreign Devils," *Foreign Policy* 38 (Spring 1980): 25; Pfau, "The Legal Status of American Forces in Iran," *The Middle East Journal* 28 (Spring 1974): 147.

120. *Foreign Relations of the United States, 1961–1963*, 17: 590.
121. *Foreign Relations of the United States, 1961–1963*, 17: 593.
122. *Foreign Relations of the United States, 1961–1963*, 17: 593–94.
123. *Foreign Relations of the United States, 1961–1963*, 17: 594.
124. *Foreign Relations of the United States, 1961–1963*, 17: 594–95.
125. *Foreign Relations of the United States, 1961–1963*, 17: 595.
126. *Foreign Relations of the United States, 1961–1963*, 17: 596–97.
127. *Foreign Relations of the United States, 1961–1963*, 17: 597.
128. *Foreign Relations of the United States, 1961–1963*, 17: 598–99.
129. *Foreign Relations of the United States, 1961–1963*, 17: 600–601.
130. *Foreign Relations of the United States, 1961–1963*, 17: 601–604.

131. *Foreign Relations of the United States, 1961–1963*, 17: 605.
132. *Foreign Relations of the United States, 1961–1963*, 17: 605.
133. *Foreign Relations of the United States, 1961–1963*, 17: 606–607.
134. *Foreign Relations of the United States, 1961–1963*, 17: 608–10.
135. *Foreign Relations of the United States, 1961–1963*, 17: 659.
136. *Foreign Relations of the United States, 1961–1963*, 17: 659–60.
137. *Izvestiya* 20 April 1962.
138. *Izvestiya* 20 April 1962.
139. *Foreign Relations of the United States, 1961–1963*, 17: 720, n. 1.
140. *Foreign Relations of the United States, 1961–1963*, 17: 720.
141. *Foreign Relations of the United States, 1961–1963*, 17: 720–22.
142. *Foreign Relations of the United States, 1961–1963*, 17: 725.
143. *Foreign Relations of the United States, 1961–1963*, 17: 726.
144. *Foreign Relations of the United States, 1961–1963*, 17: 726–27.
145. *Foreign Relations of the United States, 1961–1963*, 17: 727.
146. *Foreign Relations of the United States, 1961–1963*, 17: 727, n. 2.
147. *Foreign Relations of the United States, 1961–1963*, 17: 748–49.
148. *Foreign Relations of the United States, 1961–1963*, 17: 749.
149. *Foreign Relations of the United States, 1961–1963*, 17: 749–51.
150. *Foreign Relations of the United States, 1961–1963*, 18: 21, n. 1.
151. *Foreign Relations of the United States, 1961–1963*, 18: 10–11.
152. Ladjevardi, ed., *Khatirat-i Ali Amini* (The Memoirs of Ali Amini), 132–35.
153. Ladjevardi, ed., *Khatirat-i Ali Amini* (The Memoirs of Ali Amini), 135–36.
154. *Foreign Relations of the United States, 1961–1963*, 18: 11.
155. *Foreign Relations of the United States, 1961–1963*, 18: 16, n. 1.
156. Ladjevardi, *Khatirat-i Ali Amini* (The Memoirs of Ali Amini), 134.
157. *Ittila'at* and *Kayhan*, 19 July 1962.
158. *Foreign Relations of the United States, 1961–1963*, 18: 16.
159. *Foreign Relations of the United States, 1961–1963*, 18: 21–22.
160. *Foreign Relations of the United States, 1961–1963*, 18: 22–23.
161. Bill, *The Eagle and the Lion*, 140–41.
162. *Foreign Relations of the United States, 1961–1963*, 18: 72.
163. Department of State *Bulletin* 47, no. 1213 (24 September 1962): 458–59.
164. Department of State *Bulletin* 47, no. 1213 (24 September 1962): 458–59.
165. Ramazani, *Iran's Foreign Policy, 1941–1973,* 311–14; Ramazani, "Iran's White Revolution: A Study in Political Developmnet," *International Journal of Middle East Studies* 5 (1974): 132; Ramazani, "Iran's Changing Foreign Policy: A Preliminary Discussion," *The Middle East Journal* 24, no. 4 (Autumn 1970): 428, 433.
166. *Ittila'at Hava'i*, September 15, 1962.
167. *Foreign Relations of the United States, 1961–1963*, 18: 97–98.
168. U.S. Congress, House Committee on Armed Services, *Hearings on Military Posture*, 88th Congress, 1st Session, 1963, 276–84, as cited in Ramazani, *Iran's Foreign Policy, 1941–1973*, 318, n. 16.

180   Chapter Five

169. Geoffrey Jukes, *The Indian Ocean in Soviet Naval Policy* (London: The International Institute for Strategic Studies, May 1972), as cited in Ramazani, *Iran's Foreign Policy, 1941–1973*, 318, n. 15.

170. *Foreign Relations of the United States, 1961–1963*, 18: 99.

171. *Foreign Relations of the United States, 1961–1963*, 18: 100–105.

172. Raymond Garthoff, *Intelligence Assessment and Policymaking: A Decision Point in the Kennedy Administration* (Washington, D.C.: Brookings Institution, 1984), 12; Giglio, *The Presidency of John F. Kennedy*, 192–93; Philip Nash, *The Other Missiles of October*, 106; Walton, *Cold War and Counterrevolution*, 118–19.

173. Robert Kennedy, *Thirteen Days* (New York: W. W. Norton, 1969), 24–25.

174. Kennedy, *Thirteen Days*, 39–42.

175. Kennedy, *Thirteen Days*, 48–55.

176. Department of State *Bulletin* 47, no. 1220 (12 November 1962): 741–43; Kennedy, *Thirteen Days*, 93–94; David L. Larson, ed., *The Cuban Crisis of 1962* (Boston: Houghton Mifflin, 1963), 155.

177. Department of State *Bulletin* 47, no. 1220 (12 November 1962): 745–46.

178. Saul Bakhash, *The Reign of the Ayatollahs* (New York: Basic Books, 1984), 24; Floor, "The Revolutionary Character of the Iranian Ulama," *International Journal of Middle East Studies* 12 (1980): 519, n. 47; *Iran Almanac*, 1963, 433.

179. Bakhash, *The Reign of the Ayatollahs*, 24; Floor, "The Revolutionary Character of the Iranian Ulema," *International Journal of Middle East Studies* 12 (1980): 509; Mohsen M. Milani, *The Making of Iran's Islamic Revolution* (Boulder, Colo.: West View Press, 1988), 49.

180. *Zendegi-nameh-yi Khomeini* (The Life of Imam Khomeini) vol. 1 (Tehran: 12 Moharram Publications, 1357 (1978), 65–66, as cited in Bakhash, *The Reign of the Ayatollahs*, 25, n. 8.

181. Richard, Cottam, *Nationalism in Iran* (Pittsburgh: University of Pittsburgh Press, 1964), 305–306; Floor, "The Revolutionary Character of the Iranian Ulema," *International Journal of Middle East Studies* 12 (1980): 510–11.

182. Floor, "The Revolutionary Character of the Iranian Ulema," *International Journal of Middle East Studies* 12 (1980): 510–11.

183. Martin Sicker, *The Bear and the Lion: Soviet Imperialism in Iran* (New York: Praeger, 1988), 93–94.

184. *Ittila'at* and *Kayhan*, 9 January 1963; Lambton, "*Land Reform in Iran*," in Yarshater, ed., *Iran Faces the Seventies*, 21–22; Nikki Keddie, *Roots of Revolution* (New Haven, Conn.: Yale University Press, 1981), 156; Milani, *The Making of Iran's Islamic Revolution*, 46; Bill, *The Eagle and the Lion*, 148.

185. Farmanfarmayan, "Politics During the Sixties," in Yarshater, ed., *Iran Faces the Seventies*, 104; *Foreign Relations of the United States, 1961–1963*, 18: 328, n. 2.

186. Farmanfarmayan, "Politics During the Sixties," in Yarshater, ed., *Iran Faces the Seventies*, 105.

187. *Foreign Relations of the United States, 1961–1963*, 18: 328, n. 2.

188. *Ittela'at*, 26 January 1962; Farmanfarmayan, "Politics During the Sixties," in Yarshater, ed., *Iran Faces the Seventies*, 105–106; *Kayhan*, 26 January 1962;

Muhammad Reza Pahlavi, *The White Revolution* (Tehran: Imperial Pahlavi Library, 1967), 4.

189. Department of State *Bulletin* 47, no. 1236, 4 March 1963, 316; *Foreign Relations of the United States, 1961–1963*, 18: 334.

190. Pfau, "The Legal Status of American Forces in Iran," *The Middle East Journal* 28 (Spring 1974): 149; Ramazani, *Iran's Foreign Policy, 1941–1973*, 363.

191. United Nations, Treaty Series, *Treaties and International Agreements Registered or Filed and Reported with the Secretariat of the United Nations* 500, no. 731, "Vienna Convention on Diplomatic Relations," 18 Aril 1961, 95–126.

192. *Ittila'at* and *Kayhan*, 16–23 November 1963; Sicker, *The Bear and the Lion*, 94.

Conclusion

This study offers a fresh analysis of the origins, development, and end of the U.S.-Soviet Cold War rivalry and tensions in Iran from 1945 to 1962. The orthodox account of the Iranian crisis of 1945–46, which depicts an aggressive Soviet Union relentless on its quest to subjugate Iran by establishing autonomous regimes in Azerbaijan, does not fully consider the strategic importance of Iran to the Soviet Union, the British, and then the U.S. presence in Iran, and the Shah's use of Third Power Strategy to counterbalance the powers against one another. The revisionist view that the United States was to blame for the Cold War confrontation in Iran because of its economic interests is not a strong argument by itself. Archival documents reveal that between 1941 and 1953, the United States did not have well-defined interests in Iran. Rather, Iran served as a buffer for U.S. oil interests in Saudi Arabia and the Persian Gulf. The postrevisionists, while taking traditional and revisionist arguments into account, have not yet clearly discussed the interests of the powers involved in the crisis and how those interests affected the course of the Cold War rivalry in Iran. They have not fully analyzed the role played by the Shah and the Iranian government and have shown themselves less than objective about Soviet actions in the aftermath of the Iranian crisis.

Aside from the above three schools of thought, there have been other scholars, who have tried to analyze the Iranian crisis of 1945–46 from a unique perspective. Some have focused extensively on the United States promoting its strategic interests in the region as the main reason why the Soviets reacted the way they did in northern Iran. These scholars have discussed U.S. strategic interests in the region hand in hand with U.S. economic interests, which bring their arguments very close to the revisionist review. In the past decade, a small number of scholars have used recently declassified documents from the archives of the former Soviet Union to attempt to understand the Soviet role in this conflict more clearly. Interestingly enough, all of the above arguments still tend to fall within the parameters of the revisionist and postrevisionist schools of thought.

As I have argued, while Soviet actions in northern Iran served as a catalyst for the U.S.-Soviet confrontation in Iran, a combination of internal and external factors also fueled the Iranian crisis of 1945–46. Internal factors included: the grievances of the Azeris and the Kurds against the Iranian government and their desire for more autonomy; the activities of the communist Tudeh Party, which eventually supported Azeri and Kurdish aspirations to establish autonomous regimes in northern Iran; and the Shah's decision to employ a Third Power Strategy to counterbalance the powers against one another. External factors included: the Anglo-Soviet occupation of Iran in 1941; the beginning of U.S. involvement in Iran in 1942 as part of the Allied war effort; and continuous Soviet interference in Iranian affairs.

In contrast to the traditionalists, revisionists, and postrevisionists, whose focus is limited to the origins of the Cold War, this study has attempted to present a more comprehensive analysis of how the U.S.-Soviet confrontation in Iran began, developed, and came to an end. This study also differs from several books written on U.S.-Iranian relations that are concerned primarily with the outbreak of the Islamic Revolution of 1979 and its aftermath. For the most part, these scholars trace the beginning of U.S. involvement in Iran to 1942, and mention the Iranian crisis of 1945–46 and the oil nationalization crisis of 1951 as the highlights of the superpower rivalry in Iran. Their main emphasis, however, is the period of the 1970s, when the Iranian people began to rise up against the Shah's regime and the United States for its support of the Shah.

Scholars who have written about U.S.-Iranian relations since the Islamic Revolution of 1979 have focused on Iran's support of radical Islamic groups and its continuing defiance of the United States and the international community in pursuing its nuclear agenda. There are several gaps in their coverage of political events, and the analysis of the Cold War context is conspicuously lacking. This study has attempted to reconstruct this Cold War context in Iran by filling in two major gaps: the years 1948–50, during which the Cold War tensions increased; and 1954–62, during which the Shah and his government were on the verge of a second Cold War crisis but were able to sidestep the difficulties presented by U.S.-Soviet rivalry and eventually play a direct role in bringing the Cold War tensions in Iran to an end.

This study began with an analysis of the historical context of the Cold War rivalry in Iran by focusing on the roots of Anglo-Russian competition that had persisted since the nineteenth century. Initially, the British viewed Iran as a buffer to their interests in India, but by the early twentieth century, their focus was exclusively on oil. Russian interest in Iran in the nineteenth century was primarily territorial. Through a series of wars, the Russians had managed to annex territory from the Caucasus and parts of Central Asia formerly controlled by the Iranian Qajar monarchy. In the twentieth century, Soviet interest also turned to oil, but its zone of interest was limited to northern Iran, where oil was not found in abundance as in the southern part of the country, which was under British influence.

The analysis of the historical context identified patterns of Anglo-Russian behavior in Iran in the early twentieth century that were repeated decades later. The British and the Russians divided Iran into spheres of influence in 1907 in order to protect their interests from external threats of powers such as Germany. In 1941, once again in order to safeguard their interests and to provide a supply route to the Soviet Union during World War II, the British and the Soviets occupied Iran. In addition, as early as 1920, the Soviets began to aid the Jangali movement, led by Mirza Kuchik Khan, with the aim of transforming Iran's northern province of Gilan into an autonomous republic. The Jangali movement was crushed by Reza Khan, who later established the Pahlavi dynasty and became the Shah of Iran. In 1945, the Soviets once again encouraged and aided separatist movements in northern Iran, this time in the Azerbaijan province, which led to the Iranian crisis of 1945–46.

Within this historical context, the United States became involved in Iran in 1942, eventually supplanting Britain's position of influence. In 1942, the British favored a U.S. role in securing the Persian Gulf and the supply route through Iran to ensure the safe delivery of war supplies to the Soviet Union. Therefore the British convinced the Shah and the Iranian government that it was in Iran's best interest to have American troops and advisers in Iran to help bring order to the unstable conditions that had resulted from the Anglo-Soviet occupation. In 1942, when the United States began to send its advisers and troops to Iran, it had no special interests in the country and viewed it as a buffer state to its oil interests in Saudi Arabia and the Persian Gulf region.

Muhammad Reza Shah turned to the United States to counterbalance Anglo-Soviet influence in Iran, and in doing so, pursued a Third Power Strategy. Between 1943 and 1944, the Iranian government indicated its willingness to grant an oil concession to the United States. The idea never materialized due to Soviet opposition and Iran's subsequent decision not to grant any concessions. It was not until the aftermath of the 1953 coup that the United States began to openly identify with its oil interests in Iran, as U.S. oil companies earned a major share to market Iranian oil. Within the framework of this historical context, I shall now turn to the five themes I presented in the introduction to trace how the superpowers played out their Cold War rivalries in Iran and their policies affected Iran's postwar political and economic development.

The first theme focused on the role of the Iranian crisis of 1945–46 in initiating the Cold War confrontation between the United States and the Soviet Union. As I have shown, this crisis became one of the major international conflicts that touched off the Cold War between the two superpowers. When the Soviets acted on their expansionist policy and encouraged separatist movements in the Iranian province Azerbaijan in 1945, U.S. opposition initiated the first phase of the Cold War confrontation in Iran. The Truman administration's support of the Iranian government before the U.N. Security Council resulted in Soviet withdrawal. Whether Truman ever gave Stalin an ultimatum, there is no doubt that Stalin feared U.S. military strength and nuclear capability, which at that time were well beyond Soviet levels, or that he felt the humiliation before the international community. At the same time, the Soviet Union had entered an agreement with the Iranian government to establish a joint oil company in northern Iran, most of whose benefits would go to the Soviets. The agreement, however, was not ratified by the Majlis.

The second theme focused on Soviet policy toward Iran in the aftermath of the Iranian crisis of 1945–46. Stalin did not pursue his expansionist policy in Iran between 1948–49; instead, he launched a hostile propaganda campaign against the Shah and the Iranian government, criticizing the Shah for giving up the control of his country to American advisers and military personnel. By 1950, realizing that their hostile propaganda had ironically brought the United States and Iran closer together, the Soviets took a more conciliatory approach, sending delegates to Iran to discuss trade missions and past border issues in an attempt to resume better relations. This change in Soviet policy coincided with the oil nationalization dispute and persisted after Stalin's death in 1953. Khrushchev criticized Stalin's past policies and tried to improve relations with the Iranian government, but Iran's decision to join the Baghdad Pact in 1955 dimmed those prospects. Despite this setback, the Soviets invited the Shah for a state visit in 1956; the Shah, by this time disenchanted by his membership in the Baghdad Pact and the lack of U.S. military and economic aid, agreed.

When the Soviets offered to negotiate a non-aggression pact with the Shah, the Eisenhower administration intervened with an offer to negotiate its own bilateral defense agreement, which the Shah immediately signed. This action provoked another hostile Soviet propaganda campaign against the Shah that continued well into the early 1960s. The Iranian government, fearful that these campaigns would instigate pro-Soviet riots in the country, considered taking its case before the U.N. Security Council with U.S. support but it refrained from doing so and instead turned to enacting measures to stabilize the Iranian economy. In the early 1960s, the Soviet government reverted to a more conciliatory approach toward Iran. I will discuss this issue in conjunction with the fifth point, which focused on the end of Cold War tensions in Iran.

The third theme focused on U.S. policy toward Iran and how it tried to prevent the spread of communism in Iran. During the Iranian Crisis of 1945–46, the Truman administration provided strong diplomatic support for Iran, especially at the U.N. Security Council. Strong U.S. support of the Iranian case at the U.N. Security Council eventually led to Soviet withdrawal from northern Iran, and although the Soviets continued their hostile propaganda against Iran, they never again encroached upon Iranian territory. Following the Iranian Crisis of 1945–46, the Truman administration encouraged Iran to carry out economic reforms as part of its strategy to contain the spread of communism. The United States sent engineering firms to Iran to carry out development surveys. These efforts, in turn, enabled the Iranian government to draw up a comprehensive development plan known as the First Seven-Year Plan. While encouraging reform, the Truman administration kept its financial aid on a small scale, making it clear that the Iranians had to put their house in order if they were to expect further aid from the United States.

Given the lack of U.S. aid, the Iranian government turned to its oil revenues to finance its development plans, precipitating the oil nationalization dispute of 1951. This dispute set the Iranian government against the British, who were in charge of the AIOC and the revenues Iran received from the sale of its oil. The Truman administration tried to negotiate with Prime Minister Muhammad Musaddiq, the leader of Oil Nationalization Movement, by sending several envoys to mediate the dispute but to no avail.

Eisenhower, however, was not as patient as his predecessor. Eisenhower was concerned that Musaddiq's inability to reach a settlement had strengthened the communist Tudeh Party, which could overthrow Musaddiq and take control of the country. Earlier, the British had approached the Truman administration to propose a joint effort to overthrow Musaddiq, but no action was taken. In 1953, however, the Eisenhower administration agreed as part of its strategy to prevent Iran from falling to communism. The CIA and the MI6 engineered a coup in Iran, which overthrew Musaddiq's government and restored the Shah's regime.

The Eisenhower administration's policy centered on two goals: 1) keeping the Shah's regime and the Iranian economy intact after the 1953 coup through increased U.S. financial assistance; and 2) realigning Iran more closely to the West, which was achieved when Iran joined the Baghdad Pact in 1955. During its second term, the Eisenhower administration realized that the increased U.S. aid to Iran in the aftermath of Musaddiq's downfall had not produced concrete results. The Iranian government still struggled with a persisting budget deficit. The Eisenhower administration advised the Iranian government to take serious steps toward reform and cut back its financial aid to stress the gravity of the situation. These efforts proved effective. Between 1957 and 1960, the Iranian government took preliminary steps, experimenting with the idea of a two-party system and attempting to stabilize the economy as prescribed by the IMF and other international agencies.

Although the Eisenhower administration's policy toward Iran was successful in holding back the spread of communism in the country, the CIA-engineered coup that overthrew Musaddiq and restored the Shah's rule tarnished U.S. prestige in the eyes of many Iranians for decades to come and were used against the United States in anti-Shah demonstrations in 1979.

The Kennedy administration established an Iran Task Force to monitor events in Iran and produce reports on U.S. aid to Iran. The Kennedy administration's policy toward Iran called for a strict regimen of social and economic reforms instead of military buildup. It emphasized land reform, which was meant to build more political support for the Shah. The Kennedy administration made it very clear that the Shah could not expect any economic aid if he did not go ahead with the reforms. At the same, it offered a five-year military aid package to the Shah to keep him content.

Between 1961 and 1963, the Shah laid the foundation for a comprehensive reform program known as the White Revolution. He reluctantly appointed Ali Amini to carry out the task of reform. Amini's popularity did not last long, and he was unable to cope with Iran's budget deficit. The United States, continuing to push for reform, pressured Iran in 1962 to extend its diplomatic immunity to all U.S. personnel in Iran. The Shah's pro-Western reforms and his eventual granting of immunity to all American personnel stationed in Iran unleashed a fury never before experienced in Iranian history that was to haunt the Shah and the United States for decades to come. While communism had been contained, nationalist forces were gathering under the banner of religion and the leadership of Ayatollah Khomeini, to oppose the Shah and the United States. The end result was the Islamic Revolution of 1979, which overthrew the Shah and ended decades of U.S. influence in Iran.

The fourth theme focused on whether British policy influenced the course of Cold War tensions in Iran after the 1945–46 crisis. This study has shown that between 1941 and 1950, the British maintained a strong influence over the Iranian government. This is understandable given Britain's economic stake in its oil interests in southern Iran. The United States initially respected Britain's position in Iran and did not challenge it. At the same time, the British requested U.S. involvement in Iran to facilitate the Allied war effort. In the aftermath of the Iranian crisis, the British joined the United States to support the Iranian government against the Soviets. The British, however, were in no position to challenge the Soviets. Due to financial difficulties, the British could no longer provide aid to Greece and Turkey and had to relinquish those responsibilities to the United States, although they maintained their stronghold in Iran.

The British were unhappy about the fact that the Iranians had hired U.S. engineering firms to conduct surveys in Iran as part of Iran's plan to pursue economic development projects. These projects were to be funded by Iran's oil revenues, which were controlled by the British. In order to show some good will and at the same time deflect attention from the question of oil, the British offered to send a team of economic advisers and engineers to carry out research and draw up development plans in Iran, as their U.S. counterparts had done. The British failed to achieve any concrete results, as the U.S. teams had more financial resources available to them for this task and were on better terms with the Iranian government. In addition, the U.S. decision to enter a 50-50 oil agreement with Saudi Arabia, known as the Saudi-Aramco deal, eventually undermined the British position in Iran, since the Iranians demanded the same treatment from the British in 1951.

The British, for the most part, had kept a low profile after the Iranian crisis of 1945–46. But when the Iranians, led by Musaddiq, decided to nationalize the oil industry, the British resisted fiercely. They decided to overthrow Musaddiq's government in a covert operation with the help of the United States. The British used the communist threat in Iran to gain U.S. support for their plans. Their decision led the United States to take actions it would regret decades later, as it was forever linked to the overthrow of Musaddiq's government. In the aftermath of the 1953 coup, the United States effectively assumed Britain's place in Iran. Primary sources show that between 1954 and 1963, the British role in Iran became minimal. The only visible activity was their participation in regional defense pacts, such as the Baghdad Pact in 1955, where it gave some assurances to the participant countries that a Western power was present in this endeavor.

The fifth theme focused on how the Shah and his government's policies affected the course of the Cold War rivalry in Iran. Caught between the British and the Soviets, and later the United States and the Soviets, the Shah and his government had three options: 1) to become pro-Soviet; 2) to become pro-West; or 3) to become neutral. Given past Soviet expansionist aims and years of mistrust, the Shah espoused the second option and employed a Third Power Strategy to counterbalance British and Soviet influence in Iran. The Shah turned to the United States as the third power. His use of Third Power Strategy further heightened Cold War tensions in Iran.

For a brief moment from 1951 to mid-1953, Iran took a neutral stand in its relations with the superpowers. This was due to Prime Minister Musaddiq's rise to power and his policy of Negative Equilibrium, which sought to end foreign influence in Iran. Musaddiq's ideals, however, fell short: while advocating neutrality in public, in private he turned to the Truman administration for financial aid. Musaddiq also allowed the Tudeh Party, previously banned by the Shah, to resume its activities. Musaddiq in fact warned the United States about a possible communist takeover in order to obtain U.S. sympathy, but the tactic backfired and influenced the Eisenhower administration to accept the British proposal to overthrow his government.

In the aftermath of Musaddiq's fall, the Shah once again gravitated toward the West and pursued a pro-Western stance for Iran, promoting what he called Positive Nationalism, as opposed to Musaddiq's Negative Equilibrium. The Shah stressed the importance of maintaining close ties with the United States, which had helped Iran modernize. In the early 1960s, the Shah unveiled a six-point reform program known as the White Revolution, which was to be implemented over the next few years. By 1962, the Shah, deeply affected by the growing Cold War tensions as well as the lack of U.S. aid, decided to pursue an Independent National Policy. As part of this policy in September 1962, the Shah and his government gave a pledge to the Soviet Union not to allow the establishment of any foreign missile bases in Iran. This pledge led to a thaw in Iranian-Soviet relations and helped bring an end to Cold War tensions in Iran. The Shah, however, had lost sight of the fact that Iran lacked a political outlet by which the people could exercise their individual liberties without fear of a crackdown on their political activities. His preoccupation with a military buildup to the exclusion of the economic reform ended up hurting him and the Iranian people. The Shah's fear of a Soviet attack never materialized, and his army could not defend him from the Islamic Revolution of 1979 led by Ayatollah Khomeini.

Without taking sides or assigning blame, this study has argued that the origins and development of the Cold War rivalry in Iran were a product of complex external and internal factors. The United States, the Soviet Union, and Great Britain pursued their interests and their rivalries in Iran. But the following also contributed to the Cold War confrontation in Iran: the Shah and his government applying different measures such as the Third Power Strategy, Negative Equilibrium, and Positive Nationalism; the Tudeh Party and the threat of imminent communist takeover; and the role played by opposition groups such as the National Front and the clergy in opposing the Shah.

Preoccupied by the communist threat and the Cold War tensions of the postwar era, the Shah and the United States failed to see the dangers unfolding within Iran. The combination of both internal and external factors discussed in this study had helped laid the foundation for the Islamic Revolution of 1979. The Shah's regime was overthrown by Ayatollah Khomeini, who then established an Islamic Republic. The Islamic Republic severed its ties not only with the United States but also with the Soviet Union. In November 1979, Khomeini's followers attacked the American Embassy and took several Americans hostage. The hostages were released a year later on the day Ronald Reagan was inaugurated president.

It was not until the mid-1980s that the Soviet leader Mikhail Gorbachev made an attempt to improve relations with Iran. The two sides gradually entered into a number of trade agreements. The Russians began to help build and equip Iran's nuclear facility in Bushehr, which in time became a major source of friction between Iran, the United States, and the international community. Following the September 11, 2001 tragedy, Iran condemned any acts of terrorism and even offered to help the United States in its war on terror against the Taliban regime in Afghanistan. In 2007, Iran and the United States entered into direct talks over the violence in Iraq, which had persisted since the overthrow of Saddam Hussein's regime by U.S. forces in 2003. This was the first time the two sides had come face-to-face after nearly thirty years of diplomatic impasse.

Today, U.S.-Iranian relations remain at a standstill over Iran's decision to continue its uranium enrichment program. The Islamic Republic is fearful of the Bush administration's insistence on spreading democracy in the Middle East and prospects of a regime change in Iran. Russian-Iranian relations, on the other hand, have improved considerably over the years. Vladimir Putin visited Iran in 2007 and publicly supported Iran's right to develop its nuclear energy. President George W. Bush and Vladimir Putin's terms will come to an end in 2009 and 2008, respectively. It remains to be seen how the next American and Russian presidents will deal with the Islamic Republic and whether there will be any further improvements in their relations.

Bibliography

ARCHIVAL SOURCES

U.S. Department of State, Record Group 59, Decimal File, National Archives, College Park, Md.
U.S. Department of State, Record Group 59, Post and Lot Files, National Archives, College Park, Md.
U.S. Department of State, Record Group 84, Foreign Service Post Files, National Archives, College Park, Md.

ORAL HISTORY COLLECTIONS

Harvard University, Iranian Oral History Project, Houghton Library, Cambridge, Mass.
General Hasan Alavi-Kia.
Khodadad Farmanfarmaian.
Abul Hasan Ibtihaj.

PUBLIC DOCUMENTS, DOCUMENTARY COLLECTIONS, AND OFFICIAL PUBLICATIONS

Alexander, Yonah, and Allan Nanes, eds. *The United States and Iran*. Frederick, Md.: Aletheia Books, 1980.
Hurewitz, J. C., ed. *Diplomacy in the Near and Middle East: A Documentary Record, 1914–1956*. 2 vols. Princeton, N.J.: Princeton University Press, 1956.
Motter, T. H. Vail. *The United States Army in World War II: The Middle East Theater, The Persian Corridor and Aid to Russia*. Washington, D.C.: Department of the Army, 1952.
Royal Institute of International Affairs. *Documents on International Affairs, 1959*. London: Oxford University Press, 1963.

United Nations. Secretariat. *Treaty Series.* Vol. 457, No. 6586 (1963).
——. Treaty Series. Vol. 500, No. 731 (1964).
U.S. Congress. House of Representatives. *Assistance to Greece and Turkey: Hearings Before the Committee on Foreign Affairs.* 80th Congress, 1st Session, 1947.
——. *Hearings Before the Committee on Government Operations.* 85th Congress, 1st Session, 1957.
U.S. Congress. Senate. *Congressional Record, 1947–1963.*
——. *Legislative Origins of the Truman Doctrine: Hearings Held in Executive Session Before the Committee on Foreign Relations.* 80th Congress, 1st Session, 1973.
——. *Operation of Article VII: Hearing Before a Sub-Committee of the Committee on Armed Services.* 86th Congress, 1st Session, 1959.
——. *Hearings on Military Posture Before the House Committee on Armed Services.* 88th Congress, 1st Session, 1963.
U.S. Department of State. *Bulletin, 1945–1963.*
——. *Current Economic Developments,* No. 264, 24 July 1950.
——. *Foreign Relations of the United States, 1943.* Diplomatic Papers. Vol. 4. *The Near East and Africa.* Washington, D.C.: Government Printing Office, 1964.
——. *Foreign Relations of the United States, 1945.* Diplomatic Papers. Vol. 2. *General Political and Economic Matters.* Washington, D.C.: Government Printing Office, 1967.
——. *Foreign Relations of the United States, 1945.* Diplomatic Papers. Vol. 8. *The Near East and Africa.* Washington, D.C.: Government Printing Office, 1969.
——. *Foreign Relations of the United States, 1946.* Vol. 6. *Eastern Europe and the Soviet Union.* Washington, D.C.: Government Printing Office, 1969.
——. *Foreign Relations of the United States, 1946.* Vol. 7. *The Near East and Africa.* Washington, D.C.: Government Printing Office, 1969.
——. *Foreign Relations of the United States, 1948.* Vol. 5. *The Near East, South Asia, and Africa.* Washington, D.C.: Government Printing Office, 1975.
——. *Foreign Relations of the United States, 1949.* Vol. 4. *Western Europe.* Washington, D.C.: Government Printing Office, 1975.
——. *Foreign Relations of the United States, 1949.* Vol. 6. *The Near East, South Asia, and Africa.* Washington, D.C.: Government Printing Office, 1977.
——. *Foreign Relations of the United States, 1950.* Vol. 5. *The Near East, South Asia, and Africa.* Washington: Government Printing Office, 1978.
——. *Foreign Relations of the United States, 1952–1954.* Vol. 2. *National Security Affairs.* Washington, D.C.: Government Printing Office, 1984.
——. *Foreign Relations of the United States, 1952–1954.* Vol. 10. *Iran, 1951–1954.* Washington, D.C.: Government Printing Office, 1989.
——. *Foreign Relations of the United States, 1955–1957.* Vol. 12. *The Near East Region, Iran, and Iraq.* Washington, D.C.: Government Printing Office, 1991.
——. *Foreign Relations of the United States, 1958–1960.* Vol. 12. *The Near East Region, Iran, Iraq, and the Arabian Peninsula.* Washington, D.C.: Government Printing Office, 1993.
——. *Foreign Relations of the United States, 1961–1963.* Vol. 17. *The Near East, 1961–1962.* Washington, D.C.: Government Printing Office, 1994.

———. *Foreign Relations of the United States, 1961–1963*. Vol. 18. *The Near East, 1962–1963*. Washington, D.C.: Government Printing Office, 1995.
———. *Foreign Relations of the United States*, Diplomatic Papers. *The Conferences at Cairo and Tehran, 1943*. Washington, D.C.: Government Printing Office, 1961.
———. *Foreign Relations of the United States*, Diplomatic Papers. *The Conferences at Malta and Yalta, 1945*. Washington, D.C.: Government Printing Office, 1955.
———. *Foreign Relations of the United States*, Diplomatic Papers. *The Conference of Berlin (Potsdam), 1945*. Vols. 1 and 2. Washington, D.C.: Government Printing Office, 1960.
———. *United States Treaties and Other International Act Series 1650–1699*. Washington, D.C.: Government Printing Office, 1947.
———. *United States Treaties and Other International Agreements*. Vol. 4, No. 2809. Washington, D.C.: Government Printing Office, 1953.
———. *United States Treaties and Other International Act Series*. No. 4189. Washington, D.C.: Government Printing Office, 1959.
———. *United States Treaties and Other International Act Series*. No. 4930. Washington, D.C.: Government Printing Office, 1961.

IRANIAN PERIODICALS AND NEWSPAPERS

Azerbaijan
Azhir
Bakhtar-i Imruz
Bi su-yi Ayandeh
Dad
Dunya
Iran Almanac
Iran Times
Ittila'at
Ittila'at Havai
Kayhan
Khavar-i Now
Majaleh-yi Masael-i Iran
Mardum
Mizan Newsletter
Rahbar
Shahid

PERIODICALS AND NEWSPAPERS IN OTHER LANGUAGES

Christian Science Monitor
Current Digest of the Soviet Press

Moyen-Orient
New York Times
Pravada
Saturday Evening Post
Soviet News
Soviet Weekly
The Times of London
U.S. News and World Report
Washington Post

IRANIAN BOOKS AND ARTICLES

Alavi, Buzurg. *Panjah va Seh Nafar* (The Fifty-Three Individuals). Tehran: Amir Kabir, 1358/1979.

Arsanjani, Hasan. *Yadashtha-yi Siyasi dar Vaqaye'i Si-yi Tir 1320* (Political Notes Regarding the Events on 21 July 1952). Tehran: Pejman, 1355/1976.

Bakhtiar, Timur. *Kitab-i Siyah Darbareh-yi Sazman-i Afsaran-i Tudeh* (A Black Book about the Organization of Army Officers in the Tudeh Party). Tehran: Kayhan Press, 1334/1955.

Buzurg-Mehr, Jalil. *Dr. Muhammad Musaddiq va Residigi-yi Farjami dar Divan-i Kishvar* (Dr. Muhammad Musaddiq and the Investigation in the Supreme Court). Tehran: Shirkat-i Sahami-yi Intishar, 1367/1988.

Fardust, Husein. *Zuhur va Sughut-i Saltanat-i Pahlavi* (The Rise and Fall of the Pahlavi Dynasty). Tehran: Ittila'at, 1368/1989.

Fateh, Mustafa. *Panjah Sal Naft-i Iran.* (Fifty Years of Iranian Oil). Tehran: Sherkat-i Sahami-yi Chap, 1335/1956.

Ghani, Cyrus. *Iran: Bar Amadan-i Reza Khan Bar Uftadan-i Qajar va Naqsh-i Ingilis-ha* (Iran: The Rise of Reza Khan, the Fall of the Qajars, and the Role of the British). Tehran: Niloofar, 1377/1998.

Ibtihaj, Abu al-Hasan. *Khatirat-i Abu al-Hasan Ibtihaj* (The Memoirs of Abu al-Hasan Ibtihaj). 2 vols. Tehran: Ilmi, 1371/1992.

Iskandari, Iraj. *Khatirat-i Siyasi Iraj Iskandari* (Political Memoirs of Iraj Iskandari). Tehran: Ilmi Press, 1368/1989.

Janzadeh, Ali. *Musaddiq* (Musaddiq). Tehran: Hangam, 1358/1979.

Kambaksh, Abdul Samad. *Nazar-i bi Junbish-i Kargari va Komunisti dar Iran* (A Survey of the Labor and Communist Movement in Iran). Stockholm: Salzland Press, 1975.

Katouzian, Homayoun. *Musaddiq va Nabard-i Qudrat dar Iran* (Musaddiq and the Struggle for Power in Iran). London: I. B. Tauris, 1990.

Kayustuvan, Hussein. *Siyast-i Muvazaneh-yi Manfi dar Majlis-i Chahardahom* (The Policy of Negative Equilibrium in the Fourteenth Majlis). Vol. 1. Tehran: Mozaffar, 1327/1948.

Khamahi, Anvar. *Panjah Nafar va Seh Nafar: Khatirat-i Anvar Khamahi* (Fifty-Three Individuals: The Memoirs of Anvar Khamahi). Tehran: Hafteh, 1363/1984.

Kianuri, Nur al-Din. *Khatirat-i Nur al-Din Kianuri* (The Memoirs of Nur al-Din Kianuri). Tehran: Ittila'at Press, 1371/1992.

Ladjevardi, Habib, ed. *Khatirat-i Ali Amini* (The Memoirs of Ali Amini). Cambridge, Mass.: Harvard University, Center for Middle Eastern Studies, 1995.

———, ed. *Khatirat-i Shahpur Bakhtiar* (The Memoirs of Shahpur Bakhtiar). Cambidge, Mass.: Harvard University, Center for Middle Eastern Studies, 1996.

Mahdavi, Abdul Reza Hushang. *Tarikh-i Ravabit-i Khariji-yi Iran az Payan-i Jang-i Jahani-yi Duvum ta Suqut-i Regim-i Pahlavi* (A History of Iran's Foreign Relations From the End of the Second World War to the Fall of the Pahlavi Regime). Tehran: Pishgam, 1368/1989.

Mahdi-Nia, Ja'far. *Zindigi-yi Siyasi-yi Qavam ul-Saltaneh* (The Political Life of Qavam ul-Saltaneh). Tehran: Panus and Pasgard, 1370/1991.

Maleki, Khalil. *Tarikhcheh-yi Jibhe-yi Milli* (A History of National Front). Tehran: Taban Press, 1333/1954.

Manshur, Muhammad Ali. *Siyasat-i Dowlat-i Shoravi dar Iran* (The Soviet Policy in Iran). Tehran: n.p., 1327/1948.

Najmi, Nasser. Musaddiq, Mubariz-i Buzurg (Musaddiq,The Great Warrior). Tehran: n.p., 1359/1980.

Nejati, Gholam Husein, ed. *Dar Kenar-i Pedaram: Khatirat-i Dr. Ghulam Husein Musaddiq* (By My Father's Side: The Memoirs of Dr. Ghulam Hussein Musaddiq). Tehran: Rasa, 1369/1990.

———. *unbish-i Milli Shudan-i San'at-i Naft-i Irani va Kudeta-yi 28 Murdad* (The Movement For the Nationalization of the Iranian Oil Industry and the Coup of 28 Murdad). Tehran: Shirkat-i Sahami-yi Intishar, 1364/1985.

Pesyan, Najafgholi. *Marg Bud Bazgasht Ham Bud.* (There was Death and Return). Tehran: Shirkat-i Sahami-yi Chap, 1326/1947.

Qasemi, Ahmad. *Hizb-i Tudeh-yi Iran chi Miguyad va chi Mikhahad?* (What Does the Tudeh Party Say and What Does It Want?). Tehran: Tudeh Press, 1321/1943.

Shifteh, Nasrollah. *Zindigi-Nameh va Mubarizat-i Siyasi-yi Dr. Muhammad Musaddiq* (The Life and Political Struggles of Dr. Muhammad Musaddiq). Tehran: Kumesh,1370/1991.

Zia-Zarifi, Hasan. *Hizb-i Tudeh va Kudeta-yi 28 Murdad 1332* (The Tudeh Party and the August 19 Coup d'Etat of 1953). Tehran: n.p., 1358/1979.

ENGLISH BOOKS, ARTICLES, AND SECONDARY SOURCES

Abrahamian, Ervand. "Communism and Communalism in Iran: The Tudeh and the Firqah-i Dimukrat." *Intenational Journal of Middle Eastern Studies* 1, no. 4 (1970): 291–316.

———. *Iran Between Two Revolutions*. Princeton, N.J.: Princeton University Press, 1982.

Acheson, Dean. *Present at the Creation*. New York: W. W. Norton, 1969.

Alvarez, David. "The Missouri Visit to Turkey: An Alternative Perspective to Cold War Diplomacy." *Balkan Studies* 15, no. 2 (November 1974): 225–36.

Amirie, Abbas, and Hamilton A. Twitchell, eds. *Iran in the 1980s*. Tehran: Institute for International Political and Economic Studies, 1978.

Amirsadeghi, Hussein, ed. *The Security of the Persian Gulf*. New York: St. Martin's Press, 1981.

Amirsadeghi, Hussein, and R. Ferrier, eds. *Twentieth Century Iran*. London: Heinemann, 1977.

Amuzegar, Jahangir. *Technical Assistance in Theory and Practice: The Case of Iran*. New York: Praeger, 1966.

Amuzegar, Jahangir and M. Ali Fekrat. *Iran: Economic Development under Dualistic Conditions*. Chicago: University of Chicago Press, 1971.

Ansari, Ali. *Confronting Iran: The Failure of American Foreign Policy and the Next Great Crisis in the Middle East*. New York: Basic Books, 2006.

Arfa, Hassan. *Under Five Shahs*. Edinburgh: R. and R. Clark, 1964.

Ausland, John C. *Kennedy, Khrushchev, and the Berlin-Cuba Crisis, 1961–1964*. Oslo: Scandinavian University Press, 1996.

Avery, Peter. *Modern Iran*. New York: Praeger, 1965.

Axelgard, Frederick, W. "U.S. Support for the British Position in Pre-Revolutionary Iraq." In *The Iraqi Revolution of 1958: The Old Social Classes Revisited*, 77–94, ed. Robert A. Fernea and William R. Louis. London: I. B. Tauris, 1991.

Azimi, Fakhreddin. *Iran: The Crisis of Democracy, 1941–1953*. London: I. B. Tauris, 1989.

Bakhash, Shaul. "The Failure of Reform: The Prime Ministership of Amin al-Dawla, 1897–8." In *The Qajar Iran: Political, Social, and Cultural Change, 1800–1925*, 14–34, ed. Edmund Bosworth and Carole Hillenbrand. Edinburgh: Edinburgh University Press, 1983.

———. *The Reign of the Ayatollahs: Iran and the Islamic Revolution*. New York: Basic Books, 1984.

Baldwin, George. *Planning and Development in Iran*. Baltimore: The Johns Hopkins Press, 1967.

Bamberg, J. H. *The History of the British Petroleum Company. Vol. 2: The Anglo-Iranian Years, 1928–1954*. Cambridge: Cambridge University Press, 1982.

Banani, Amin. *The Modernization of Iran, 1921–1941*. Stanford, Calif.: Stanford University Press, 1961.

Barraclough, Geoffrey. *Survey of International Affairs 1959–1960*. London: Oxford University Press, 1964.

Bayne, E. A. *Persian Kingship in Transition*. New York: American Universities Field Staff, 1968.

Behrooz, Maziar. *Rebels with a Cause: The Failure of the Left in Iran*. London: I.B. Tauris, 2000.

———."Tudeh Factionalism and the 1953 Coup in Iran." *International Journal of Middle East Studies* 33, no. 3 (August 2001): 363–82.

Berman, Ilan, ed. *Taking on Tehran: Strategies for Confronting the Islamic Republic*. Lanham, Md.: Lexington Books, 2007.

Bernstein, Barton J. *Politics and Policies of the Truman Administration*. Chicago: Quadrangle Books, 1970.

Bharier, Julian. *Economic Development in Iran, 1900–1970*. London: Oxford University Press, 1971.

Bill, James. *The Eagle and the Lion: The Tragedy of American-Iranian Relations*. New Haven: Yale University Press, 1988.

. *The Politics of Iran: Groups, Classes, and Modernization*. Columbus, Ohio: Charles E. Merrill, 1972.

Bill, James, and William Roger Louis, eds. *Musaddiq, Iranian Nationalism, and Oil*. Austin: University of Texas Press, 1988.

Bostock, Frances, and Geoffrey Jones. *Planning and Power in Iran: Ebtehaj and Economic Development under the Shah*. London: Frank Cass, 1989.

Brinkley, Douglas, ed. *Acheson and the Making of U.S. Foreign Policy*. New York: St. Martin's Press, 1993.

Bullard, Sir Reader. *The Camels Must Go*. London: Faber and Faber, 1961.

Byrnes, James F. *All in One Lifetime*. New York: Harper & Brothers, 1958.

———. *Speaking Frankly*. New York: Harper & Brothers, 1947.

Campbell, John C. *Defense of the Middle East: Problems of American Diplomacy*. New York: Harper & Bros., 1958.

Carr, C. D. "The United States-Iranian Relationship, 1948–1978: A Study in Reverse Influence." In *The Security of the Persian Gulf*, 57–84, ed. Hossein Amirsadeghi. New York: St. Martin's Press, 1981.

Chaqueri, Cosroe. *The Soviet Socialist Republic of Iran, 1920–1921*. Pittsburgh: University of Pittsburgh Press, 1995.

Chubin, Shahram, and Sepehr Zabih. *The Foreign Relations of Iran*. Berkeley: University of California Press, 1974.

Churchill, Winston. *The Grand Alliance*. London: Cassell, 1950.

Cleveland, William. *A History of the Modern Middle East*. Boulder, Colo: Westview Press, 2004.

Cottam, Richard. "American Policy and the Iranian Crisis," *Iranian Studies* 13 (1980): 279–305.

———. *Iran and the United States: A Cold War Case Study*. Pittsburgh: University of Pittsburgh Press, 1988.

———. *Nationalism in Iran*. Pittsburgh: University of Pittsburgh Press, 1964.

———. "The United States, Iran, and the Cold War." *Iranian Studies* 3, no. 1 (Winter 1970): 2–22.

DeNovo, John. *American Interests and Policies in the Middle East, 1900–1939*. Minneapolis: University of Minnesota Press, 1963.

Diba, Farhad. *Mosaddeq, A Political Biography*. London: Croon Helm, 1986.

Doenecke, Justus. "Iran's Role in Cold War Revisionism." *Iranian Studies* 5, nos. 2 &3 (Spring–Summer 1972): 96–111.

———. "Revisionists, Oil, and Cold War Diplomacy." *Iranian Studies* 3, no. 1 (Winter 1970): 23–33.
Druks, Herbert. *Harry S. Truman and the Russians, 1945–1953*. New York: Robert Speller and Sons, 1966.
Eagleton, William. *The Kurdish Republic of 1946*. Oxford: Oxford University Press, 1963.
Eden, Anthony. *Full Circle*. Boston: Houghton Mifflin, 1960.
Elwell-Sutton, L. P. *Persian Oil: A Study in Power Politics*. London: Lawrence and Wishart, 1955.
———. "Political Parties in Iran." *Middle East Journal* 3, no. 1(January 1949): 45–62.
Emami-Yeganeh, Jodi. "Iran vs Azerbaijan (1945–1946): Divorce, Separation or Reconciliation?" *Central Asian Survey* 3, no. 2 (1984): 1–27.
Fakiolas, Efstathios. "Kennan's Long Telegram and NSC-68: A Comparative Theoretical Analysis," *East European Quarterly* 31, no. 4 (Winter 1998): 415–434.
Farmanfarmayan, Hafiz. "Politics During the Sixties." In *Iran Faces the Seventies*, ed. Ehsan Yarshater. New York: Praeger, 1971.
Fatemi, Faramarz. *The U.S.S.R. in Iran*. London: Thomas Yoseloff, 1980.
Fatemi, Nasrollah S. *Oil Diplomacy: Powderkeg in Iran*. New York: Whittier, 1954.
Fawcett, Louise. *Iran and the Cold War: The Azerbaijan Crisis of 1946*. Cambridge: Cambridge University Press, 1992.
Feis, Herbert. *From Trust to Terror: The Onset of the Cold War, 1945–1950*. New York: W.W. Norton, 1970.
Fernia, Robert A., and William. Roger Louis, eds. *The Iraqi Revolution of 1958: The Old Social Classes Revisited*. London: I. B. Tauris and Co., 1991.
Ferrier, R. W. "The Anglo-Iranian Oil Dispute." In *Musaddiq: Iranian Nationalism and Oil*, 168–74, ed. James Bill and William R. Louis. Austin: University of Texas Press, 1988.
———. *The History of the British Petroleum Company: The Developing Years, 1901–1932*. Vol. 1. Cambridge: Cambridge University Press, 1982.
Fesharaki, Fereidun. *Development of the Iranian Oil Industry: International and Domestic Aspects*. New York: Praeger, 1976.
Fleming, Denna. *The Cold War and its Origins, 1917–1950*. Vol. 1. London: George Allen and Unwin Ltd., 1961.
Floor, Willem. "The Revolutionary Character of the Iranian Ulema." *International Journal of Middle Eastern Studies* 12, no. 4 (1980): 501–24.
Frye, Richard. *Iran*. New York: Holt, 1953.
Gaddis, John L. "The Emerging Post-Revisionist Synthesis on the Origins of the Cold War." *Diplomatic History* 7 (Summer 1981): 171–90.
——— *Strategies of Containment: A Critical Appraisal of Postwar American National Security Policy*. New York: Oxford University Press, 1982.
Ganji, Babak. *Politics of Confrontation: The Foreign Policy of USA and Revolutionary Iran*. London: Tauris Academic Studies, 2006.
Gardner, Lloyd. *Architects of Illusion*. Chicago: Quadrangle, 1970.
———. *Economic Aspects of New Deal Diplomacy*. Madison: University of Wisconsin Press, 1964.

Garthoff, Raymond L. *Assessing the Adversary: Estimates by the Eisenhower Administration of Soviet Intentions and Capabilities.* Washington, D.C.: Brookings Institution, 1991.

——. *Intelligence Assessment and Policymaking: A Decision Point in the Kennedy Administration.* Washington, D.C.: Brookings Institution, 1984.

Gasiorowski, Mark J. "The 1953 Coup d'Etat in Iran." *International Journal of Middle East Studies* 19, no. 3 (August 1987): 261–86.

——. *U.S. Foreign Policy and the Shah: Building a Client State in Iran.* Ithaca, N.Y.: Cornell University Press, 1991.

Ghods, Muhammad Reza. *Iran in the Twentieth Century.* Boulder, Colo.: Lynne Rienner, 1989.

Giglio, James N. *The Presidency of John F. Kennedy.* Lawrence: University Press of Kansas, 1991.

Goode, James F. *The United States and Iran, 1946–1951: The Diplomacy of Neglect.* London: Macmillan, 1989.

——. *The United States and Iran: In the Shadow of Musaddiq.* London: Macmillan, 1997.

Grayson, Benson Lee. *United States–Iranian Relations.* Lanham, Md.: University Press of America, 1981.

Halle, Louise J. *The Cold War as History.* New York: Viking Press, 1955.

Harbutt, Fraser. *The Iron Curtain.* New York: Oxford University Press, 1987.

Harris, George. *Troubled Alliance: Turkish American Problems in Historical Perspective, 1945–1971.* Washington, D.C.: American Enterprise Institute, 1972.

Hasanli, Jamil. *Iran at the Dawn of the Cold War: The Soviet–American Crisis over Iranian Azerbaijan, 1941–1946.* Lanham, Md.: Roman & Littlefield Publishers, 2006.

Hess, Gary. "The Iranian Crisis of 1945–1946 and the Cold War." *Political Science Quarterly* 89, no.1 (March 1974): 117–46.

Hooglund, Eric. *Reform and Revolution in Rural Iran.* Austin: University of Texas Press, 1982.

Houghton, David. *U.S. Foreign Policy and the Iran Hostage Crisis.* Cambridge: Cambridge University Press, 2001.

International Engineering Company Incorporated. *Report on Program for the Development of Iran.* San Francisco: MKI, 1947.

Jones, Joseph M. *The Fifteen Weeks.* New York: Viking Press, 1955.

Jukes, Geoffrey. *The Indian Ocean in Soviet Naval Policy.* London: International Institute for Strategic Studies, 1972.

Karshenas, Massoud. *Oil, State, and Industrialization in Iran.* Cambridge: Cambridge University Press, 1990.

Katouzian, Homayoun. *Musaddiq and the Struggle for Power in Iran.* London: Tauris, 1990.

——, ed. *Musaddiq's Memoirs.* London: Jebhe, 1988.

—— *The Political Economy of Modern Iran: Despotism and Pseudo-Modernism, 1926–1979.* New York: New York University Press, 1981.

Kazemzadeh, Firuz. *Russia and Britain in Persia, 1864–1914.* New Haven: Yale University Press, 1968.

Keddie, Nikki R. *Roots of Revolution: An Interpretative History of Modern Iran.* New Haven: Yale University Press, 1981.

Kennan, George F. *Memoirs, 1925–1950.* Boston: Bantam, 1967.

———. "The Sources of Soviet Conduct." *Foreign Affairs* 25, no.4 (July 1947): 566–82.

Kennan, George F. and John Lukacs. *George F. Kennan and the Origins of Containment, 1944–1946.* Columbia, Mo.: University of Missouri Press, 1997.

Kennedy, Robert. *Thirteen Days.* New York: W. W. Norton, 1969.

Kingston, Paul W. *Britain and the Politics of Modernization in the Middle East, 1945–1958.* Cambridge: Cambridge University Press, 1996.

Kirkendall, Richard S., ed. *The Truman Period as a Research Field: A Reappraisal, 1972.* Columbia, Mo.: University of Missouri Press, 1974.

Kolko, Gabriel. *The Politics of War.* New York: Random House, 1968.

Kolko, Gabriel, and Joyce Kolko. *The Limits of Power: The World and United States Foreign Policy, 1945–1954.* New York: Harper & Row, 1972.

Kuniholm, Bruce. "Loy Henderson, Dean Acheson, and the Origins of the Truman Doctrine." In *Acheson and the Making of U.S. Foreign Policy*, ed. Douglas Brinkley. New York: St. Martin's Press, 1993.

———. *The Origins of the Cold War in the Near East: Great Power Conflict and Diplomacy in Iran, Turkey, and Greece.* Princeton, N.J.: Princeton University Press, 1980.

———. "Rings and Flanks: The Defense of the Middle East in the Early Cold War." In *The Cold War and Defense*, 111–36, ed. Keith Neilson and Ronald Haycock. New York: Praeger, 1990.

Kunz, Diane B., ed. *The Diplomacy of the Crucial Decade.* New York: Columbia University Press, 1994.

Ladjevardi, Habib. *Labor Unions and Autocracy in Iran.* Syracuse, N.Y.: Syracuse University Press, 1985.

Lambton, Ann K. "Land Reform and the Rural Cooperative Societies." In *Iran Faces the Seventies*, 5–43, ed. Ehsan Yarshater. New York: Praeger, 1971.

Larson, David L., ed. *The Cuban Crisis of 1962.* Boston: Houghton Mifflin, 1963.

Lawson, Fred. "The Iranian Crisis of 1945–46 and the Spiral Model of International Conflict." *International Journal of Middle East Studies* 21, no.3 (1989): 307–26.

Leffler, Melvyn. *A Preponderance of Power: National Security, the Truman Administration, and the Cold War.* Stanford, Calif.: Stanford University Press, 1992.

Lenczowski, George, ed. *Iran under the Pahlavis.* Stanford, Calif.: Hoover Institution Press, 1978.

———. *Russia and the West in Iran, 1918–1948.* Ithaca, N.Y.: Cornell University Press, 1949.

Lippmann, Walter. *The Coming Tests with Russia.* Boston: Little, Brown, 1961.

Lytle, Mark H. *The Origins of the Iranian-American Alliance, 1941–1953.* New York: Holmes & Meier, 1987.

Mark, Eduard. "Allied Reactions in Iran, 1941–47: The Origins of a Cold War Crisis." *Wisconsin Magazine of History* 59, no. 1 (Autumn 1975): 51–63.

Marlowe, John. *Iran*. London: Pall Mall Press, 1963.
McFarland, Stephen. "A Peripheral View of the Origins of the Cold War: The Crises in Iran, 1941–1947." *Diplomatic History* 4, no. 4 (Fall 1980): 333–51.
McGhee, George. *Envoy to the Middle World: Adventures in Diplomacy*. New York: Harper & Row, 1983.
Milani, Mohsen M. *The Making of Iran's Islamic Revolution*. Boulder, Colo.: West View Press, 1988.
Millspaugh, Arthur C. *Americans in Persia*. Washington, D.C.: Brookings Institution, 1946.
Mottahedeh, Roy P. "Iran's Foreign Devils." *Foreign Policy* 38 (Spring 1980): 19–34.
Nash, Philip. *The Other Missiles of October*. Chapel Hill: University of North Carolina Press, 1997.
Neilson, Keith, and Ronald Haycock, eds. *The Cold War and Defense*. New York: Praeger, 1990.
Nollau, Gunther and Hans Wiehe. *Russia's South Flank: Operations in Iran, Turkey, and Afghanistan*. New York: Praeger, 1963.
Oney, Earnest. "The Eyes and Ears of the Shah." *The Intelligence Quarterly* 1, no. 4 (February 1986): 1–3.
Pahlavi, Ashraf. *Faces in a Mirror: Memoirs from Exile*. Englewood Cliffs, N.J.: Prentice-Hall, 1980.
Pahlavi, Muhammad Reza. *Answer to History*. New York: Stein & Day, 1980.
———. *Mission for My Country*. New York: McGraw-Hill, 1961.
———. *The White Revolution*. Tehran: Imperial Pahlavi Library, 1967.
Pfau, Richard. "Containment in Iran, 1946: The Shift to an Active Policy." *Diplomatic History* 1, no. 4 (Fall 1977): 359–72.
Pfau, Steven. "The Legal Status of American Forces in Iran." *Middle East Journal* 28, no.2 (Spring 1974).
Plan Organization of Iran. *Review of the Second Seven-Year Program*. Tehran: Economic Bureau, 1960.
———. *The Second Seven-Year Development Plan of Iran*. Tehran: Public Relations Bureau, 1335/1956.
Plate, Thomas. *Secret Police: The Inside Story of a Network of Terror*. New York: Doubleday and Co., 1981.
Pollack, Kenneth. *The Persian Puzzle: The Conflict Between Iran and America*. New York: Random House, 2004.
Powers, Francis Gary. *Operation Overflight*. New York: Holt, 1970.
Raine, Fernande. "The Iranian Crisis of 1946 and the Origins of the Cold War." In *The Origins of the Cold War: An International History*, 93–110, eds. Melvyn Leffler and David Painter. Oxon, U.K.: Routledge, 2005.
———. "Stalin and the Creation of the Azerbaijan Democratic Party in Iran, 1945." *Cold War History* 2, no. 1 (October 2001): 1–38.
Ramazani, Rouhollah K. "The Autonomous Republic of Azerbaijan and the Kurdish People's Republic: Their Rise and Fall." In *The Anatomy of Communist Takeovers*, 448–74, ed. Thomas Hammond. New Haven: Yale University Press, 1975.

———. *The Foreign Policy of Iran, 1500–1941.* Charlottesville: University of Virginia Press, 1966.
———. Iran's Changing Foreign Policy: A Preliminary Discussion," *The Middle East Journal* 24, no. 4 (Autumn 1970): 421–37.
———. *Iran's Foreign Policy, 1941–1973.* Charlottesville: University of Virginia Press, 1975.
———."Iran's White Revolution: A Study in Political development," *International Journal of Middle East Studies* 5 (1974): 124–39.
Reardon, Steve L. "Frustrating the Kremlin: Acheson and NSC 68." In *Dean Acheson and the Making of U.S. Foreign Policy,* 159–72, ed. Douglas Brinkley. New York: St. Martin's Press, 1993.
Ricks, Thomas M. "U.S. Military Missions to Iran, 1943–1978: The Political Economy of Military Assistance." *Iranian Studies* 12 (Summer 1979): 163–94.
Roosevelt, Archie. "The Kurdish Republic of Mahabad." *The Middle East Journal* 1, no. 3 (July 1947): 247–69.
Roosevelt, Kermit. *Countercoup: The Struggle for the Control of Iran.* New York: McGraw-Hill, 1979.
Rossow, Robert. "The Battle of Azerbaijan." *Middle East Journal* 10 (Winter 1956): 17–32.
Rubin, Barry. *Paved with Good Intentions: The American Experience and Iran.* New York: Oxford University Press, 1980.
Schlesinger, Arthur. *One Thousand Days.* London: André Deutsch, 1965.
Shuster, Morgan. *The Strangling of Persia.* Washington, D.C.: Mage, 1987.
Shwadran, Benjamin. *The Middle East, Oil, and the Great Powers.* New York: Praeger, 1955.
Sick,Gary. *All Fall Down: America's Tragic Encounter with Iran.* New York: Random House, 1985.
Sicker, Martin. *The Bear and the Lion: Soviet Imperialism in Iran.* New York: Praeger, 1988.
Slavin, Barbara. *Bitter Friends, Bosom Enemies: Iran, the United States, and the Twisted Path to Confrontation.* New York: St. Martin's Press, 2007.
Spalding, Elizabeth. *The First Cold Warrior: Harry Truman, Containment, and the Remaking of Liberal Internationalism.* Lexington, Ky.: University Press of Kentucky, 2006.
Spanier, John W. *American Foreign Policy Since World War II.* New York: Praeger, 1960.
Stocking, George. *Middle East Oil: A Study in Political and Economic Controversy.* Nashville, Tenn.: Vanderbilt University Press, 1970.
Taylor, A. J. P. *Struggle for Mastery in Europe.* Oxford: Clarendon Press, 1954.
Truman, Harry S. *Memoirs: 1945: Year of Decisions.* Vol. *1.* New York: Signet, 1955.
———. *Memoirs: Years of Trial and Hope, 1946–52.* Vol. 2. New York: Signet, 1956.
Ullman, Richard H. *Anglo-Soviet Relations, 1917–1921: The Anglo-Soviet Accord.* Vol. 3. Princeton, N.J.: Princeton University Press, 1973.
——— *Anglo-Soviet Relations, 1917–1921: Intervention and the War.* Vol. 1. Princeton, N.J.: Princeton University Press, 1961.

Upton, John M. *The History of Modern Iran: An Interpretation.* Cambridge, Mass: Harvard University Press, 1960.
Walton, Richard J. *Cold War and Counterrevolution.* New York: Viking Press, 1972.
Wilber, Donald N. *Iran, Past and Present.* Princeton: Princeton University Press, 1976.
Woodhouse, Christopher M. *Something Ventured.* London: Granada, 1982.
Yaniv, Avner. *Deterrence Without the Bomb: The Politics of Israeli Strategy.* Lexington, Mass.: D. C. Heath, 1987.
Yapp, Malcolm. *The Making of the Modern Near East, 1792–1923.* New York: Longman, 1987.
Yarshater, Ehsan, ed. *Iran Faces the Seventies.* New York: Praeger, 1971.
Yegorova, Natalia. *The Iranian Crisis of 1945–46: A View from the Russian Archives*, working paper no. 15, Woodrow Wilson International Center for Scholars, www.wilsoncenter.org/topics/pubs/ACFB51.pdf, accessed September 7, 2007.
Yeselson, Abraham. *United States-Persian Diplomatic Relations, 1883–1921.* New Brunswick, N.J.: Rutgers University Press, 1956.
Zabih, Sepehr. *The Communist Movement in Iran.* Berkeley: University of California Press, 1966.
———. *The Mossadegh Era.* Chicago: Lake View Press, 1982.
Zonis, Marvin. *The Political Elite of Iran.* Princeton, N.J.: Princeton University Press, 1971.

Index

Note: page numbers followed by n refer to notes, with note number.

Abadan oil refinery, Iranian seizure of, 73
Acheson, Dean: and oil nationalization crisis, 70, 71, 72–73, 74, 80; and Shah's state visit, 52; and U.S. aid, 43–44, 51
Adalat Committee, 29
Afghanistan: and Anglo-Russian Convention of 1907, 10; as threat to Iran, 138, 139, 145–46
Afshartus, Mahmud, 83
Ahmad Shah, 12
AIOC. *See* Anglo-Iranian Oil Company
airspace, Iranian, Soviet violations of, 124–25
Ala, Hussein: as ambassador to U.S., 33, 35, 36; appointment as Prime Minister, 102; on Eisenhower Doctrine, 109, 110; intelligence provided to U.S., 82; problems faced by, 66–67; resignation of, 110; on Soviet diplomacy, 102; at UN, 38, 39; U.S. aid requests, 52
Alam, Assadollah: as ally of Shah, 165; appointment as Prime Minister, 165, 166; and Mardom Party, 110–11; meeting with Johnson (Lyndon), 167; National Front and, 171; opposition to, 170–71, 172
Alavi-Kia, Hasan, 107, 112, 149
Allen, George V.: appointment as ambassador, 39; assessments of Qavam, 39, 41; assurances of U.S. support, 41–42; on GENMISH, 49; and Iranian aid requests, 40, 42, 44; and Iranian Crisis of 1945–46, 40–41; on Iranian sovereignty, 45; and Majlis elections of 1946–47, 42–43; on Shah's constitutional reforms, 48
Amini, Ali: as ambassador to U.S., 104, 114, 115; appointment as Prime Minister, 149, 188; and Iranian economy, 163, 164–65; and land reform, 155; on military spending, 156–57; opposition to, 150–51, 152, 155, 156; problems faced by, 163, 165–66, 188; reform efforts, 149, 151; relationship with Shah, 150, 154, 164, 165–66; requests for U.S. aid, 164; resignation of, 165; response to unrest, 152, 155, 156; Shah's concessions to, 149; Soviet propaganda against, 150–51, 152,

207

163; U.S. evaluations of, 150–51, 152, 155–56; U.S. support for, 150, 154, 160, 165; and White Revolution, 154–55; and World Bank loan, 106
Amory, Robert, 141
Anglo-Iranian Oil Company (AIOC): agreement of 1933, 63, 64; compensation for oil nationalization, 99; and financing of economic development, 45; history of, 63; and International Oil Consortium, 99; offers of aid to Iran, 65; renegotiation of oil agreement, 51, 64, 65; Soviet-inspired worker unrest, 39–40; Supplemental Agreement of 1949, 51, 53, 65
Anglo-Persian Oil Company (APOC), 63
Anglo-Russian Convention of 1907, 10–11
Anglo-Soviet occupation of Iran, vi; and Cold War in Iran, 9; Iranian response, 9, 14, 15; purpose of, 9, 13, 185; Soviet withdrawal, 28, 36, 37–38, 187; and U.S. involvement in Iran, 16–18; withdrawal agreement and negotiations, 15, 20–22, 35
Ansari, Massud, 126
antitrust law, and International Oil Consortium, 98
APOC. *See* Anglo-Persian Oil Company
Aqelvi, Farajollah, 49
Arabian-American Oil Company (Aramco), 50/50 oil agreement with Saudi Arabia, 62, 65, 69, 189
Arab League, and Baghdad Pact, 101
Aramco. *See* Arabian-American Oil Company
Arani, Taqi, 14
Ardalan, Ali Qoli, 73, 117, 124
Arfa, Hasan, 20, 34, 39
ARMISH. *See* United States Mission to the Iranian Army

Arsanjani, Hasan, 77, 115, 149, 155, 157, 166
article VI. *See* Russo-Persian Treaty of 1921
Atlantic Charter, Truman and, 20
Attlee, Clement, 71, 72
Autonomous Republic of Azerbaijan, 33
Azerbaijan: return to Iranian control, 43; Soviet control of (*see* Iranian Crisis of 1945–46)
Azeris: causes of revolt, 28, 29; recognition of National Assembly of Azerbaijan, 39; Soviet support of, 1–2, 22, 28, 29, 30, 32. *See also* Democratic Party of Azerbaijan; Iranian Crisis of 1945–46
Azhir (Alarm), 30

Baghdad Pact: administrative structure, 103; creation of, 100–102; Iran and, 102–3, 113, 116, 187; Iraqi withdrawal from, 103, 118; Second Baghdad Pact Conference, 104; Soviet reaction to, 103, 105, 186; U.S. and, 103. *See also* Central Treaty Organization (CENTO)
Bakhtiar, Shahpur, 152
Bakhtiar, Timur, 99, 107, 145, 149
Bakhtiari tribal leaders, opposition to Musaddiq, 80, 82
balance-of-trade payments, 115, 142, 147
Baqai, Mozaffar, 83
Battle Act. *See* Mutual Security Act
Bayar, Celâl, 102–3
Bayat, Morteza Qoli, 19, 21
Beckett, Sir Eric, 77
Behbahani, Muhammad, 156
Berlin blockade, 51
Berlin Wall, 152
Berry, Lampton, 114
Bevin, Ernest, 34
bilateral agreements, U.S.: with Turkey and Pakistan, 124. *See also* U.S.-Iranian bilateral agreement

Black, Eugene, 120
BMEO. *See* British Middle East Office
border disputes and agreements with Soviet Union, 83, 85, 100, 102, 110–11, 172–73
Borujerdi, Hussein, 139
Bowles, Chester, 156–57
Brezhnev, Leonid, 172–73
British Foreign Office: concerns about Mansur, 54; and oil nationalization crisis, 69; and overthrow of Musaddiq, 81
British influence in Iran: on Majlis, 21; Reza Shah's resistance to, 12; U.S. as counterbalance to, 15; U.S. response to, 18. *See also* Anglo-Soviet occupation of Iran
British influence in Iraq, decline of, 118
British Middle East Office (BMEO), 45
Brownell, Herbert, 98
budget deficits: under Alam, 166; under Amini, 152, 163, 165; under Eqbal, 111, 113; impact of, 116, 120; under Musaddiq, 76, 79; under Qavam, 77; Shah's lack of interest in, 165; U.S. aid and, 94, 104, 108, 109, 113, 187; U.S. policy on, 166–67
Bullard, Sir Reader, 14, 17, 34
Bundy, McGeorge, 163
Bureau of Near Eastern Affairs, report of Iran policy, 52–53
Byrnes, James, 31, 33, 35, 37, 42

Cabell, Charles, 139
Caspian Fishery, Soviet designs on, 81
Cassady, John, 103
censorship in Iran, 150
CENTO. *See* Central Treaty Organization
Central Intelligence Agency (CIA): concerns about Tudeh Party, 82; and creation of SAVAK, 78, 106; Eisenhower administration reliance on, 80; and overthrow of Musaddiq, 63, 80, 81, 83, 85, 86, 187; report on Amini government, 150–51; report on Iran's prospects, 119
Central Treaty Organization (CENTO): and Iranian Army requirements, 161; and Iranian security, 148; origin of, 103, 118; Soviet threats against, 140; and U-2 incident, 140; U.S. support for, 126, 127
Chamoun, Camille, 117
Chapin, Selden: appointment as ambassador, 102; and Baghdad Pact, 102, 103; replacement of, 116; report on Shah's visit to Soviet Union, 105; and U.S. aid, 113, 115
China, communist takeover of, 53
Churchill, Winston: as First Lord of Admiralty, 63; on Iranian oil concessions, 20; and oil nationalization crisis, 74, 76, 79; on Soviet occupation of Iran, 22; and Tehran Conference, 18; on U.S. aid to Iran, 76
CIA. *See* Central Intelligence Agency
clergy: anti-Shah activism, 172, 173, 188; and Cold War, 190; concern about anti-Shah demonstrations, 156; and land reform, 139, 155; opposition to Local Council Elections bill, 170–71; opposition to White Revolution, 172
Cold War, Iran's strategic importance in, 108
Cold War, origins of: Iran as case study in, 2; scholarly disagreement on, 1
Cold War in Iran: ending of, 169, 190; origins of, vi, 1–2, 190
communist parties, Persian ban on, 14. *See also* Tudeh Party
communist threat: and Cold War, 1; and Democratic Party of Iran, 39; fall of China, 53; fall of Czechoslovakia, 51; National Security Council assessment of, 139; SAVAK as response to, 107; Shah's fear of, 95, 118, 120, 123, 137, 139, 147,

190. *See also* containment policy; Eisenhower Doctrine; Soviet expansionism; Truman Doctrine; U.S. military aid, Shah's requests for; U.S. policy in Iran
Compagnie Française des Pétroles, 97, 99
Connolly, Donald, 16
Constantinople Agreement of 1915, 10
Constituent Assembly (1949), 50
constitutional reform, by Shah, 48–50
containment policy: under Eisenhower, 63, 94, 187–88; under Kennedy, 137, 144–45, 188; origins of, 35; rearmament program, 53; under Truman, 55, 187. *See also* Eisenhower Doctrine; Truman Doctrine
Cuban Missile Crisis, 113, 126, 168–70
Czechoslovakia, fall to communists, 51

D'Arcy, William Knox, 63
Dean, Sir Patrick, 81
Defense Department, U.S.: and diplomatic immunity for U.S. military personnel, 158–60; Middle East defense strategy, 101; and Qum airfield construction, 112–13; report on U.S. military aid, 139
Democratic Party of Azerbaijan, 29–30, 31, 32, 33
Democratic Party of Iran, 39, 40
Democratic Party of Kurdistan, 29, 31, 33
Derakhshesh, Muhammad, 149
Development Loan Fund (DLF): and economic stabilization program, 142; loan requirements, 114; loans to Iran, 113, 115, 116–17, 121, 126, 144
Dez Dam, 138
Dillon, Douglas, 120
diplomatic immunity for U.S. military personnel, 158–60, 172, 188
DLF. *See* Development Loan Fund
Dobrynin, Anatoly, 169–70

Dooher, Gerald, 37–38, 54
Dreyfus, Louis, 16, 18
Dulles, Allen, 80, 81, 83, 121
Dulles, John Foster: appointment as Secretary of State, 80; on Baghdad Pact, 101; death of, 125; and IRBMs to NATO, 113; meeting with Muhammad Reza Shah, 117; and oil nationalization crisis, 96–97; and overthrow of Musaddiq, 83; and Qum airfield construction, 112; on Soviet-Iranian nonaggression pact, 121, 122; on Tudeh Party, 85; and U.S. aid, 98, 104, 116; visit to Iraq, 113–14
Dunya (World), 14

earthquake of September 1962, 167
economic reforms: Eisenhower administration insistence on, 94, 109, 141, 187–88; First Seven-Year Plan, 50, 105, 187; German assistance, 12–13; IMF stabilization measures, 115, 137, 161, 188; Kennedy administration insistence on, 137, 146, 147, 148, 151, 154, 157, 160, 161, 162, 167, 168, 169, 188; Majlis resistance to, 17, 79; necessity of, 108, 119; under Qavam, Ahmad, 44–45; Second Seven-Year Development Plan, 105, 108, 163; Third Economic Plan, 147, 152, 156, 158, 161, 164; Truman administration insistence on, 43, 187; U.S. assistance for, 12, 15, 17–18, 54, 112, 158, 164, 187. *See also* economic stabilization program; land reform; oil revenues, and funding of economic reforms
economic stabilization program, 138–45, 188; IMF measures, 115, 137, 161, 188; impact of, 162; measures taken, 142; U.S. assistance for, 141–42, 143–44
economy of Iran: destabilizing factors in, 116; deterioration of, 163–65;

National Security Council reports on, 165; and social unrest, 50
Eden, Anthony, 20, 22, 74, 80, 96
education reform, Shah's interest in, 154
Egypt: antimonarchy propaganda from, 95, 117, 142, 148; relations with Iran, 142; Shah on, 160
Eisenhower, Dwight D.: appearance before Majlis, 127; election of, 80; and IRBMs to NATO, 113; meetings with Shah, 117, 127; meeting with Eqbal, 126–27; meeting with Khrushchev, 126; and overthrow of Musaddiq, 86; at Paris Summit (1960), 141; and Shah's visit to Soviet Union, 105; on Soviet-Iranian nonaggression pact, 122; support for Iran, 126–27; support of Shah, 125–26; and U.S. aid, 83, 84, 104, 125, 127, 138, 139; visit to Iran, 127
Eisenhower administration: aid, 94, 96, 98, 99–100, 104, 109, 111, 137, 187; insistence on economic reforms, 94, 109, 141, 187–88; Iran policy, 94, 187–88; and oil nationalization crisis, 62–63, 187; overthrow of Musaddiq, 63; reliance on CIA, 80
Eisenhower Doctrine, 95, 107, 126; House Joint Resolution 117 addendum, 109; Iranian reaction to, 107–8, 110
election reform, Shah's support of, 143
Entesar, Masoud, 140
Entezam, Nasrollah, 103
Eqbal, Manuchehr: anticorruption campaign, 119; appointment as Prime Minister, 110; and land reform, 127, 138; meeting with Eisenhower, 126–27; political reforms, 110, 111, 114; problems faced by, 111; requests for U.S. aid, 113; resignation of, 143
Ertegun, Mehmet, 37
Exim Bank. *See* Export-Import Bank

Export-Import Bank: and economic stabilization program, 142; loan requirements, 42, 43, 114; loans to Iran, 41, 54, 76, 106, 113, 144

Fardust, Hussein, 150
Farmanfarmayan, Khodadad, 112, 151
Fedaiyan Islam, 66, 67–68
Firqah-i-Dimukrat-i Azerbaijan. *See* Democratic Party of Azerbaijan
First Seven-Year Plan, 50, 105, 187
Firuz, Mozafar, 40
Five Year Military Program, 169, 188
Flag of Islam. *See* Parcham-i Islam
FOA. *See* U.S. Foreign Operations Administration
Food for Peace, 145
Ford Foundation, 112
Foreign Assistance Act of 1961, 146
Fulbright program, 53
Furughi, Muhammad Ali, 14, 15

Garner, Robert, 74–75
Gaud, William, 160, 161
Gellman, Waldemar, 103
GENMISH. *See* United States Mission to the Iranian Gendarmerie
Germany: aid to Persia, 13; Anglo-Russian fear of, 10–11, 13–14; relations with Iran pre-World War II, v, 12–13
Gilan Soviet Republic, 11–12, 185
gold, Iranian, Soviet return of, 54, 83, 85, 100, 102
Gorbachev, Mikhail, and Soviet-Iranian relations, 191
Grady, Henry F., 54, 69, 70, 72, 73
Great Britain: aid to Turkey and Greece, 43, 188–89; and Baghdad Pact, 102, 104, 189; diplomatic relations with Iran, 80, 96–97; exploitation of Qajar monarchy, 10; fear of German influence, 10–11, 13–14; history of involvement in Persia/Iran, 10–11, 184–85, 188–89; influence in Iraq,

118; and Khuzistan labor unrest, 40; oil interests in Iran, v, 9, 15, 22, 44, 184–85 (*see also* Anglo-Iranian Oil Company); overthrow of Musaddiq, 63, 80–81, 84, 85; response to oil nationalization crisis, 62, 66–68, 69–70, 72–74, 79–81, 189; on Shah's constitutional reforms, 48, 49; support of Zahedi, 96; treaty of alliance with Iran (1942), 15; and Treaty of Brussels, 51; in World War II, v, 9, 15. *See also* Anglo-Soviet occupation of Iran; *entries under* British
The Great Game, 10
Greece: and NATO, 51, 100; U.S. aid to, 43–44, 52, 100, 189
Gromyko, Andrei, 36, 37, 140, 170
Gulf Oil, 97, 99

Hakimi, Ibrahim: appointments as Prime Minister, 21, 46; and GENMISH, 49; and Iranian Crisis of 1945–46, 33; resignation, 34
Hamilton, Fowler, 158
Harriman, Averell: as ambassador to Soviet Union, 32; on Iranian Progress, 147; and oil nationalization crisis, 72, 73; Shah's meeting with, 162; visit to Iran, 146
Harvard University, economic advisors from, 112, 164
Hazir, Abdul Hussein, 47
Heald, Sir Lionel, 77
Hedayat, Khosrow, 124, 144
Hekmat, Ali Asghar, 120, 124
Henderson, Loy: and aid to Turkey and Greece, 43–44; appointment as ambassador, 73; biography, 73; Eisenhower administration and, 80; and oil nationalization crisis, 79; and overthrow of Musaddiq, 83, 86, 98; replacement of, 102; on Tudeh Party, 78, 82; and U.S. aid, 75, 76, 77, 82–83, 96, 98
Herter, Christian, 125, 126, 139

Hizb-i Mardom. *See* Mardom Party
Hizb-i Milliyun. *See* Milliyun Party
Hizb-i Tudeh. *See* Tudeh Party
Holmes, Julius: appointment as ambassador, 151; and economic deterioration in Iran, 164–65; and humanitarian aid, 167; on Iranian budget deficits, 166; and Shah's state visit, 159; and threats to Amini government, 154, 163; and U.S. aid, 157–58, 169
Hoover, Herbert, Jr., 96
hostage crisis, 191
House Joint Resolution 117, 109
humanitarian aid, 167
Hurley, Patrick, 18

IBRD. *See* International Bank for Reconstruction and Development
Ibtihaj, Abul Hasan: as director of Iranian National Bank, 42, 49; loan requests, 121; as Plan Organization director, 102, 106, 112, 115, 120, 123–24; on U.S. role in Iran, 153
ICA. *See* International Cooperation Administration
ICBMs. *See* Intercontinental Ballistic Missiles
IMF. *See* International Monetary Fund
Independent National Policy, 167–68, 190
India, and Baghdad Pact, 104
Intercontinental Ballistic Missiles (ICBMs): missile gap, 144; Soviet testing of, 113, 126
Intermediate Range Ballistic Missiles (IRBMs), in Turkey, 113, 126, 138, 168, 169, 170
International Bank for Reconstruction and Development (IBRD), 74
International Cooperation Administration (ICA), 111, 112–13
International Court of Justice, oil nationalization crisis and, 68, 71, 74, 77, 78, 79–80

International Monetary Fund (IMF): and economic stabilization program, 142; loans to Iraq, 144; stabilization measures, 115, 137, 161, 188
International Oil Consortium, 97–99
International Oil Consortium Agreement of 1954, 99
Iranian-American Cultural Society, 45
Iranian Army: Joint Chiefs of Staff evaluations of, 161, 162–63; purging of Tudeh Party members from, 99; Shah's views on size of, 162, 163, 165 (*see also* U.S. military aid, Shah's requests for); U.S. efforts to reduce, 158, 161–63; U.S. policy on, 98, 100, 116, 118, 151, 158, 161; U.S. training, 17
Iranian Crisis of 1945–46, 28–55; Iranian complaint to UN, 2, 21, 28, 34, 36–38, 186; Iranian response, 32, 33; and origin of Cold War, vi, 1–2, 186; origins of, 22, 28–32, 183–84, 185, 186; scholarly views on, 2–3, 183–84; settlement of, 34–46; Soviet blocking of Iranian forces, 1–2, 28, 32, 33; Soviet goals, 1, 31; Soviet justifications, 31–35; Soviet negotiations, 36–37; Soviet retaliation for Security Council defeat, 39–40; Soviet withdrawal, 28, 36, 37–38, 187; U.S. response, 2, 21, 31, 32, 33, 35–36, 38, 41, 187
Iranian National Oil Company, 71
Iranian nuclear program: Russian views on, v, 191; scholarly analysis of, 3; U.S. views on, v, 191
Iranian-Soviet aviation company, Soviet pressure for, 41
Iran Party, 171
Iran Task Force, 147, 149–50, 152, 153, 155–56
Iran Teachers Association, 149
Iraq: antimonarchy propaganda from, 95; and Baghdad Pact, 101–2, 103, 104, 118; relations with Iran, 160; as threat to Iran, 119, 127, 138, 139, 145–46
Iraqi Revolution, 118–19
IRBMs. *See* Intermediate Range Ballistic Missiles
Iskandari, Iraj, 40, 41
Islamic Republic: establishment of, 173, 190; relations with U.S., 173, 190–91
Islamic Revolution of 1979, 2–3, 173, 188, 190
Israel, Iranian support for, 142
Ittila'at (newspaper), 42

Jangali movement, 11, 185
Jernegan, John D., 47, 100
Johnson, Lyndon B., 144, 167
Joint Chiefs of Staff, U.S.: evaluation of Iranian Army, 161, 162–63; report on military aid, 116
Joint U.S.-Iranian Economic and Social Development Commission, 81

Kashani, Abul Qassim, 65, 77–78, 81, 83
Kavtaradze, Sergei, 19
Kennan, George, 30–31, 35
Kennedy, John F.: and Cuban Missile Crisis, 170; election of, 137, 144; on Iranian budget deficits, 166–67; meetings with Shah, 160–62; support for Iran, 148, 151; and U.S. aid, 159, 165; and Vienna Conference (1961), 151; on White Revolution, 172
Kennedy, Robert, 169–70
Kennedy administration: aid, 137, 146–47, 155, 157, 161, 166, 167, 168; and Cuban Missile Crisis, 170; foreign policy, 144–45; humanitarian aid, 167; insistence on reforms, 137, 146, 147, 148, 151, 154, 157, 160, 161, 162, 167, 168, 169, 188; Iran policy, 151, 171, 188; support of Amini, 150
Khomeini, Ruhollah: arrest of, 173; establishment of Islamic Republic, 173, 190; and Islamic Revolution of

1979, 190; rise to prominence, 170, 188
Khrushchev, Nikita: attacks on Shah's regime, 123; Berlin Wall, 152; and Cuban Missile Crisis, 169–70; at Paris Summit (1960), 141; relations with Iran, 126, 186; rise to premiership, 82; on stability of Shah's regime, 147–48, 151; state visit to U.S., 125–26; and U-2 incident, 140; and Vienna Conference (1961), 151
Khuzistan province, Soviet-inspired labor unrest in, 39–40
Kianuri, Nur al-Din, 19, 25n18, 99
Kirk, Alan, 54
Komala (Committee) party, 31
Kuchik Khan, Mirza, 11, 185
Kupal, Sadiq, 48
Kurdish People's Republic, 33
Kurds: causes of revolt, 28, 29; establishment of Kurdish People's Republic, 33; Shah's concerns about, 160; Soviet support of, 1–2, 22, 28, 29, 31. *See also* Democratic Party of Kurdistan; Iranian Crisis of 1945–46

land reform, 127, 137, 138–39, 155; clergy's exemption from, 139; opposition to, 138, 139, 155; political impact of, 139; Shah's interest in, 127, 138, 139, 154, 162; U.S. advice on, 157
Lapin, Sergei, 171
League of Nations, 63
Lebanon, unrest in, 117
Lend-Lease program in Iran, 17, 32
Lenin, Vladimir Ilyich, 11
Le Rougetel, Sir John, 48, 49, 53
Lippmann, Walter, 147–48
loans: from Development Loan Fund, 113, 115, 116–17, 121, 126, 144; efforts to obtain, 42, 43; from Export-Import Bank, 41, 54, 76, 106, 113, 144; Export-Import Bank loan requirements, 42, 43, 114; from International Monetary Fund, 144; Iranian requests for, 114, 151; Musaddiq requests for, 75; from U.S., 99–100, 102, 109, 150; from World Bank, 105–6, 108, 120, 125, 138; World Bank loan requirements, 42, 43
Local Council Elections bill, 170–71, 172

MAAG. *See* Military Assistance Advisory Group
Mahdavi, Parviz, 114
Majlis: Amini dissolving of, 149; and economic reform, 17, 50, 79; Eisenhower appearance before, 127; elections of 1946–47, 42–43; elections of 1960, 137, 143, 149; elections of 1961, 137, 145, 149; elections suspension by Shah (1961), 154; establishment of, 10; foreign influence, 21; Hakimi administration and, 21; and Iranian Crisis of 1945–46, 34; and land reform, 127, 138, 139; Musaddiq dissolution of, 85; and oil nationalization crisis, 66–68, 99; Pishihvari candidacy, 30; raising of Reza Khan to Shah, 12; and Shah's anticorruption campaign, 119; Shah's dissolution of (1953), 97–98; Shah's power to dissolve, 48, 50; and Soviet oil concession, 28, 45–46, 64, 65; special powers granted to Musaddiq, 78, 81; and Supplemental Agreement of 1949, 51, 53, 64; and World Bank loan, 106
Maki, Hussein, 78, 81
Maleki, Khalil, 30
Mansur, Hasan Ali, 14, 53, 54
Mao Zedong, 53
MAP. *See* Mutual Assistance Program
Mardom Party (People's Party): creation of, 110, 111, 114; and election of

1960, 143; and election of 1961, 145; platform, 110, 111
Marshall, George C., 43, 48, 49, 51
Mason, Edward S., 112, 163–64
Maximov, Mikhail, 31–32
McElroy, Neil, 144
McGhee, George, 52, 69, 70, 74
McNamara, Robert, 160–61, 170
Menderes, Adnan, 141
Meyer, Armin, 150, 154
MI6, overthrow of Musaddiq, 63, 80, 85, 187
Middle East Command, 100
Middle East defense, U.S. policy on, 100–101
Middleton, George, 79
Military Assistance Advisory Group (MAAG), 53
Military Mission for the Iranian Army (ARMISH). *See* United States Mission to the Iranian Army
Milliyun Party (Nationalist Party): creation of, 110, 111; and election of 1960, 143; and election of 1961, 145; platform, 110, 111
Millspaugh, Arthur, 12, 15, 17–18
Molotov, Vyacheslav, 20
Morris, Leland, 16
Morrison, Herbert, 67–68
Morrison-Knudsen International Engineering Company, 43, 48, 50
Moscow Conference of Foreign Ministers, 33
MOSSAD, and creation of SAVAK, 78, 106
Muhammad, Qazi, 31, 33
Muhammad Reza Shah: Amini and, 149, 150, 154, 164, 165–66; assassination attempt against, 50; assumption of Shahdom, 14; cost of military spending by, 116; dissolution of Majlis (1953), 97–98; on Iranian Crisis of 1945–46, 43; on Iraq, 160; on Iraqi Revolution, 118, 119; on Kurds, 160; and Musaddiq, 70, 82, 85–86, 98; and NATO, 51; obsession with military budget, 162, 163, 165, 190 (*see also* U.S. military aid, Shah's requests for); and oil nationalization crisis, 70; overthrow of, 173; planned departure from Iran (1953), 82; power to dissolve Majlis, 48, 50; Qarani plot against, 115; on Qum airfield, 115–16; and SAVAK, 78, 106–7; State Department assessment of regime, 53, 108; suspension of elections, 154; threats to regime of, 94–95, 139, 141; and withdrawal of Allied troops, 21; and World Bank loan, 106; on Zahedi, 102

Muhammad Reza Shah, and foreign policy: Baghdad Pact, 102–3, 104; fear of communism, 95, 118, 120, 123, 137, 139, 147, 190; Independent National Policy, 167–68, 190; international concerns of, 117, 160; Positive Nationalism policy, 95, 117, 190; support of Israel, 142; Third Power Strategy, 24n11, 185, 189; U-2 incident, 140

Muhammad Reza Shah, and reform: anticorruption campaign, 119; constitutional reform, 48–50; economic reform, 105, 109–10, 137, 142, 147, 151, 162; education reform, 154; election reform, 143; land reform, 127, 138, 139, 154, 162; political reform, 78, 95, 110; social reform, 154; and White Revolution, 137, 154, 171, 173, 188, 190

Muhammad Reza Shah, and Soviet Union: Soviet-Iranian nonaggression pact negotiations, 95, 121–23; Soviet propaganda attacks, 49, 78, 95, 122, 123, 124, 125, 163, 168, 186; state visits to Soviet Union, 102, 104–5, 109, 186

Muhammad Reza Shah, and United States: ARMISH, 49; disappointment with U.S. support, 51, 52, 95, 104, 113, 120, 137–38, 139, 147, 157–58, 162, 168, 186; GENMISH, 48–49; meetings with Eisenhower, 117, 127; meetings with Kennedy, 160–62; meeting with Johnson (Lyndon), 167; pro-Western stance, 94, 95, 189, 190; requests for U.S. aid, 40, 44, 47, 49, 52, 102, 104, 110, 112, 113, 114, 115, 116, 119, 122–23, 125, 127, 138, 139, 157, 160, 162, 165, 169; response to Truman Doctrine, 44; state visits to U.S., 50, 52, 100, 115, 117, 156–57, 158, 159–62; suspicions of U.S., 115; U.S. support for, 108, 116, 118, 142, 146–47, 156, 158, 167; and U.S. military aid, 75

Murray, Wallace, 21, 31, 32, 35–36, 37, 39

Musaddiq, Muhammad: appointments as Prime Minister, 67, 77, 78; arrest of opposition, 83, 86; biography, 64; dissolution of Majlis, 85; and land reform, 138; and National Front, 64; Negative Equilibrium policy, 62, 64, 74, 117, 189–90; and oil nationalization crisis, 62, 66, 67–68, 70, 71–75, 79–80, 187; opposition to, 78; overthrow of, 63, 80–81, 83–84, 85–86, 187, 188, 190; reform program, 79; resignation, 77; severing of diplomatic relations with Britain, 80; special powers granted to, 78, 81, 82; and Supplemental Agreement of 1949, 64; trial and sentencing of, 98; Tudeh Party and, 63, 67–68, 76, 78, 84, 86, 190; U.S. support for, 74; and U.S. aid, 75, 76, 81, 82–83, 84, 190; and wartime moratorium on oil concessions, 19–20, 64

Mutual Assistance Program (MAP), 52, 116, 117–18

Mutual Security Act of 1954 (Battle Act), 75, 76, 124

NAC. *See* North Atlantic Council
Nasser, Gamal Abdel, 117, 142, 160
Nassiri, Nimatollah, 85–86
National Assembly of Azerbaijan, Iranian recognition of, 39
National Bank of Iran, aid requests, 42
National Freedom Movement, 171
National Front: alliance with clergy, 172; antigovernment demonstrations, 151–52; anti-Shah activism, 78, 171, 172; and Cold War, 190; creation of, 64–65; and election of 1961, 145; and oil nationalization, 69; opposition to Qavam government, 77–78; popularity of, 143; SAVAK monitoring of, 106; support of Musaddiq, 81, 85; suppression of, 110, 156, 171; Tudeh Party and, 78, 82, 145; U.S. views on, 151, 155–56; and White Revolution, 155, 171
Nationalist Party. *See* Milliyun Party
National Revolt of July 21, 77–78
National Security Council, U.S.: on Amini, 166; on Iranian economy, 163–64, 165; NSC-68 report, 53; on Soviet-Iranian nonaggression pact, 121; on Soviet-Iranian relations, 142; on threats to Iranian regime, 139, 141; on U.S. aid, 166; on U.S. policy in Iran, 52, 68–69, 98, 108–9, 142, 149–50
NATO. *See* North Atlantic Treaty Organization
Negative Equilibrium policy, 62, 64, 74, 117, 189–90
Nehru, Jawaharlal, 104
New York Mirror (newspaper), 16
Nicholas II, Tsar of Russia, 11
Nixon, Richard M., 80, 97, 126, 144
North Atlantic Council (NAC), 113
North Atlantic Treaty Organization (NATO): establishment of, 51; Greece in, 51, 100; missile installation in Turkey, 113, 126, 138, 168, 169, 170; Turkey in, 51, 100

North Korea, aggression toward South Korea, 53
Nouri-Esfandiary, Fatollah, 46, 47
NSC-68 report, 53
nuclear program, Iranian, v, 3, 191
nuclear test ban treaty, Soviet offer of, 169

OCI. *See* Overseas Consultants Incorporated
oil, Iranian: consortium to sell, 97–99; in World War II, 13
oil concessions: British, 63 (*see also* Anglo-Iranian Oil Company); Majlis rejection of Soviet concession, 28, 45–46, 64, 65; Soviet pressure to obtain, vi, 9, 28, 35, 36, 37, 38, 41, 42, 43, 45–46, 64; U.S. acquisition of, 15, 16; U.S. interest in, 1, 9, 31, 185; U.S.-Soviet competition for, 19–20, 185; World War II moratorium on, 19–20, 64
oil nationalization crisis of 1951–1953, 2–3, 62–86; British blockade of Iranian oil, 73, 79–80; British response, 62, 66–68, 69–70, 72–74, 79–81, 189; financial consequences of, 105, 137; and International Court of Justice, 68, 71, 74, 77, 78, 79–80; Iranian demands, 72, 79–80; Majlis oil committee report, 66; nationalization, 66–68; origins of, 52, 55, 62–65, 69, 187; resolution of, 96–100; Security Council intervention, 73–74; Soviet response, 62, 69, 70; U.S. response, 62, 68–74, 79–81; World Bank mediation, 74–75, 76
oil revenues, and funding of economic reforms, 50–51, 55, 109, 120, 123, 147, 187. *See also* Oil Supplemental Agreement of 1949
Oil Supplemental Agreement of 1949, 51, 53, 54, 64
oil workers strikes, following nationalization of oil industry, 66–67

Operation AJAX, 81, 84, 85
Operation Boot, 80
Ottoman Empire, relations with Germany, 10
Overseas Consultants Incorporated (OCI), 45, 48, 50

Pahlavi, Ashraf, 85
Pahlavi Dynasty, establishment of, 12
Pakistan: and Baghdad Pact, 101, 103, 104; U.S. aid to, 159; U.S. bilateral agreement with, 124
Pakravan, Hasan, 107
Parcham-i Islam (Flag of Islam), 50
Peace Corps, 144–45
Pegov, Nikolai, 120–21, 126
People's Party. *See* Mardom Party
Persia: economic reform efforts, 12–13; and Gilan Soviet Republic, 11–12; origin of name, 22n1; and World War I, 10
Persian Gulf Command headquarters, 18
Persian Gulf Service Command, 16
Pierce, James, 49
Pishihvari, Ja'far, 29–30, 33, 41, 43
Plan Organization: creation of, 50; Economic Bureau, 112; funding of, 105–6, 115, 117, 121, 125, 138, 151; leadership change, 123–24; and oil revenues, 147; and Third Economic Plan, 157; U.S. support of, 164
Point IV program, 51, 53, 54, 55
political reforms: under Eqbal, 110, 111, 114; necessity of, 108, 119; Shah and, 78, 95, 110; U.S. encouragement of, 109. *See also* two-party system
political stabilization efforts, 148–67
Positive Nationalism policy, 95, 117, 190
postrevisionist views of Cold War origins in Iran, 2, 183–84
Potsdam Conference (1945), 22
Powers, Francis Gary, 140
Presbyterian missionaries in Iran, 15

press, Soviet, on Democratic Party of Azerbaijan, 30
pro-Western stance: Shah's adoption of, 94, 95, 189, 190; U.S. encouragement of, 101, 105
Prudhomme, Hector, 75
Putin, Vladimir, 191

Qajar monarchy: Anglo-Russian exploitation of, 10, 185; D'Arcy oil concession, 63; fall of, 12
Qarani, Vali, 115
Qasim, Abd al-Karim, 118, 119, 160
Qavam, Ahmad: Allen (George) assessment of, 39, 41; appeasement of Soviets, 34–35, 39, 42; appointments as Prime Minister, 16, 34, 45, 77; cabinet changes, 40, 41; and Democratic Party of Iran, 39; economic reforms, 44–45; and Iranian Crisis of 1945–46, 34–38, 39, 40–41; and Khuzistan labor unrest, 40; and Majlis elections of 1946–47, 42; and oil nationalization crisis, 77; opposition to, 77–78; political alignment, 16–17, 39; public opinion on, 41; requests for U.S. aid, 41; resignations, 18, 46, 78; and Soviet oil concession, 45–46
Qods-Nakhai, Hussein, 148
Qum airfield construction, 112–13, 115–16

Ra'd (newspaper), 12
Radford, Arthur W., 123
Radio Moscow, 125, 127
Ramsey, Fred, 47
Rashidian brothers, 80
Razmara, Ali: appointment as Prime Minister, 54; assassination of, 66; and nationalization of oil industry, 65, 66; reform program, 54; Soviet relations, 54; and Supplemental Agreement of 1949, 65; U.S. support for, 54

rearmament program, 53
reforms: under Amini, 149, 151; education reform, Shah's support of, 154; election reform, Shah's support of, 143; under Musaddiq, 79; under Razmara, 54. *See also* constitutional reform; economic reforms; political reforms; social reforms; White Revolution
Regime of the Soviet-Iranian Frontier and the Procedure for the Settlement of Frontier Disputes and Incidents (1957), 110–11
regional defense pact: U.S. recommendation of, 98, 100. *See also* Baghdad Pact
revisionist view of Cold War origins in Iran, 1–2, 183–84
revolution of 1906, 10
Reza Shah: abdication, 14; and adoption of Iran as name, 22n1; anticommunist activities, 29; assumption as Shah, 12; coup of 1921, 12; dissatisfaction with APOC agreement, 63; economic reforms and, 12–13, 15; and Gilan revolt, 11–12, 185; as prime minister, 12; response to Anglo-Soviet influence, 12, 13; Third Power Strategy, 12, 24n11, 184; Tudeh Party and, 14; U.S. media on, 16; and World War II, vi
Richards, James P., 109
Ridley, Clarence, 17
Rieber, Torkild, 75
Rockwell, Stuart W., 163, 164
Rolin, Henry, 77
Roosevelt, Franklin D., 18, 20
Roosevelt, Kermit, 81, 83–84, 85
Rossow, Robert, 35
Rountree, William, 117, 124
Royal Dutch-Shell, 97, 99
Rusk, Dean: on Amini government, 154; appointment as Secretary of State, 144; on economic deterioration in

Iran, 164; on Iranian defense, 145–46, 148, 161; meetings with Shah, 160; and U.S. aid, 151, 161, 164, 169
Russia: Anglo-Russian Convention of 1907, 10–11; Bolshevik Revolution, 11; Constantinople Agreement of 1915, 10; expansionist policy, 10; exploitation of Qajar monarchy, 10; fear of German influence, 10–11; history of interest in Iran, 184–85; in Iran, U.S. as counterbalance to, 15. *See also* Soviet Union
Russian Soviet Federated Socialist Republic, establishment of, 11
Russo-Persian Treaty of 1921, 12; Article VI, 12, 34, 35, 47, 70; and Baghdad Pact, 103; and CENTO, 140; Iranian cancellation of Article VI, 124; Soviet offers to cancel, 83, 121–23; and U.S. aid, 47; and U.S. involvement in Iran, 119–20

Sadchikov, Ivan, 36, 83
Sadr, Muhsin, 21
Saed, Muhammad, 19, 20, 51, 53
Said, Nuri al-, 118
Saleh, Allahyar, 171
Sanjabi, Karim, 65
Saudi Arabia: Aramco 50/50 oil agreement, 62, 65, 69, 189; U.S. oil concession, 1
SAVAK: creation of, 78, 106; discovery of procommunist Army officers, 139; functions, 106–7; public perception of, 107, 150; and Qarani plot, 115; Soviet propaganda against, 125; structure, 107; suppression of National Front, 171
Schwarzkopf, H. Norman, 17, 48, 49, 85
Seaboard Oil Company, 16
Second Baghdad Pact Conference, 104
Second Seven-Year Development Plan, 105, 108, 163
Seitz, John, 119
Semeonov, Vladimir, 121

Shahbaz II exercises, 140
Shah of Iran. *See* Muhammad Reza Shah; Reza Shah
Sharif-Emami, Ja'far, 143–44, 149
Shayesteh, Muhammad, 20
Shepherd, Sir Francis, and oil nationalization crisis, 53, 65, 66, 67, 69, 71, 73
Sheridan, Joseph P., 17, 18
Shuster, Morgan, 15
Sinclair Oil Company, 15
Skrine, Sir Claremont, 40
Smith, Walter Bedell, 37, 84
Smith-Mundt program, 53
social reforms: necessity of, 108; U.S. insistence on, 146, 147, 154, 167, 169; U.S. pressure for, 43
social unrest in Iraq, U.S. failure to address, 118
Socony-Vacuum Oil Co., 97, 99
Soviet expansionism: Berlin blockade, 51; as cause of Cold War, 1–2, 183; fall of Czechoslovakia, 51; Greece and Turkey, 44; and Iranian policy, 189; strategies, 30–31; Truman's response to, 20. *See also* containment policy
Soviet influence in Iran: on Majlis, 21; pressure to obtain oil concessions, vi, 9, 28, 35, 36, 37, 38, 41, 42, 43, 45–46, 64; Reza Shah's resistance to, 12; U.S. response to, 18. *See also* Anglo-Soviet occupation of Iran; Soviet-Iranian relations; Soviet propaganda attacks
Soviet interests in Iran: history of, 10; World War II and, v–vi, 9. *See also* Russo-Persian Treaty of 1921
Soviet-Iranian agreement of December 2, 1954, 102
Soviet-Iranian agreement of December 19, 1962, 171
Soviet-Iranian non-aggression pact: negotiation of, 120–23, 186; U.S. response, 121–22, 186

Soviet-Iranian oil company, Soviet pressure for, 28, 35, 36, 37, 38, 186
Soviet-Iranian relations: border disputes and agreements, 83, 85, 100, 102, 110–11, 172–73; Brezhnev visit, 172–73; deterioration of, 126; Gorbachev and, 191; improvements in, 54, 63, 83, 85, 105, 163, 171, 186–87, 190; Iranian nuclear program and, v, 191; Iranian pledge not to allow foreign missile bases, 137, 141, 142, 167–70, 190; negotiations for nonaggression pact, 120–23, 186; Putin and, 191; Shah's Independent National Policy and, 168; U.S.-Iranian bilateral agreement and, 119, 121, 122–23, 168. *See also* Soviet influence in Iran
Soviet military: airspace intrusions, 124–25; blocking of Iranian forces in Iranian Crisis, 1–2, 28, 32, 33; prevention of Iranian action in Mazandaran, 20
Soviet oil concession: Majlis rejection of, 28, 45–46, 64, 65; Soviet pressure to obtain, vi, 9, 28, 35, 36, 37, 38, 41, 42, 43, 45–46, 64; U.S.-Soviet competition for, 19–20, 185
Soviet policy in Iran, State Department on, 53
Soviet propaganda attacks: after Iranian rejection of non-aggression pact, 122–26, 168, 186; after Iranian rejection of oil concession, 28, 46–48; against Amini administration, 150–51, 152, 163; Iranian response, 95, 124, 186; against Musaddiq administration, 62; against Saed administration, 19; against Shah, 49, 78, 95, 122, 123, 124, 125, 163, 168, 186; U.S. reaction to, 126–27; against U.S. involvement, 46, 49, 119–20, 122, 123, 124, 127, 186
Soviet Union: border disputes and agreements, 83, 85, 100, 102, 110–11, 172–73; and Caspian Fishery, 81; claims on Turkish territory, 33, 35, 37; economic influence on Persia, 13; establishment of, 11; fear of German influence, 13–14; fomenting of revolt in Iran, 149–52; Gilan invasion of 1920, 11; and Gilan Soviet Republic, 11–12, 185; history of involvement in Persia, 10–13; and Majlis elections of 1946–47, 42–43; military insecurity of, 169; nonaggression pact negotiations, 95; reaction to Baghdad Pact, 103; resentment of U.S. involvement in Iran, 15, 19, 32, 119, 121, 122–23, 168; response to oil nationalization crisis, 62, 69, 70; response to Shah's U.S. visit, 163; support of Tudeh Party, 69, 78; testing of ICBMs, 113; treaty of alliance with Iran (1942), 15; treaty right to intervene in Iran, 12, 34; in World War II, v–vi, 9. *See also* Anglo-Soviet occupation of Iran; Iranian Crisis of 1945–46; *entries under* Soviet
Sputnik, U.S. reaction to, 113, 126
Stalin, Joseph: death of, 82; and Iranian Crisis of 1945–46, 22, 33–35, 37, 186; and Tehran Conference, 18
Standard Oil of California, 97, 99
Standard Oil of New Jersey, 19, 97, 99
Standard-Vacuum Oil, 19
State Department, U.S.: on Amini, 163; and diplomatic immunity for U.S. military personnel, 160; and economic stabilization program, 142; and Iranian Crisis of 1945–46, 32, 35; on Iranian role in Middle East defense, 101; on Iran's prospects, 108, 119; on Mansur, 54; on Muhammad Reza Shah's regime, 53; NSC-68 report, 53; and oil nationalization crisis, 69, 72; and overthrow of Musaddiq, 80, 83–84; and Shah's constitutional reforms,

Index

48, 49; on Soviet propaganda, 125; on Tabataba'i, 67; Truman's reliance on, 21, 80; on U.S. aid, 112, 116, 117–18, 158; on U.S. policy, 40, 41–42, 50, 52–53, 108, 151
Stettinius, Edward, 20, 36, 37, 38
Stokes, Richard, 72
students: anti-British demonstrations, 97; antigovernment demonstrations, 145, 148, 156; communist influence on, 148; and National Front, 65, 143, 156; and Plan Organization, 112
Suhaili, Ali, 14, 15, 16, 18, 19
Supplemental Agreement of 1949, 51, 53, 54, 64, 65

Tabataba'i, Sayyid Zia al-Din, 12, 67
Talbot, Philip, and Iranian defense, 148
Taqizadeh, Sayyid Hasan, 34
Tass, anti-Shah propaganda, 123
Taylor, Maxwell, 159
teachers strike, 148–49
technical aid: administration of, 111; in Eisenhower administration, 96, 100, 109, 111; in Kennedy administration, 155; in Truman administration, 51, 54–55, 75, 76, 81; U.S. House report on, 108
Tehran Conference (1943), 18–19
Tehran Declaration of 1943, 20, 32–33
Texas Oil, 97, 99
Thant, U, 170
Third Economic Development Plan, 147, 152, 156, 158, 161, 164
Third Power Strategy, 12, 24n11, 184, 185, 189
Thornburg, Max, 48
Tibet, and Anglo-Russian Convention of 1907, 10
Timmerman, Stephen, 17
trade: trade deficits, 115, 142, 147; US-Iranian trade agreement of 1943, 142
traditionalist view of Cold War origins in Iran, 1, 183

Trans-Iranian Railway, 13
Treaty of Brussels (1948), 51
Tripartite Declaration of 1943, 18
Tripartite Treaty of 1942, 15, 21, 34, 35
Trotsky, Leon, 11
Truman, Harry S.: assumption to presidency, 20; and Atlantic Charter, 20; and attempted assassination of Shah, 50; and Iranian Crisis of 1945–46, 33, 38; and oil nationalization crisis, 70, 71–72, 74, 76, 79, 187; rearmament program, 53; and Shah's state visit, 52
Truman administration: aid, 51, 54–55, 75, 76, 81, 187; containment policy, 55, 187; insistence on economic reforms, 43, 187; and Iranian Crisis of 1945–46, 2, 21, 186; Iran policy, 20–21, 31, 36; reliance on State Department, 21, 80; response to oil nationalization crisis, 62; stance toward Soviet Union, 35; and U.S. withdrawal from Iran after World War II, 22
Truman Doctrine, 43–44
Tudeh Party: anti-American protests, 78, 84–85; antigovernment protests, 20, 156; anti-Shah activism, 78, 86, 94, 114, 143, 152–53; attempted assassination of Shah, 50; and Cold War, 190; criticism of U.S. aid, 84–85; Democratic Party of Azerbaijan and, 30; dissolution of, 153; in exile, 111, 114, 139, 143, 152–53; government crackdowns on, 20, 29, 50, 96, 99; and Iranian Crisis of 1945–46, 184; labor actions, 39–40; Musaddiq and, 63, 67–68, 76, 78, 84, 86, 190; National Front and, 78, 82, 145; and National Revolt of July 21, 78; and oil nationalization crisis, 62, 72; opposition to Qavam government, 77–78; origin of, 14; outlawing of, 50; party congresses, 14; Pishihvari and, 29–30;

222   Index

program and goals, 14, 40; Qavam
  cabinet positions, 40, 41; SAVAK
  monitoring of, 106; Soviet support
  of, 69, 78; State Department on, 53;
  support of Soviet Union, 19, 29, 39,
  82; suppression of, 110, 111; U.S.
  concerns about, 36, 78, 82, 85, 187
Turkey: and Baghdad Pact, 101–2, 104;
  and NATO, 51, 100; NATO missiles
  in, 113, 126, 138, 168, 169, 170;
  overthrow of Menderes government,
  141; Soviet claims on Turkish
  territories, 33, 35, 37; U.S. aid to,
  43–44, 52, 100, 159, 189; U.S.
  bilateral agreement with, 124; U.S.
  support for, 37
two-party system: introduction of, 95,
  110–11, 114, 188; Shah on, 110

U-2 flights over Cuba, 170
U-2 incident, 126, 140–41
United Nations: Iranian complaint
  against Soviets in Azerbaijan, 2, 21,
  28, 34, 36–38, 186; Iranian protest of
  Soviet propaganda, 124, 125; and oil
  nationalization crisis, 73–74; Soviet
  retaliation for Iranian complaint,
  39–40
United States (U.S.): and Baghdad Pact,
  104, 118; economic interests in Iran,
  1–2, 183; history of involvement
  in Iran, 15–18; oil concession in
  Iran, 1, 9, 15, 16, 19–20, 31, 185;
  oil concession in Saudi Arabia, 1;
  response to Iranian Crisis of 1945–
  46, 2, 21, 31, 32, 33, 35–36, 38, 41,
  187; response to oil nationalization
  crisis, 62–63, 68–74, 79–81; in
  World War II, vi, 9, 16–18, 185. See
  also entries under U.S.
United States Mission to the Iranian
  Army (ARMISH), 17, 43, 45, 46, 49
United States Mission to the Iranian
  Gendarmerie (GENMISH), 17, 41,
  48–49

U.S. advisors: economic, 12, 15, 17–18,
  54, 112, 164; military and law
  enforcement, 17, 43, 45, 46, 49; in
  World War II, 16–18, 185
U.S. aid: Amini requests for, 164;
  Baghdad Pact and, 102–3;
  conditions for, 158; for economic
  stabilization program, 142; in
  Eisenhower administration, 94, 96,
  99–100, 104, 109, 111, 137, 187;
  Eqbal requests for, 113; following
  resolution of oil nationalization
  crisis, 99–100; to Greece, 43–44;
  in Kennedy administration, 137,
  146–47, 155, 157, 161, 166, 167,
  168; limits on, 50–51, 55, 109;
  Musaddiq and, 75, 76, 81, 82–83,
  84, 190; National Bank of Iran
  requests for, 42; National Security
  Council recommendations, 69;
  oil nationalization crisis and, 79;
  Qavam's requests for, 41; requests
  for, 51–55, 104–5, 114, 120, 145–46,
  148; Shah's disappointment with, 52,
  95, 104, 113, 120, 137–38, 147, 168,
  186; Shah's requests for, 40, 47, 49,
  115, 122–23, 165; State Department
  recommendations, 41–42, 53; in
  Truman administration, 51, 54–55,
  75, 76, 81, 187; Tudeh critique of,
  84–85; to Turkey, 43–44, 52, 100,
  159; U.S. House Committee on
  Government Operations report on,
  108; in World War II, 18; Zahedi's
  request for, 95–96. See also technical
  aid; U.S. advisors; U.S. military aid
U.S. Commercial Cooperation, 17
U.S. Defense Department. See Defense
  Department, U.S.
U.S. embassy hostages, 191
U.S. Foreign Operations Administration
  (FOA), 96
U.S. foreign policy. See containment
  policy; U.S. policy; U.S. policy in
  Iran

U.S. House Committee on Government Operations, report on U.S. aid, 108
U.S. involvement in Iran: as counter to Anglo-Soviet influence, 15; history of, 15–18; Soviet resentment of, 15, 19, 32, 119, 121, 122–23, 168
U.S.-Iranian bilateral agreement: Ibtihaj critique of, 153; and Iranian security, 139; negotiation of, 122, 123, 124, 186; signing of, 124, 186; Soviet response to, 119, 121, 122–23, 168; U.S. proposal of, 119
U.S.-Iranian economic cooperation agreement (1961), 155
U.S.-Iranian Mutual Defense Assistance agreement (1950), 53
U.S.-Iranian relations: Anglo-Soviet occupation and, 9; history of, 15–18; Ibtihaj critique of, 153; Iranian nuclear program and, v, 191; under Islamic Republic, 173, 190–91; post-September 11th, 191; pre-Islamic revolution, v; pre-World War II, vi; scholarly views on, 2–3; since Islamic Revolution, 184. *See also* Independent National Policy; Negative Equilibrium policy; Positive Nationalism policy; Third Power Strategy
U.S. Joint Chiefs of Staff. *See* Joint Chiefs of Staff
U.S. military activities in Iran: as cause of Cold War in Iran, 2; diplomatic immunity for U.S. military personnel, 158–60; post-World War II military personnel, 21; post-World War II withdrawal, 21, 22; in World War II, vi, 9, 16–18, 185
U.S. military aid: to Baghdad Pact, 103; conditions for, 158, 161; Department of Defense report on, 139; in Eisenhower administration, 98; Five Year Military Program, 169, 188; to Greece, 100; to Iran, 118; Iranian requests for, 120; in Kennedy administration, 158, 161, 162, 169, 188; limits on, 101; Musaddiq rejection of, 75, 76; National Security Council recommendations, 69; to Pakistan, 159; Qavam's requests for, 41; rearmament program and, 53; Saed's requests for, 52; Shah's disappointment with, 51, 52, 95, 113, 120, 139, 147, 157–58, 162, 186; Shah's requests for, 47–48, 49, 52, 110, 112–19, 127, 138, 160, 162, 165; Soviet objections to, 46, 77; State Department recommendations, 41–42, 116, 117–18; in Truman administration, 42, 45, 47, 76; Tudeh critique of, 84–85; to Turkey, 100, 159
U.S. National Security Council. *See* National Security Council, U.S.
U.S. policy: as cause of Cold War in Iran, 2; on Middle East defense, 100–101
U.S. policy in Iran: in Eisenhower administration, 94, 187–88; on Iranian Army, 98, 100, 116, 118, 151, 158, 161; Iran Task Force reports on, 149–50, 152, 153, 155–56; in Kennedy administration, 151, 171, 188; National Security Council reports on, 52, 68–69, 98, 108–9, 142, 149–50; State Department reports on, 40, 41–42, 50, 52–53, 108, 151; in Truman administration, 20–21; in World War II, 18
U.S. State Department. *See* State Department, U.S.

Venezuela, oil industry in, 65
Vienna Conference (1961), 151
Vyshinsky, Andrei, 34

Wailes, Edward: on Amini government, 150; appointment as ambassador, 116; and economic reform, 151; and Iranian defense, 148; and Majlis

elections of 1960, 143; meeting with Shah, 151; replacement of, 151; and Soviet-Iranian non-aggression pact, 121; and U.S. aid, 146
Warne, William, 81
war on terror, Iran and, 191
White Army, Soviet pursuit of, 11
White Revolution: implementation of, 154–55, 188, 190; motivation for, 137, 171; name of, 154; opposition to, 155, 170–73; referendum on, 171–72; six points of, 172
Wiley, John: appointment as ambassador, 47; replacement of, 54; and Shah's constitutional reforms, 49; and U.S. aid, 47, 51
Williams, Murat, 114
women, voting rights of, 170–71, 172
Woodhouse, Christopher Montague, 80–81
Workers' and Toilers' Union, 39–40
World Bank: and economic advisors, 112; loan requirements, 42, 43; loans to Iran, 105–6, 108, 120, 125, 138; and oil nationalization crisis, 74–75, 76; and Third Economic Development Plan, 152, 156

World War I, Persian role in, 10
World War II: Iranian support of Allies, 14–15, 18–19; Iran's strategic importance in, v–vi, 13, 16; U.S. advisors, 16–18, 185; U.S. involvement in Iran, vi, 9, 16–18, 185; U.S. policy in Iran, 18; U.S. postwar withdrawal, 21, 22. *See also* Anglo-Soviet occupation of Iran

Yakubov, Ahad, 32
Yalta Conference (1945), 20

Zahedi, Ardeshir, 81–82
Zahedi, Fazlollah: appointment as Prime Minister, 95; arrest of, 86; kidnapping and murder of Afshartus, 83; negotiations with Soviets, 100; and oil nationalization crisis, 96–100; and overthrow of Musaddiq, 80, 81–82, 85; problems faced by, 95; request for U.S. aid, 95–96; resignation, 102; resistance to reform, 102; resumption of diplomatic relations with Great Britain, 96–97; suppression of dissent, 96, 97, 99; U.S. and British support for, 84